RED RAG
TO A BULL

A passionate and informative record of one man's attempt to restore a small Scottish farming and sporting estate, at a time when the political class, the media and the educational establishment are dominated by people who have lost all sense of the countryside as the heart of the British way of life. Blackett is devoted to wildlife, and describes in fascinating detail his battle to maintain ecological equilibrium on his patch of land at a time when almost everything necessary to achieve that end has been denounced or even criminalised at the behest of people who know nothing whatsoever about the matter. His book belongs with the tradition established by H. Rider-Haggard and A.G. Street – a frank, honest and beautifully observed account of the 'return of the native'. Blackett shows us how to rediscover the land beneath the layers of priggishness and plastic that have been deposited upon it by urban disdain. And when the peasants next march on London to confront the nonentities in Parliament, they will surely each be carrying a copy of this book in their pockets.

Sir Roger Scruton, *FBA, FRSL*

What a brilliant, enlightening and amusing book, about the real countryside. Jamie Blackett presents the reader with the realities of rural life, hitting nails on the head left, right and centre – and only missing twice.

Those with mud on their boots and the countryside in their hearts will love it. Those with Bambi on the TV and soya in their cupboards will have problems as their prejudices are exposed; but they should/must read it nevertheless – enlightenment!

Red Rag to Bull has messages for everybody concerned with rural Britain today. It should be read by politicians, bureaucrats, ramblers, wildlife-lovers, townies, blow-ins and bumpkins like me. What a read!

Robin Page

Jamie Blackett was accused of being a right-wing version of me – and he took it as a compliment! Having read *Red Rag to a Bull* – so do I!

George Galloway

RED RAG TO A BULL

Rural Life in an Urban Age

Jamie Blackett

Quiller

Also by Jamie Blackett

The Enigma of Kidson: The Portrait of a Schoolmaster

Copyright © 2018 Jamie Blackett

First published in the UK in 2018
by Quiller, an imprint of Quiller Publishing Ltd

Reprinted 2020

British Library Cataloguing-in-Publication Data
A catalogue record for this book is available from
the British Library

ISBN 978 1 84689 288 2

Jacket designed by Edward Bettison
Typeset by Arabella Ainslie

Printed in the Czech Republic

Quiller
An imprint of Quiller Publishing Ltd
Wykey House, Wykey, Shrewsbury SY4 1JA
Tel: 01939 261616
Email: info@quillerbooks.com
Website: www.quillerpublishing.com

In memory of Annabel,
the bravest of the brave

It was the best of times, it was the worst of times, it was the age of wisdom, it was the age of foolishness, it was the epoch of belief, it was the epoch of incredulity, it was the season of Light, it was the season of Darkness, it was the spring of hope, it was the winter of despair, we had everything before us, we had nothing before us, we were all going direct to Heaven, we were all going direct the other way — in short, the period was so far like the present period, that some of its noisiest authorities insisted on its being received, for good or for evil, in the superlative degree of comparison only.

Charles Dickens, *A Tale of Two Cities*

Contents

Acknowledgements

I WOULD like to thank the 'expert witnesses' who appear in the book: David Cameron, David Mundell, Owen Paterson, Matt Ridley and John Mackenzie of Gairloch for being so generous with their time and very patient with my amateurish interviewing technique.

I have been fortunate to be able to ask a number of kind people to read various drafts and give me feedback, and I am very grateful to my aunt Cicely McCulloch, Pedro Landale, Jeremy and Char Culham and Lesley Andrews for their help and encouragement.

The effort would have been wasted if Andrew Johnston of Quiller Publishing had not taken a gamble on a hastily scribbled synopsis and I am immensely grateful to Andrew and Gilly and their team at Quiller for giving the book the attention to detail and quality of production that only a small independent publisher can bring; also particularly the editor, Andrew's brother Barry Johnston, whose advice has been invaluable. I am sure I am not alone in feeling grateful that this particular branch of the Johnston family has given up rustling cattle in Annandale and gone into publishing.

Most of all I should thank our wonderful team here, especially David McWilliam, Graham Kennedy, John Rippon, Kate and Hayley Nichol, and Karen McKie for their forbearance and for doing all the hard work while I have been abstracted by the book. And last, but in all ways first, my wife Sheri, who has put up with being married to a soldier, then a farmer and now, worst of all, also a writer.

Thank you.

Jamie Blackett
Arbigland
September 2018

Introduction

EVERY GENERATION moans about change. I have taken consolation in thinking about how my forebears have dealt with the challenges of their times. The first of my family to live here at Arbigland, General William Stewart, who bought this estate in 1852, soon after the repeal of the Corn Laws, showed considerable optimism by investing in land when the pessimists were predicting a collapse in prices. He had a relatively easy time as they stayed up, kept artificially high by the Crimean War and the American Civil War. It was his nephew, my great-uncle Kit, who had to keep going through the agricultural depression that followed tariff reform, with falling commodity prices and rents.

My great-grandfather Willie never had much chance to make a go of things, blown off his horse – his hunter, actually – by shrapnel at the First Battle of Ypres in 1914. It fell to his widow, Prudence, to hang on through the hard times in the twenties and thirties, so that her son Bill, my grandfather, could keep the flame alive. He probably had it easiest, although he lost five years of his youth away at the war, and he gradually took the land back in hand, as tenancies were given up, and forged a single, modern agricultural business out of eight farms, increased to eleven and several large blocks of forestry in the hills by the time he finished. He built up a renowned dairy herd and took full advantage of the agricultural boom, as farmers dug for Britain and fed the nation in the decades that followed.

His eldest son, Archie, never had a chance to make his mark, drowned punt gunning in 1970 shortly after taking over, though he left behind his paintings, which are wonderful evocations of the Solway and the geese and ducks that he loved. It fell to my father, Beachie, to hang on, the estate shrunk again by death duties, as the Chancellor of the Exchequer, Denis Healey, 'squeezed the rich until the pips squeaked'. My siblings and I led a carefree life that seemed in retrospect to revolve around ponies, building dams on the beach, and daily walks with our nanny, the saintly Mrs Kennon. But off-stage there were regular crisis talks going on in the estate office, as my father tried valiantly to modernise the dairying operation and make it pay.

Farming became reliant on the Common Market and subsequently the European Union. Like many of his generation, he was encouraged to get out of dairying – with a 'golden milkshake' from Brussels – and was paid to grub up the hedges and become a barley baron. His big crisis came in the nineties, when the Lloyds insurance market went bust after three hundred years of providing a steady income for landowners, and took him with it.

So, every generation has had to adapt to changing circumstances, and one shouldn't complain. But, notwithstanding Dickens's wise words at the beginning of this book, I think us baby-boomers have had to put up with more changes than most, and one can be forgiven for thinking that we live in a time of revolution unlike any other for the last three centuries. My predecessors could at least be sure of which country they were living in, but devolution and the current proposals for Scottish independence could yet take us back to pre-1707.

Every century has had its levellers threatening landowners, but no government in Britain[1] has struck at the whole concept of land ownership like the Scottish Government with its land reform legislation. And Brexit seems set to have the most profound impact on agriculture – for good or ill – since that repeal of the Corn Laws in 1846. Globalisation happened in agriculture over one hundred years ago, but farming is also being changed more rapidly than ever by revolutions in green energy, digital technology and biochemistry.

Old men in the parish, my father among them, can remember Clydesdale horses ploughing the fields, yet it is now possible to grow and

---

1   I have said Britain rather than the United Kingdom, as the nineteenth-century Irish Land Reform Acts were more Draconian – more about them later.

harvest a field of wheat without humans, let alone horses. Communities are changing as well; after nearly a millennium, this village is without a church or a shop, and fewer people in the countryside now have a direct link with the land than ever before – from more than twenty to fewer than five in one generation since the seventies on this estate alone.

Whereas those who went before me spent all their free time in the sporting field, the authoritarian state has taken its cudgel to hunting and coursing, and threatens shooting with a thousand indirect laws, and the salmon is fast disappearing from our rivers, no one quite knows why. The flora and fauna of the countryside have probably always been in a state of flux, but my ancestors would be shocked by the disappearance of some species, possibly not unconnected with the rapid population growth of some others. They all had to deal with the weather but according to the scientists, we have experienced greater climate change than past generations.

To varying degrees, they were largely left to get on with things by the government, in peacetime anyway. But during my time, I have been aware of the Big State making its lupine presence felt. I have a recurring image at the back of my mind; it is as though we are clinging to the outer branches of one of the trees in the policies that rocks and sways in the wind, while at its foot the Big State howls and snarls at us, like a particularly malevolent troll trying to shake us out of the tree.

Sometimes it sends laughing hyenas from its leviathan departments with new regulations or tax demands, or proposals for 'rafts' of legislation. At other times it hurls abuse at us, occasionally in a broad Glaswegian accent, calling us wicked lairds and quislings for the English and such like, or else in the nasal whine of the home counties, with threats of dire consequences for non-compliance, or a Belgian accent, confusing us with weird directives. Now and then he allows his nauseating brother Big Business to come and bully us. He robs us of our gold left at the bottom of the tree, and then leaves us on hold for hours listening to inane telephone music if we dare to complain.

It is a daunting time to be running an estate and in other ways exhilarating; the best of times, the worst of times, sometimes terrifying, but at all times fascinating. I always wish that I could talk to all the previous lairds to get their take on what is happening. Alas, I can't do that; all I get is tantalising glimpses of what they thought and did from what they left behind on paper, their game books and account books and so on, and the archaeological evidence on the ground.

Future generations will have this book as a kind of history of here, now, like a time capsule buried in a school playground. Maybe they will take it off some dusty shelf and take comfort from finding that their problems are nothing new. It might help them to understand how we coped with those challenges and to recognise why we took the decisions that we did, good and bad. And I hope they will conclude that we did our best.

Prologue

IT WAS what we call a dreich day in Galloway and my cap had reached saturation point, so that the water started running off and down my neck, and formed a pond in the small of my back.

'You'll need to hurry, Sian, I don't think we can hold him much longer,' I said, with as much sangfroid as I could muster.

The bull was getting disgruntled. We were all less than gruntled. It had been a long day and we were cold and hungry; tired, too, as every step in the mud seemed to suck a little more of our strength away.

Sian, one of our vets, was leaning over the fence of the corral, trying to stick a needle filled with TB-testing serum into a tonne of angry bull. He was angry, because we had taken his wives away from him, and he was facing a long winter of enforced celibacy. Next to me, Davie smouldered with volcanic rage. He had just given me a frank assessment of my personal qualities. As his employer, I was perhaps less indignant about this than I might have been.

It was over twenty years since someone had bestowed the c-word on me. Then it had been our drill instructor at the Guards Depot, the menacing figure of Lance Sergeant Nelson, a man of few words, all of them obscene. Nellie had a face disfigured by glass from a Glasgow bar fight, so when he stuck it close to mine and spat a stream of violent invective in my ear, while simultaneously administering the knobbly end of his picquet cane to my knuckles, I paid rapt attention; and prayed earnestly that when he next bawled, 'Squad will move to the right in threes ... right TURN!', I would turn right, and not left again.

Davie would have made a good soldier, I reflected. The Vikings who populated the land west of the River Nith in the ninth century had left behind a genetic patrimony of red hair and belligerence, and an impenetrable dialect. Davie is bred true to type. I was secretly quite pleased to be working with a man who was able to express his opinions freely, with admirable brevity and clarity. He was also right; this was not one of my better ideas and I should have found the money from somewhere to invest in a little health and safety.

With blind optimism, I had left the comfortable self-importance of my job as a Chief of Staff in the Army and was now standing up to my shins in mud, holding one end of a gate that was pinning a coiled spring of taurine lethality in the corner of the pen. Sooner or later, we were going to have to let go and, the laws of physics being what they are, sooner rather than later.

'OK, that's you, boy.' Sian retreated to safety outside the pen.

Davie and I looked at each other and there was a telepathic pulse of that mutual understanding of comrades in arms. His mood had changed suddenly. He had a glint in his eye and a devil-may-care grin on his face.

'I doot we're gan to have to run for it.'

I nodded, 'On the count of three, then? One, two, three, Fuuuuuuuuuck!'

We turned and fled. It is astounding how fast you can run through mud in wellies when there is a bull, normally the most placid and ponderous of creatures, trying to kill you. And even more astonishing, how fast a bull can move when he puts his mind to it. We shot up the sides of the pen like squirrels up a tree and the bull's head butted the soles of Davie's boots impotently, just as he cleared the top.

Landing in a heap in the briars on the other side, the adrenalin fizzed out in peals of laughter. There is nothing quite as funny as a near-death experience.

Shortly after that I invested in some heavy-duty cattle handling equipment. The bull was 'put away'.

Coming Home

CHAPTER ONE

LIKE THE wild geese and the salmon, I had felt the pull to return to Galloway. In twenty years of soldiering, I had carried some migratory impulse within me that had gradually become more insistent, until it had become so irresistible that hard logic and finances – that were, shall we say, jejune, they sound better that way – had been unable to stop me. In truth, it had sustained me. In hot deserts and steamy jungles, I had clung to the belief that one day I would walk the bogs for snipe again, with the ice thawing beneath my feet and the clear January skies filled with goose music, before retreating to the library fire.

Shivering in a sleeping bag on snow-doused hillsides, I had consoled myself with thoughts of riding across hot stubbles, with the clean smell of straw in the swath and the afternoon lullaby of pigeons cooing in the woods being carried on the breeze. I longed to build sand dams on the beach with my children, as I had done as a child, and feel for cockles with our toes in black Solway mud, before walking back up through shady rhododendron glades for tea.

The urge first started to become unbearable when I was serving in South Armagh, in Northern Ireland. The helicopter swerved and lurched out of the sky with its precious cargo of young men, keeping the landing site a secret until the last minute from the assumed terrorist with his heavy machine-gun, just across the Irish border. As it landed we thudded out, half-jumping, half-falling, and energised by a parting blast of hot air and an intoxicating lungful of aviation fuel vapour, we ran, crouching low below the down-draught from the blades, before diving into fire positions on the dewy grass.

As the helicopter climbed away to safety, and we shook ourselves down and set off on patrol, it struck me forcibly that it was spring. It had not yet been spring on the north German plain, where we had been training days before. And in the base that would be home for the next six months, where I had been dropped unceremoniously by the same helicopter the night before, it could have been any season for all we knew, as there were no windows and, even on the helipad that served as our prison exercise yard outside, we could only see the sky above the high tin-sheet walls.

Looking around me, it seemed as though the pilot had misread his map and I was back in Galloway. The banks were bright with yellow gorse flowers and white showers of blackthorn blossom, and the air was filled with spring songs, larks and yellowhammers, and the urgent yet soothing baaing sound of a lambing field somewhere in the valley below. The patchwork of fields and the bright green of the spring grass were the same, the heathery mass of Slieve Gullion, with its evergreen skirt of conifers, could have been Criffel, the hill that sits above us at home.

The only difference was that I couldn't see the sea and the landscape was studded with hacienda-style bungalows, proof that local planning officers valued their kneecaps more than vistas or vernacular style. Around me was familiar rural life, tractors muck spreading, milk tankers doing the rounds of small farms, and sheep being gathered. But it was as if we were invisible.

The people looked straight through us as we trudged past, melting inside our body armour, creaking under the weight of our packs, our eyes stinging with salty sweat leaking from under our berets. Only the old man mending his fence with his collie gave us a shy smile without lifting his head. And whereas the locals walked freely through the gates, we had to fight our way through the thickest part of the blackthorn hedges, like ghosts through walls, in order to avoid being blown up by IEDs,[2] cursing in a most unspiritual manner.

All through that spring and summer, as I walked through that

---

2   Improvised explosive devices.

countryside, in it but not of it, I longed to swap day jobs with the local farmers. Men who seemed no different from our neighbours at home yet, surreally, were often trying to kill us. And I realised that I couldn't put off turning my sword into a ploughshare for much longer.

I agonised, procrastinated, and finally, with the arrogance of youth and a song in my heart, I followed my instincts and became a farmer a few years later. It has not been easy, a butterfly seems to flap its wings in the Amazonian rainforest and the farmers of West Dumfriesshire are in the swamp up to their necks, but I wouldn't have swapped this life for any other.

The vicissitudes of business have always been outweighed by the opportunity to live in a paradise among trees and hedges, birds and wild animals, that are oblivious to man's attempts to complicate life. And there is infinite variety. As a landowner, farmer, builder, tourism operator and – I hope – conservationist, I have been close to the front line on many of the key issues facing the countryside today.

Driving north up the M6 and crossing the River Esk, in the Debatable Land that blurred the borders of England and Scotland for centuries, one becomes aware of the prominent peak of Criffel, backlit by the late afternoon sun, rising like a blue-black half-moon out of the sea. My spirits always rise then, as I know that we will shortly be turning off and driving west through Dumfriesshire.

Half an hour on, driving from Annandale into Nithsdale, we can see Arbigland for the first time. The estate stretches like a blue finger in the distance, pointed at the Lake District fells from the foot of Criffel into the silver expanse of the sea. Arbigland is a corruption of Ard Beg Land, which means a small peninsula in Gaelic, not that Gaelic has been spoken here much since the twelfth century. Further away on the English side, St Bee's Head arcs round, and the two headlands frame the Irish Sea beyond; and on the horizon, you can sometimes detect a few clouds sitting above a faint outline of mountains, which is the Isle of Man.

If you look very carefully at the Arbigland peninsula, you can see a dip in the green line of trees, which is the big house, a square matchbox on the horizon. So many journeys, so many memories jostle at that point on the road; eager anticipation of the holidays ahead, with Annabel and Edward, my sister and brother, curled up beside me in the back of our parents' ancient car with our Jack Russell, Trump, warm at our feet.

We have been driving for days, it seems, from Berkshire and our term-time life, playing pub cricket[3] up busy A roads through yet-to-be-bypassed towns and up the miraculous new motorways, stopping frequently for urinary emergencies, carsickness, Trump walking, and to eat hard-boiled eggs and cold sausages in the new service-station car parks.

Later, driving home on leave as a young officer in a variety of old bangers with different girlfriends beside me, and then with Sheri as fiancée, then as wife, and later with our children Oliver and Rosie now in the back.

'That must mean we're neely there.'

'Still a bit of a way to go, we have to go all the way round by Dumfries, remember.'

'Aaaaaaa-aw. I wish we had a boat and could go straight across. Why can't we, Dad?'

Or of going the other way, back south to school, with my nose pressed to the window and a lump in my throat, straining my eyes and imagining that I can see my pony in his field behind the house.

On through the brown sandstone terraces of Dumfries, past Rabbie Burns's final resting place at St Michael's Kirk, we drive across the river, once an international border, hearing the first seagulls, and head towards the Solway Coast.

---

3   Do children still play pub cricket? The batsman scores runs from the number of legs on pub signs you pass and you are out if you pass one with none. Thus, The Dog and Partridge is a six and The Wheatsheaf takes your middle stump out.

From there the road meanders over the Whinny Hill to Scotland's most romantic village, New Abbey, with its ruined Sweetheart Abbey, where Queen Devorgilla of Galloway buried her husband's heart. And then as the road tops a knowe, just past Drumburn, we see Arbigland again, a tapestry of woods and fields along a hog's back, with the village of Carsethorn clustered around its harbour at the sea end and the vast panorama of the Lake District mountains across the Solway behind.

Turning off in Kirkbean with its classical Georgian kirk, more like a Massachusetts church, we carry on and across the humpback bridge over the burn that forms our march, and onto Arbigland, up the Smithy Hill and into the trees, where so often a couple of roe deer jump out in front of the car. We turn into the main avenue down a funnel of rhododendrons, and through the old gates with their stone falcons – the family crest – on pillars either side, the crunch of gravel and we are there. Home.

I have so many memories of the big house that if I ever lost my sight, I could move round it with all my other senses, the creak of floorboards, the banshee howl of the wind around the chimneys on a windy night, the smell of wax floor polish and pipe smoke, and of damp and dog coming from the basement, the feel of the draughts and of threadbare Persian rugs on polished floors.

My parents moved there when I was five and my mental map of the big house and its surroundings gradually took form and expanded from that time. My room was at the top of the stairs and here my siblings and I were confined for epidemics of whooping cough and chickenpox; I still have a few pockmarks where I disobeyed my parents and picked the itchy spots. We were seen by Dr Milne-Redhead, who did regular home visits in those days from his house in Mainsriddle. He would be given a glass of sherry in the library for his trouble once he had seen us. If he had a surgery, I never saw it.

Through one window I could see my pony in his field, and every evening I would watch the rooks flying backwards and forwards across the front of the house, from an old beech tree in the policies to an equally venerable chestnut tree by the tennis court. To and fro they would go, cawing incessantly, about what I never could fathom. In the Easter holidays, they moved down to their rookery round the pond in the garden, and I would watch them building their nests, stealing twigs from each other's piles high in the tops of the branches.

Out of the other window, as the last of the sun streamed from the back of Criffel, I could count the cows in the field above the house, red-and-white Ayrshires and one black-and-white one, a harbinger of the herd's conversion to Friesians in the early seventies.

In those early days we lived mostly on the middle two floors; the basement had the estate office in it and the gunroom, but both of these were out of bounds to children, otherwise it was a rabbit warren of redundant kitchens and storerooms filled with curiosities. The attic was likewise full of jumble beyond a green baize door, where presumably the long-vanished maids had slept. Closer inspection revealed trunks full of old clothes and military uniforms and these were to become our dressing-up boxes.

Every morning we would go for a walk with Mrs Kennon, known to us as 'Kenny'. The baby of the family, Ed, in his pushchair, was both her favourite and, as a troublesome toddler, the cause of most of her work, and he was referred to as 'an awfi' boy'. Most mornings we would go to the home farm and watch the cows being milked in their byres, and pick up a creamy churn of unpasteurised milk to take back to the house. This would be decanted into a large shallow bowl for the cream to be skimmed off by Mum.

Sometimes we would walk the other way along the West Avenue where Kenny, whose real name was Nancy, lived with her husband, Jock, who was our forester. He presided over the sawmill and, as many forestry workers did in those days, he had a missing finger from putting his hand too close to the circular saw blade as he fed the logs through. This was an object of fascination to us children.

Next to their cottage is God's Acre, the little family cemetery, a garden in full bloom from snowdrop time until the last hydrangea head has faded, where we Blacketts find our final repose and our dogs lie around the walls, in sure and certain knowledge that we will be reunited in the next life.

But best of all, we would walk down the Broad Walk, a carriage drive that goes from the house down through the gardens to the sea. There we would spend hours building fortresses in the sand, then filling the moats by diverting the stream that runs down from the pond and through a natural rill formed by the rocks and across the sandy bay.

We would clamber over the Devil Stone, a large egg-shaped granite boulder with serrations across its middle. These were probably caused by someone trying to split the rock, and the stone was almost certainly left there by a glacier in the last Ice Age; but we much preferred the legend that the Devil had taken a mouthful of rock out of Criffel and, finding it too hot, spat it out so that it landed on the beach with his teeth marks on it.

Sometimes we would catch shrimps in the rock pools and take them back up to the house to form an aquarium in an old hip bath in the attic. They never lived very long in there, alas.

As we grew older, we came to appreciate the finer points of the big house, which is a good example of a Georgian mansion, 'built in the Adam style' by a polymath of the Scottish Enlightenment, William Craik, in 1755. As children we tried hard to work out how he had managed to put the large Grecian urns, each of which must weigh nearly a ton, on the corners, three storeys up, using block-and-tackle pulleys pulled by oxen or horses. Dad would say, 'One day they will fall down and squash somebody underneath.' So we always gave them a wide berth on windy days.

We lived mainly in the nursery wing unless we had a house party, when the house would come alive and we would sit either in the library in winter, or in the blue drawing-room in summer, and on rare, special occasions use the drawing-room, which doubled as a ballroom, for reel parties. Then the house would revolve around the dining-room.

Here, around the walls, portraits of the ancestors demonstrated the changing hairstyles through the centuries, from great-uncle Nisbet Balfour, home from the American War of Independence in his redcoat and his powdered wig; to Christopher Blackett, whose ponytail is just visible on the velvet collar of his Regency buck's coat; and my great-grandfather Willie in his Boer War service dress, with his luxurious cavalry moustache swept up at either end. It all meant that when Oliver arrived back from his gap year with a millennial's beard, we were able to observe that what goes around comes around.

It was in the dining-room that Dad was giving a guided tour to a party of tourists, when they stood gawping, open-mouthed with bemusement as, behind his back outside, a large inflatable doll, of the kind said to be much befriended by sailors, floated vacuously on the breeze while Ed lowered it from an upstairs window.

The dining-room looks out to sea at either end, and at shooting lunches the low winter sun came flooding in with extra intensity after bouncing off the water. But it is the dinner parties I remember most. Creeping downstairs with Annabel to listen at the door; then progressing to 'butling duties', learning how to lay the table and pour the drinks and, finally, at last, being allowed to be one of the grown-ups. Memories of laughter-filled nights around the table with the candlelight glowing on the silver, and on velvet smoking jackets and silk evening dresses, and on faces pink with wine.

Lest I am giving the impression that we lived in great comfort, I should perhaps set the record straight. It was Arctic. On winter nights, we would all huddle round the nursery fire, then run up to freezing cold, damp bedrooms, where I would dive into bed to avoid the wolf that was known to live underneath it.

A family friend told me the other day that when they stayed with us, they had to bribe their children with bags of sweets to stay upstairs, in a bedroom where they could see their breath condensing before them. And, when it rained, we would have to race round putting containers everywhere to catch the drips coming through the ceilings. During one prolonged wet spell, my father announced with a degree of pride, perhaps betraying his Anglo-Irish ancestry, that we were now 'a ten-bucket house'.

But, having told you all about it, the big house no longer forms part of this story, as it doesn't belong to us anymore. It was sold in 2000, along with the stable yard and the gardens, and it now sits brooding reproachfully at the heart of the estate, on it but no longer of it, like an elephant in the room, a large white one in retrospect.

The new owners, since moved on, were very nice and we have been back inside a number of times. It is a disconcerting feeling seeing it redecorated and refurnished, like coming downstairs and seeing one's mother dressed up to go to a vicars' and tarts' party in fishnet stockings and suspenders.

The catalyst for the sale of the big house was the recession of the early nineties and the collapse of the Lloyds insurance market, a catastrophe for many landowners, who had relied on it as a steady return on their land. These two events hit my father particularly hard.

In Greek tragedies, hubris is followed by nemesis, and we now sought the next phase: catharsis, my father and stepmother moving back to his wartime childhood home at Nethermill; and my family and I, in time, to the House on the Shore, the dower house of the estate, which sits in the bay at the bottom of the gardens.

I must have been about five or six when it first dawned on me that I would one day be something called 'the Laird'. I think I gleaned this from either Alice or Primrose, who appeared most mornings to help my mother in the house. I didn't really understand what it meant at first, but then I gathered that this was what Dad was sometimes called, so I was able to work out the job description from there.

Further career advice was gained from my grandfather, a terrifying giant known to the family as Gaffer, and to everyone else locally as the Major. Gaffer had been the Army heavyweight boxing champion and had once taken to the ring with the world champion, Primo Carnera, and even in his dotage he put the fear of God into most people. Having handed over the estate, he exercised a non-executive presence from behind the steering wheel of his old white Volvo, as he drove around, fag in mouth, keeping an eye on things and voicing his displeasure at any lapse in standards.

For the last decade of his life, Gaffer occupied a large armchair in what came to be known as the Oval Office, a small study at the end of the House on the Shore. Behind his chair, a shotgun sat propped up against the wall, so that he could wage war on the rabbits and any other unwelcome fauna foolish enough to come within range on the lawn outside. Beside him was a revolving bookcase bulging with books, mostly history, on which sat *The Times*, a large tumbler full of pink gin at lunch-time, or whisky in the evening, a silver ashtray and a packet of Embassy cigarettes. Here he would hold audiences with passing friends and relations and, during the school holidays, often with a teenaged me.

These were treasured hours spent discussing farming, history, politics and current affairs, and listening as he imparted advice on life. He would tell me never to mix whisky with soda as it hardened the arteries,[4] that three drinks a day were enough for any man, and that he only ever had one glass of gin at lunch-time and two glasses of whisky in the evening. But as each measure was enough to floor most mortals, I'm not sure this was strictly objective. He also told me that I need never pay for sex, as I would find enough women willing to oblige for nothing if I spoke nicely to them, which raised a number of questions in my mind that I didn't dare ask.

At least once during the holidays we discussed, 'What I Was Going to Do When I Left School'. It was during one of these conversations that I told him that, after a spell in the Army, I wanted to come home and run the estate. He gave me an uncharacteristically gentle look; I thought I detected pride and pleasure, mixed with pity and concern.

'It will be hard, you know. We are only really bonnet lairds. Do you know what a bonnet laird is?'

I shook my head.

'It's what is sometimes referred to in English history books as a hedgerow knight. Someone who has some land and an ancient name, but

---

4   Advice I have cheerfully ignored, without any apparent damage hitherto.

no money and really not much more than the clothes he stands up in, hence the bonnet.'

I nodded.

'It may be very hard. You mustn't destroy your life trying if it proves impossible.'

I remember staring fixedly at the dappled sunlight filtering through the old sycamores along the shoreline. The implicit challenge seemed to make the job that much more alluring.

The role of laird has evolved in past decades, here at any rate. The days of feudalism have long since disappeared. The buck still stops with the laird, as far as the agencies of the state and the bank manager are concerned, but deference and distance have been replaced by a more consensual camaraderie, *primus inter pares*, similar to being the abbot of a monastery or the team leader of a kibbutz.

Estates were once the standard unit of land ownership and to be found everywhere, but they have dwindled to the point where they have almost become objects of curiosity. The very word estate – the e-word – is one loaded with connotations in the modern age, not all of them positive. To some people it implies land stolen from the populace in some historical crime – the Norman Conquest, the Enclosure Acts or the Reformation – then passed down through a male-orientated system of primogeniture, and it smacks of a privileged rentier life and exploitation of tenants and labour. But, to me, an estate means something that is far more than the sum of its parts.

It means a community of people living and working together as one of Burke's little platoons; it means a balanced portfolio of businesses, with emphasis on property, tourism and silviculture as well as agriculture, and therefore a balanced landscape. It also means the preservation of architectural heritage and gardens and the conservation of habitats and wildlife, which to me are inextricably linked with the practice of various field sports.

And it means land managed for the long-term, passed down from previous generations and held in trust for generations unborn in a classic

Burkean contract, balancing the needs of the estate pensioners in their cottages, against the desire to plant trees for great-grandchildren to harvest.

A friend, who recently took over another estate, described to me an image she held in her head of three generations of a family, sitting clinging onto a log being washed down a vast river in spate. The laird is at the front of the log, with his children and grandchildren behind. He has to steer through the rapids and fend off rocks and other hazards along the way. Suddenly he falls off, or climbs to the back, and you are in the driving seat.

I suppose I'd had most of my life up to that point to think about it, but those thoughts had mostly been a hazy daydream about the perks of the job. It was only now that I had to sit down and analyse what I was going to do, and how the hell I was going to do it. I had read in a commonplace book that as one goes through life one should 'cherish the past, adorn the present and create for the future' and that struck a chord. I began to look around for things that needed cherishing, or would benefit from adorning, and I set about trying to turn dreams into creations that would bring lasting rewards.

The estate seemed like an empty opera house, with nothing much happening on the stage and no sound coming from the orchestra pit. It was a beautiful space, but dead for most of the time, the arable contract farming arrangement meaning that there was no one working on the land for months at a time, and a shortage of funds meant that I'd had to let the shoot. We had no livestock and, as the fields were covered in wall-to-wall winter cereals for eleven months of the year, not much wildlife either.

My mind was concentrated on the fact that I had a seven-figure mortgage to keep up. A large part of the estate had been sold to an insurance company in the seventies, after my uncle's death, and then leased back. We managed to buy it back, so we now owned the estate outright again, but the payments were a constant worry. The price of wheat in the early noughties was languishing at £60 per tonne, less in nominal terms than a generation before, which in practice meant that we were sometimes receiving as little as £37 per tonne after deductions for drying, storage and marketing.

After paying for labour, seeds, sprays and fertilisers, we were eating heavily into the EU single farm payment subsidy just to keep going. Without that, we were farming at a heavy loss and in fact the whole estate was barely breaking even; without contemplating providing anything for us to live on, or reinvesting anything in the business. Naïve as I was, I could sense that by growing crop after crop on the land, selling the straw and not having any muck to put back on, we were taking out more than we were putting in each year, and eventually this was going to suck us into a downward spiral from which we couldn't recover.

Most importantly it was a 'one-trick pony'. There was an arable operation that was almost entirely reliant on that most fickle phenomenon in Galloway, the weather, for its profitability. And the farmhouses and cottages were only just providing sufficient rent to maintain them. The buzzword of the time was diversification, and the government made funds available for farmers to diversify. I didn't need persuading and burnt the midnight oil putting grant applications together. Lessons learnt from business school were put to good effect, as I worked my way through SWOT[5] analyses.

The net result of all these deliberations, and a series of serendipitous opportunities, was that we changed the business from a precarious two-legged stool to one with four legs, by adding a beef herd and a tourism business to the existing arable and property enterprises. And by an extraordinary turn of events, we added a pack of foxhounds to the estate's mix and later took the shoot back in hand. Soon the stage was providing daily drama and there was operatic music coming from the pit.

What follows is a hotchpotch of recollections and reflections from the last two decades. As I took over the estate in 2000, it is a twenty-first-century view of life from the silage-pit face.

---

5   Strengths, Weaknesses, Opportunities & Threats.

Summer

CHAPTER TWO

FOR THE first nine years, I was trying to run the estate by remote control from Yorkshire. There is a choice to be made between option one: earning a good living elsewhere and pouring all one's money and free time into an estate that one seldom sees, or has time to enjoy, and being castigated for one's pains as an 'absentee landlord'. To do this one either has to let the land and risk the politicians preventing you ever getting it back again, or take a chance farming it yourself without being able to exercise hands-on control. And option two: taking a vow of poverty and going for the full-immersion farming experience, so that the children can be brought up there, which is surely the whole point.

I always wanted option two, but it took us a while to create the conditions for it to be possible. It is said that estates need two 'w's to survive: the will and the wife. The will needs to be written in such a way that the estate is not broken up when each laird dies, and each generation needs to marry a wife who has the grit to make a go of it. I was very fortunate as one of fourteen grandchildren that a large part of what had been my grandfather's estate was passed to me. And lucky beyond measure that my wife, Sheri, has supported me through thick and thin – mostly thin, in option two – and ended up doing a lot of the work to allow me to 'live the dream'. She seized the opportunity to make the House on the Shore into a family home, something that it had never been before.

The house looks out to sea, as the name suggests, so that every day is different. On clear days, we are lined up on the peaks of Skiddaw and Helvellyn across the water in the Lake District, but the endless permutations of light and tide and weather sometimes make us feel as if we are wrapped in the technicolour embrace of an abstract Turner seascape. It was built in 1936 by my formidable great-grandmother, in the bay at the bottom of the big house gardens, not far from the Devil Stone. I remember 'Grandy' as a very old lady in tweeds and a felt hat, who encouraged me to throw my Action Man with his parachute out of her upstairs drawing-room window. The oldest person I ever knew and the only Victorian.

Born before there were cars on the roads, she lived to see Neil Armstrong land on the moon on her television; her father, an Irish bonnet laird, had fought as a volunteer with Garibaldi's Redshirts in Italy, a two-step remove from me to mid-nineteenth century European history that I always find surprising to contemplate. She had built the house to her own design as her retirement home. A devotee of Lutyens's architecture and Gertrude Jekyll's gardening ideas, her vision was for a Cotswold manor house in the Arts and Crafts style, and she demolished a row of derelict cottages elsewhere on the estate to cart the stone for its walls.

With its seven sharply pointed gables, its round dovecotes and its mellow buff colour, it does indeed look as if it should be in Gloucestershire, rather than sitting on the shoreline of the Scottish Riviera; in harmony with the rocks on the beach below, which are where much of the building stone on the estate was originally quarried. Guests often say that it reminds them of a house in a Daphne du Maurier novel and in fact it has been used to simulate Cornwall as a film location. It was one of the last houses to be built before the Second World War and people often speculate whether it would ever have received planning permission (which was introduced in 1948) in the decades that have followed. It is one of the ironies of the British countryside that any beautiful houses and villages almost always predate the Act designed to keep it looking beautiful.

That first year in the House on the Shore, I saw the estate through fresh eyes. Sitting on a small, lawned, raised beach between the woods and the sea, the house allows for an intimacy with the natural world not possible in the big house, where we sat one storey up, separated from the fields by lawns and gravel. As a family, we have become attuned to frantic beckoning from one another and the imprecation, 'Come and look through the window!' as a succession of unexpected animals shows themselves.

I remember sitting mesmerised with the children on the terrace as we watched a family of young stoats playing at the end of the lawn. The stoat is said to be able to transfix its rabbit victims by putting on an act, and the baby stoats seemed to be born thespians. Or there were the times when we saw a big dog otter with its strange humpbacked gait coming down from the pond in the gardens, clambering over the rocks, then scampering over the sand and into the sea for a swim each evening.

Sometimes dolphins, or perhaps more accurately porpoises, come and put on a show below the house when the tide is right in. Best of all, our bird table outside the kitchen window attracts not only a wide range of birds, but also red squirrels doing gymnastic displays. There had not been any red squirrels at Arbigland in my childhood and we have yet to have the grey menace, though they are not far away. The reds had died out in the winter of 1947 and not returned. Then around the turn of the century there started to be sightings. Discovering that there was a healthy population living in the woods around the House on the Shore was a wonderful housewarming present.

I am admiring the lawn. Not for its neat stripes or uniform green grass, but for the opposite. I have decided that all lawns on the estate should be mown less often to let the wildflowers grow. This is helping the bees and there is one now foraging across patches of daisies, trefoils, forget-me-nots and clover. It has been controversial with some of the holiday cottage guests, who have been aggrieved that they are not like suburban bowling greens. I am pondering how to bridge this cultural chasm, when something catches my eye.

The barefaced cheek of it: the rabbit lies stretched out in the middle of the lawn, as if sunbathing. It is too far to be sure of killing it with a shotgun, and in the wrong direction to allow a safe shot with a rifle. I am a little conflicted, as part of me, probably the part that enjoyed *Watership Down*, quite likes seeing rabbits grazing in the morning dew; after all, they are keeping the sward tight and saving on mowing time. Sheri is less forgiving of the scrapes they dig, and the havoc they wreak in the herbaceous border and the vegetable garden. We wage a war of attrition, savouring the harvest of *lapin au vin* as we go. It is an ancient feud and it brings back happy memories of my grandfather, crouching in his armchair, squinting over his shotgun at any young buck who dared to nibble the very same sacred turf outside.

Suddenly a thrush alarms and the rabbit sits up, then makes a run for the fuchsia hedge along the sea wall. The movement draws my eye and then I see something else. At first it looks like a large marmalade-and-white cat, then my brain processes the image and I realise it is a fox. It sits motionless on its haunches, no doubt waiting to see if any other prey stirs, then it makes its run and pounces into the hedge, once, twice, thrice, then it frantically rootles side to side. But Bugs has jumped down onto the beach and I can see him bouncing away along the sand, and into a hole in the rocks.

The fox gives a good impression of pretending that it didn't really care about the rabbit – what rabbit? It trots back across the lawn, pauses, snaps at a passing fly, then sits down and gives itself a scratch with its hind legs. I have a chance to have a better look at her – I think it's a vixen – she's a beauty, but not in great condition. I guess she must still have cubs on her and wonder if she has an earth along the cliffs.

I love seeing foxes, which may seem counterintuitive coming from one who hunts and shoots. As we do not have any lambing here, we can afford to tolerate the odd fox, although they still need controlling. Provided we have a small, stable population, I don't think they do us too much harm, as long as we keep pheasant poults firmly out of harm's way until they can get up into the trees to roost; although I have a twinge of conscience about our lapwings and partridges.

Our inability to do anything about 'the untouchables' – the predators protected by law – means that perhaps we should kill more foxes to compensate. Foxes are territorial and by leaving them to police their own territories, we avoid having too many incomers, as the old dog fox will see them off. They are relatively solitary creatures and do not congregate in large family groups, like other predators such as the badgers and the kites. Attempting a zero-fox policy by killing them in spring and summer would be time consuming without a gamekeeper, and might actually risk bringing in more foxes, while the smaller mammals and the ground-nesting birds are at their most vulnerable.

There are no easy options for killing foxes – I don't like the idea of trapping or snaring them, and lamping them by night risks wounding them. Hunting here in the autumn and winter will tell us how many we have, and we can cull a few and disperse that year's cubs, so that the population is kept in check, but otherwise we leave them alone.

We often see foxes crossing the drive by the kennels at night. It always amuses me that they should loiter within sound and scent of hounds. Do they do it on purpose to taunt them? It certainly seems as if they are deliberately living up to their Fantastic Mr Fox image. The sound of a fox barking at night always gives me goose pimples.

Running an estate like Arbigland is like having a beautiful and capricious mistress. She is very beguiling, and you can't stop gazing at her and pinching yourself to check that she is really yours. She dazzles you with her loveliness and persuades you to spend money on her that you can ill afford. It is all too tempting to cover her in pheasant poults, or fancy new rhododendrons with which to impress your friends, just as a man might hang diamonds round the neck of a trophy wife. If you refuse to buy her that fancy new tractor, then she sulks.

I feel sympathy for the Chancellor of Exchequer battling with the spending departments, as my family, tenants and employees ask me to spend money to mend potholes or put up fences, or make helpful suggestions about 'what would look nice there'. Or as neighbours sniff that 'your hedges are looking a bit hairy this year'. The wish list always seems to exceed the overdraft limit by hundreds of thousands of pounds.

At other times, it is brutally masculine, like wrestling with a large, clown-faced jack-in-the-box. Just when you think you have him back in the box, the joker boings out again and whacks you on the nose with a cackle. I have become used to being on call the whole time, to reacting to the mobile ringing with the news that there is stock on the road, or a cow down with staggers, or a holiday cottage with no hot water; fragments of intelligence that cut through the clutter and demand action, normally just as we are sitting down to a meal.

A friend, another laird of a small estate, once told me: 'Friends from the south come to stay and look around and say, "Isn't this wonderful? How lucky you are to live in these surroundings?" And I look and say, "Yes, we are very blessed." And as I look, I see a tree that has blown over that I still haven't had time to clear up, and a cow that is bulling, which must mean that she has not held to the bull and will have to be culled, and a slate is missing off a cottage roof, and I can't enjoy the view.'

Tragically, that friend later took his own life, and ever since it has made me realise that a farmer needs to force himself to keep a sense of proportion sometimes.[6]

The piece of intelligence that gives me more of a sinking feeling than most is when the drains are backing up. The female of the species has a keener sense of smell than the male and is more apt to confront matters, particularly, and perhaps I'm being cynical here, when confronting matters means stirring the male into action.

For some reason it is generally on a Saturday morning, when I am contemplating spending a carefree afternoon on the golf course. My first instinct is to decide on a course of inaction, hoping that the problem will go away or at least contain itself until Monday when, if the blockage is serious, a tanker can come and we can jet. In order to achieve that limited

---

6   And I have tried to support the farming charity, The Royal Scottish Agricultural Benevolent Institute, which runs a helpline for the farming industry along the lines of the Samaritans, called Gatepost.

objective, I go through a process of denial.

'No, I don't think that's sewage you are smelling, it's just rotting leaves,' as I catch an all-too-familiar waft on the breeze.

'No, I'm sure that's just rainwater,' as I glimpse tell-tale grey water seeping up in a patch of nettles.

This won't cut much ice with Mrs B, who has been through this routine many times before. So I attempt to draw a line under it and move on.

'Okay, we'll just leave it for a while to see whether it clears itself. Someone has probably put too much loo paper down it.'

It is clear that this won't cut it either, as I am forcibly reminded that there are bed and breakfasters turning up later.

Mentally I calculate the half-life of decomposing, plastic-coated cotton wadding and reluctantly accept that, short of a miracle, there is very little chance of deliverance between now and tea-time.

'Okay, I'll get it sorted then.'

I pull on my septic tank maintenance uniform – coveralls and wellies – and look out my rubber gauntlets, just in case. I see the mice have had one finger. Bugger. Then I take from the potting shed the most essential tools of my trade, the rods. The rods have been handed down from my father; I have enhanced their capabilities with a collection of gadgets that go on the end, plungers for different gauges of pipe, a wheel, and a thing like a double-pronged corkscrew. They live in a discarded golf bag, a trick I learnt from an itinerant plumber.

Resolutely I advance on the offending system. It has been a while since the last offence and the critical components are hidden from view under a tangle of secondary jungle, brambles and nettles, with an under tier of wild garlic. I retreat back to the potting shed in search of the strimmer, two steps forward and one step back. The strimmer has two feeble orange shoelaces with frayed ends poking out of the drum, and I decide that the brush-cutting blade is required. The set-up time wastes valuable minutes.

Finally, no, not finally at all, after expending valuable energy on the pull-cord, the undergrowth explodes into globs of sap and stemmy bits and the air is filled with a musky vegetable smell, as the strimmer reduces the jungle to a satisfying stubble, order out of chaos. I have broken into a prickly sweat and my skin and hair are now coated in detritus, which looks and smells like a sprinkling of chopped chives. We are not often troubled by midges here, but it is at this point that every midge in the parish decides to attack my forehead.

I am now in a position to conduct my assessment. There are about a dozen septic tanks on the estate, for which I have varying shades of responsibility. Varying according to whether the cottages they serve, normally two per tank, are in-hand in the form of holiday cottages or tenanted, and in the latter case whether circumstances on the day are negotiated in such a way that the 'repairs' fall to the landlord, or the 'emptying' falls to the tenants. They come in all shapes and sizes, their architecture determined by age, engineering design and foible, often sheer cussedness, on the part of the original builder.[7]

This one is our own and therefore of particular interest, to me at any rate. For those who live in flush-and-forget townhouses on mains sewerage, I shall describe it now. Sturdy earthenware pipes converge via subterranean branch lines on the main feeder pipe to the tank. These pass through two inspection traps covered by heavy concrete covers. The tank itself is also covered by a heavy iron lid. Just short of the tank there is a plunging point, where a pipe rises vertically from a subterranean T-piece to reach the surface, and this also acts as a breather pipe.

The tank itself is about three metres long by two metres wide by two metres deep and made of reinforced concrete. It has an inflow pipe and an outflow pipe, which is three-quarters of the way up and shaped like an H, so that the water has to flow up into it and the chances of a blockage are reduced. The outflow pipe proceeds past two more rodding points and into the soakaway.

The soakaway is about ten metres of perforated pipe well below the ground in a trench of sand and rubble. The idea is that the sewage sits

---

7   One day I must discuss with my publisher whether the time is ripe for a definitive guide to the estate septic tanks of south-west Scotland.

decomposing in the bottom of the tank while the liquid – 'grey water' – rises to the surface and seeps away down the outflow into the soakaway and thence into the ground where it is absorbed by the earth.

It is an ingenious contraption that must have transformed the lives of our forebears, who were used to staggering down the garden to sit holding their noses above a festering 'long drop' cesspit. It's a wonder that the Victorians were as keen on curry as they were. The introduction of the water closet and its accompanying septic tank was a triumph of British engineering – how often do we get a whiff of sewage elsewhere in the world, especially in France. And it has put sewage out of sight, mind and smell … until it goes wrong.

It is at this point that I remember that I will need the crowbar for lifting the lids, necessitating another trip back to the potting shed; another step back.

Lifting the heavy wrought-iron lid is always one of the riskiest parts of the job, as one is in danger of losing a finger or of dropping the lid into the foul water below. The tank itself looks to be functioning healthily. There is a crust on the top halfway between Stilton rind and the foam on the top of a 'brown cow'.[8] But looks can be deceptive and it is necessary to feel its consistency with the rods, like a quality assurance inspector in a cheese factory. It's liquid and what sludge there is in the bottom feels loose enough. No need to empty the tank, so that's one line of inquiry exhausted. It can't be on the outflow either as the level is normal, one small mercy to be thankful for.

Close to, the smell is becoming more aggressive. There is something weird about the interaction between our noses and our brains. Most of our consciousness is repelled by the smells coming out of the tank, but a tiny bit gets a guilty pleasure from some of the lush notes. Is it because deep down our bodies recognise some of the 'good' bacteria our guts need for our immune systems to function? I recognise in amongst the assault on my nasal sensors the extreme halitosis caused by congealed fat in the mix, and

---

8   By this I mean the childhood treat made by adding vanilla ice cream to Coca-Cola.

say a silent fatwa against whoever has scraped hot fat down the sink, which has hardened in the pipes like furring in a blocked artery.

I lift the brick and peer down into the plunge point upstream of the tank. It's hard to tell from the level, but I think I'll give it a plunge anyway. Plunging is a pleasurable activity after all. The rod with the rubber bung on the end is selected and a couple of extension rods added. I push it down and listen for the satisfying grunts and gurgles as hydraulic forces reverberate through the system. I strain my ears for the anticipated whoosh, as the pent-up mass of water and muck frees itself and comes racing down the pipes, but no, not today, sunshine. My forehead prickles and I can feel midges from outside the parish now – they have sensed the increased carbon-dioxide levels and decided to come and join the feeding frenzy. It's going to be a long afternoon.

Moving back upstream, I lift the concrete lid on the rodding point – deep disappointment, as it has backed up and the porcelain channel of the pipe is invisible under eighteen inches of dirty water. Kneeling in the nettles, it takes valuable minutes to feel for the entrance to the pipe. Feeding the rods up, I screw extensions on and push with a well-practised clockwise motion; losing a rod or the end piece doesn't bear thinking about. Then I hit something solid.

My nose has an itch that demands action and, with difficulty, I peel my gauntlets off to blow it. I have just put them back on again when my mobile goes and I take them back off again to answer it. Someone is pocket calling me; I put them back on again. Just then Sheri turns up with a cup of tea, so gloves off again.

'Are you winning?'

This is the moment when I adopt a negative demeanour developed from observing generations of working men clearing drains. I blow out my cheeks and offer a pessimistic prognosis. 'It's just as I said, we are probably going to have to bring in a jetter, maybe even a digger. I should have followed my instincts and waited until Monday, rather than wasting time on it now.' It is traditional also at this juncture to mutter something darkly misogynistic about the suspected source of the blockage.

Glancing around as I drink my tea, I see that the tide is half in and realise that I must have been there an hour or more. The contented purring from the gulls contrasts with my predicament, and a snatch of poetry pops up in my head from some dark recess:

Live happy in the moment, take no thought
For hidden things beyond, be firm to test
And turn the edge of troubles with a jest
For bliss unmixed was never earthly lot.

Horace, *Ode XVI, Book II*

Did Horace pause from toiling at some first-century BC cesspit in Rome, lean on his spade and think what I'm thinking?

There is at least, at this point, the consolation of having located the source of the trouble. From here on in, it is a furious fight against a subterranean beast of mythology. First there is a slim opportunity for guile. The corkscrew is deployed on the end of the rods and an attempt made to capture the offending blockage and retrieve it intact. When this happens, it is the ultimate prize, like making a grand slam at bridge, or getting the jackpot on a one-armed bandit. Otherwise it is a case of pitting brute hydraulic force against it, building a rhythm as the rods are pulled and pushed backwards and forwards, pushing the sludge further down the pipe, until suddenly there is no resistance and an ecstatic cry of 'it's getting away now'. Getting away now, three of the sweetest words in the English language. And suddenly the effort all seems worthwhile.

Like visits to the dentist, these battles with the sewage monster have coalesced in my mind to create a recurring nightmare with variations caused by particularly distressing incidents. One that sticks in my mind was the time that I had to get inside the tank to repair the outflow. It so happened that my cousin, David Bland, was arriving to stay that afternoon with a friend. He came down to find me and we had a brief conversation, conducted on my part from inside the tank, to the effect that I would come and see him when I had fixed the problem and had a shower.

As they withdrew, I heard the friend say, 'Ah, the landed gentry, they are never far away from being in the shit.'

* CHAPTER THREE *

MY DAY starts with a drive round the estate before breakfast. As often as not, at least once around the circuit, I will bump into hound exercise. Sporting artists have tended to focus on Christmas card scenes of horses and hounds in a winter landscape. For me, one of the joys of being closely associated with a pack of hounds is seeing them jogging along between frothy drifts of cow parsley in the lanes on summer mornings, their sterns (never tails) waving like the barley in the breeze; Andrew and Alan creaking along with them on bicycles, in brown kennel coats and tweed caps, hunting crops over the handlebars.

I usually hear them before I see them. 'Get on, Magpie,' and a pistol crack of a whip, sounds of Arbigland that now seem as innate as the piping of the waders.

I was first taken hunting at ten years old with the (now sadly extinct) Aldenham Harriers, near my maternal grandparents' home in Hertfordshire. In the light of subsequent legislation, it is worth recording that the Master, Lady Lyell, was a High Court judge's wife and stepmother of a future Attorney General, and the Field Master was the local police inspector.

My parents were by now in the throes of getting divorced, and life had become hyphenated between my father in Scotland and my mother in Berkshire. The experience was sharpened by anticipation brought about by an abortive attempt over the Christmas holidays when, to my bitter disappointment, the meet had been cancelled by a hard frost. Mum devotedly towed my pony behind her clapped-out Datsun Sunny up and down the Chiltern Hills from Berkshire to Hertfordshire again for another attempt, a single mother's act of quiet heroism I took for granted at the time, and for which I was never able to thank her properly before she died.

The hunting gene was strong in her and she was determined to give me the opportunity. My grandfather, Jim Withycombe, who had been one of the finest polo players of his generation in his youth, was by this time an OAP, who had not been on a horse for years. With a generosity that I have only just begun to appreciate, he borrowed a hunter and came out as my minder. He must have been in agony for weeks afterwards, poor man!

I remember not being allowed to have any breakfast, 'in case I needed to be operated on later', but Granny gave me a drop of whisky in a flask to take with me 'for Dutch courage'. Then the two of us set off, my pony, the excellent Mayflower, pulling my arms from their sockets to get to the front. Hare hunting is an excellent introduction for the young, as you can see venery in the open and the hare will invariably run in a circle, so there is less danger of being left behind.

It was on that day I first watched hounds work and witnessed that magical moment when a pack of hounds feathers across the plough, until one hound hits on the scent and speaks, then others join in the harmony, and finally the whole pack is in an orchestral crescendo, baying ecstatically in full cry as they accelerate away from the horses; the huntsman sounding 'Gone Away' on his horn to the echo. No other field sport can match the spine-tingling sound of hound music.

I can remember vividly the moment when we came to a large fence that had to be jumped, as there was no way round. 'Just tuck in behind me,' said my grandfather, as he sailed over. There was no option but to follow, and in a complete funk, I 'threw my heart over', so that the rest of me had to follow. A scramble, then a glorious, soaring flight, then a mouthful of mane on landing and the two of us were galloping after the rest of the field in a reckless cavalry charge, dodging the clods of mud in their slipstream. From that moment on, I was hooked.

Bringing the hunt kennels here was the fulfilment of a daydream that had been with me since childhood. Almost as soon as I could read, my imagination was captured by a children's book called *We Hunted Hounds* by Christine Pullein-Thompson, a seminal work on the internal mechanisms of a hunt about a group of children who start their own. And from that moment on, I fantasised about having our own pack at Arbigland. The daydream stayed with me through long years in exile in the Army, punctuated by hunting with the draghounds while at Sandhurst, and then by frequent trips to Leicestershire to hunt with the Quorn and the Belvoir.

My last job in the Army was in Yorkshire, and we made many friends while hunting there, and for a time our lives revolved around the Bedale Hunt and its attendant Pony Club. When we discussed moving home one day, Sheri said, 'Why are we even contemplating moving back to Dumfriesshire? It doesn't even have a hunt anymore.' It stung, but I was forced to agree that it was a fair point.

Through my late teens, I had managed a few days with the Dumfriesshire Hunt on my father's horse. In those days the nearest meet was thirty miles away near Lockerbie. I had assumed that one day it would be there for me when I returned. I little thought that the politicians would have imposed a ban and the hunt, with its distinctive black-and-tan hounds, would have gone into what was euphemistically known in the Army as 'suspended animation'. The ban in 2002 had been the final straw, following the terrible foot-and-mouth epidemic that had swept the county the previous year.

It was also a slap in the face for the hunting and farming community, who had saved the Blair government's skin by making the awful sacrifice of slaughtering their sheep and cattle. It devastated farms across the north as the main vector for the disease was Longtown Mart near Carlisle. Lessons from previous outbreaks were ignored and infected carcasses were transported to huge funeral pyres, spreading disease as they went.[9] Hunting was suspended and hunt staff were called up and worked around the clock as part of the military operation, performing their traditional role of humanely destroying the animals. They were all moved to other parts of the country so that they did not have to kill animals belonging to their neighbours and friends.

The scars from the outbreak have yet to heal around here; it was a living nightmare for everyone involved. My father remembers driving into Dumfries for a meeting on the day of the cull. The fields were all full of

---

9   The recommendations of the Northumberland Report of 1967, made by the Duke of
     Northumberland, could not be enacted, because of an EU directive and its interpretation by
     the Environment Agencies.

cattle and sheep as usual on the way in, but on his way home there was not a sign of life anywhere, only ghostly killing fields. Fortunately, we had no stock at Arbigland of our own then, but the movement ban meant that we were unable to let any of our grass fields for grazing that year, a loss for which there was no compensation.

The ban was met with incredulity by hunting people. It followed in Scotland with indecent haste on the foot-and-mouth disaster, when morale in the countryside was rock bottom and there was disgust that kennel huntsmen went from being indispensable to the nation one minute, to expendable the next. The politicians responsible will never be forgiven.

The old Hunt had folded, but fortunately a few brave souls had kept a committee and a hunt ball going, and some die-hards had re-established a point-to-point meeting on a new course at Netherby, just over the border in England.[10] The revenue from the ball and the point-to-point was then used to pay a neighbouring pack, the Eglinton – now sadly extinct – to come and hunt, as a gun pack under the new law, in what was left of the old country (less about 30,000 acres of one estate that was no longer accessible) on about twenty days per season.

Things would probably still be muddling along in this stop–go fashion had the arrangement not reached a stop phase at the end of the summer holidays of 2005, and had we not invited an old Army friend, Tim Easby, then huntsman of the West of Yore, to bring his hounds to stay at the House on the Shore for a few days. We had three glorious days hunting in the early mornings and the evenings, in the hills and along the shore. People came from far and wide and we partied late into the night.

Whether it was the 'drink taken' or a touch of sunstroke, or the magic of listening to those hounds that awakened my daydream, I don't know, but when the Hunt Secretary, Daphne Thorne, craftily suggested that we should do something about re-establishing the Hunt, with a fit of bravado,

---

10 The reason that Netherby is in England is that when Elizabeth I and James VI were trying to fix the problems in the Debatable Land, they asked the French Ambassador to adjudicate on the border. The Grahams gave him a good lunch and asked him to put Netherby on the English side. It is a strategy that has sometimes looked prescient recently.

I boldly said that I thought I could achieve it and somehow it all began to fall into place.

We were very fortunate that Daphne, the Hunt's most important asset, had remained. Daphne and her husband, Robert, are hound people *par excellence*, with their own packs of minkhounds and bassets. Like all good hunt secretaries, she would have made an excellent chief whip of a political party, as she had an encyclopaedic knowledge of the Hunt's subscribers and supporters, actual and potential, and was ruthlessly efficient with great charm.

On one of the mornings, two young students, Hannah Hutchings and her boyfriend Callum Rae, appeared from nowhere with a couple of beagles on leads and joined in with great enthusiasm. Hannah later took over as secretary, when Daphne retired, and has exactly the same qualities. Callum subsequently took over running the Hunt Supporters' Club. Without the three of them, all that was subsequently achieved would not have been possible.

Daphne's instinct was that there would be enough support if we could offer a new hunt that was sufficiently appealing. This chimed with what I was thinking and, in what seemed a matter of minutes, I was elected onto the committee and made Hunt Chairman, on the proviso that we would take the necessary steps to form our own pack.

Despite having hunted for thirty years, my only real knowledge of how a hunt was organised came from a book written for ten-year-olds. I began to wish that I had shown more interest in the beagles at school. It was one of those crazy things that one does at forty; before that I would not have had the confidence or experience, and now I would probably think of a hundred and one reasons why it was impractical and lack the energy. Having crossed this Rubicon, I sketched out a plan and called it, rather unoriginally, Operation Phoenix.

Students of management science may have heard of a technique called telling future truths. So we called an EGM of the Hunt and confidently told everyone that we were going to have our own pack again. This was received with rather less rapture and rather more scepticism than I had hoped. We had no hounds or horses, no kennels, very little country, only a handful of subscribers and nothing like enough money.

I thought there was every possibility of making a fool of myself, but that if I was going to fail then it was in a good cause. It was a way of making a stand against what I saw as urban socialists in Westminster and Edinburgh destroying our way of life. For me, that decade will always be remembered by the civil rights marches – they were not called that at the time, but that is what they were – organised by the Countryside Alliance.

I went on several marches, so the following recollection from memory, though it is crystal clear, may be composite. The one shortly before the English ban on hunting in 2004 sticks in my mind the most, when we demonstrated in Parliament Square while the House of Commons debated the Bill. An early start from Yorkshire, via Darlington station, the train packed with Geordie terrier men with large, foxy whiskers. Then joining a solid wall of defiant rustics advancing through the streets of London.

The spin doctors later had sections of the media believe that the marchers were tweed-clad landed gentry, braying for their vested interests, the establishment being disestablished, but that is not how I recall it. There were some people like that, mostly I suspect from the M4 corridor, but the overriding impression was that the core of the march was made up of ordinary working men and women fearful for their livelihoods, something more like a modern-day Jarrow March, of the salt coming out of the earth to shake an angry Saxon fist at the neo-Normans foreseen by Chesterton:

> *They have given us into the hand of new unhappy lords,*
> *Lords without anger or honour, who dare not carry their swords.*
> *They fight by shuffling papers; they have bright dead alien eyes;*
> *They look at our labour and laughter as a tired man looks at flies.*
> *And the load of their loveless pity is worse than the ancient wrongs,*
> *Their doors are shut in the evening; and they know no songs.*

I remember a red-faced farmer's wife carrying a placard that said, 'This cow isn't mad, she's bloody livid.' There were hunt banners redolent of colliery brass bands and of the colours of old county regiments, the Old Surrey and Burstow, Spooners and West Dartmoor, Braes of Derwent, York and Ainsty, hunts that gave their names to the battleships that escorted the Atlantic convoys: Atherstone, Fernie, Cottesmore, Pytchley. We flowed into Trafalgar Square, a bucolic enactment of de Tocqueville's aphorism, 'When democracy fails, the people take to the barricades.' And as we did so, someone shouted 'Pigeon!' and everyone looked skyward and gave a great *rus in urbe* belly-laugh born of a shared sense of humour, a shared way of life.

Halfway down Whitehall, marshals reminded everyone to show their respect. As I walked past the Cenotaph, I gave a silent eyes right and thought of all those hunting men who had fought in the world wars to preserve our freedoms, of my grandfather Jim, mentioned in despatches on the beach at Dunkirk, of my great-grandfather Willie lying in the mud of Flanders, his terrified charger, who had been cubbing in Rutland only weeks previously, galloping back to the lines, stirrups flapping below an empty saddle.[11]

I thought of all those Snaffles prints: *Pass Friend*, *Killed in the Open*, *Once Upon a Time*. And I thought of my mother on her death bed only a few months before, confused by the morphine, asking me several times with pain in her eyes, 'Are they going to ban hunting?'

Was this really happening?

The last time I had been in Whitehall, in fact, I had been on a horse myself. It was the State Opening of Parliament and as adjutant of my battalion, I had been sitting dressed as if for the Battle of Inkerman in a greatcoat and bearskin on a grey horse named Fleetwood, on whom I had hunted in Rutland only weeks before. As Her Majesty drew level in

---

11 This image is based on the account of his groom, who told my grandfather years after the war that he knew his father was a casualty, as his horse arrived back in the lines with an empty saddle. He later died of his wounds in a field hospital in Poperinghe.

her state coach, the crowd gave a great roar and the pavements became a flickering blur of Union Jacks.

Fleetwood went straight up on his hind legs and for interminable seconds seemed to start toppling over backwards, his hooves slipping and sliding on the tarmac. Some instinct of self-preservation, not taught at Pony Club, made me bring the pommel of my sword down between his ears and the moment passed safely.

That time I had been there upholding the established order, rather tenuously at that precise moment, but now I was, what? Was I on a different side, there to bring the new order crashing down? It certainly felt like it, there were now twenty thousand[12] people in Parliament Square and there was an ugly mood brewing. I was no longer a serving officer, but it felt weirdly uncomfortable all the same.

Once in the square, I bumped into several friends who were still serving in the Ministry of Defence. They gleefully told me that an edict had been issued forbidding them to join the protest, but that work in the MOD had ground to a halt as the building had just about emptied. The proprieties of the British constitution seemed to be wobbling.

The crowd surged towards the Palace of Westminster. I heard people shouting, 'Sit down!' Good idea, show the world's media a Gandhi-style passive resistance in the road outside Parliament. But the police were having none of it. A hard-edged, yellow-and-blue line of police officers in riot gear pulled people to their feet and started to push us back. I had been in riots before, a real one in West Belfast, and any number of simulated ones on exercises, and I was taking a professional interest in the Met's deployment. There were no petrol bombs in this one and no intent to harm people or property, but I could feel the crowd psychology changing.

Driven by helpless anger and inarticulate frustration, the sheer weight of numbers was pushing those at the front against the police, whose

---

12 This is the Countryside Alliance estimate based on their counters' figures, the police estimate (not counted) is slightly lower. The biggest CA March had 400,000 people and is claimed to have been the biggest civil rights march in British history.

discipline suddenly gave way. Batons came raining down on the crowd and soon there was a trickle of bloodied casualties being helped to the rear; ordinary people, husbands, wives, daughters, even grandmothers. The Big State had bitten back.

Later, the news that a group of protesters led by Otis Ferry had broken into the chamber and caused the sitting to be suspended, flashed around the square with great excitement. History had been made, even if nothing had been achieved – the vote went through all the same. Coming away that evening, I passed the police's quick reaction force down a side street. Scores of mounted police in riot helmets mounted on horses, batons at their sides. I have often wondered what would have happened if the police commander had panicked and ordered them into the square.

Country people used to dodging mad cattle and catching loose horses by their bridles would not have run like football hooligans. Perhaps another Peterloo Massacre was narrowly avoided. The Independent Police Complaints Commission later found that several policemen had deliberately concealed their badges and identities as they inflicted 'serious head injuries', and if you look online you can still see photographs of grinning policemen hitting unarmed protesters. Seven policemen were charged, but later walked free.

I was worried that we would not attract enough followers for our new hunt, in a changed environment, where what we were doing was not illegal as long as we abided by the new rules, but not exactly approved of by the Big State, or the liberal – or 'illiberal' – media either. But I need not have been concerned. Historically, the people of Dumfriesshire have been natural dissidents. Prior to the Union of the Crowns in 1603, the borderlands had been a byword for lawlessness, as private armies of light cavalry rampaged across the land from Kirkcudbright to Berwick, and

Lanark to Lancaster, stealing cattle and burning houses.[13]

The Reivers, as they were known, were bound by bonds of kinship to certain prominent 'riding families' on both sides of the border. In our area the most prominent were the Maxwells, Johnstones, Bells, Irvings, Grahams, Armstrongs, Jardines and Littles. They fought the English reivers, they fought the forces of the crown in both nations, and they fought each other.

The Union put a stop to all that, as there was no longer a frontier to be exploited. These families continued to focus on cattle, but on breeding, hauling and dealing in them, rather than stealing them, although some have observed that the distinction is a narrow one. But the tradition of horsemanship carried on: to this day, if you analyse a typical mounted hunting field in Dumfriesshire, you will still find these same riding families.

Very fortunately, a scion of one the families, the Bells, in the shape of Malcolm Bell-Macdonald, had remained as Master of the rump of the old Hunt. The other half of Malcolm's name comes from the famous Highland clan who shielded Bonnie Prince Charlie on his epic escape after Culloden.

I once asked Malc if he would help me with my civic duties in Dumfries, when I was the Pursuivant for the Riding of the Marches one year. He was characteristically forthright in his reply, 'Certainly not, we still have not forgiven the Provost and Baillies of Dumfries for impounding our baggage train in 1745.' Memories run deep in Scotland.

Malcolm and I decided that we should try to persuade our friends Piet and Sue Gilroy to come into the mastership. Piet has the benefit of being 'well kennt' in the farming community in the Stewartry, and his Falstaffian figure and zest for life would ensure that hunting on the western side of the country was fun and well supported by the farmers. Sue's father, David Culham, had been a Master in the seventies and she herself was the ultimate Pony Club mum (now granny), and would be brilliant at encouraging the children of the Hunt.

---

13 For more on this colourful period of British History, see *The Steel Bonnets* by George MacDonald Fraser, HarperCollins, 1989, and *The Reivers* by Alistair Moffat, Birlinn, 2007.

It was only in her retirement speech at the Puppy Show many years later that Sue revealed that when she asked her father what he thought about her becoming a Master, he had said, 'You are mad, you will lose your man, you will lose your money and you will lose your mind!' Happily, many years later, she still has all three.

Piet and Sue were initially a little hesitant, correctly realising that it would mean a lot of hard work. So we invited the two of them and Malc to stay with us in Yorkshire to hunt with the Bedale. Piet very generously brought a bottle of malt whisky with him so, after dinner, he and Malc and I proceeded to drink it, after Sheri and Sue had gone to bed. We had just about reached the bottom when, after some persistent lobbying, he reached across the table and shook my hand and said that he and Sue would do it.

We decided to call ourselves the Dumfriesshire & Stewartry[14] Foxhounds, to reflect the names of the two counties we would be hunting over. We also registered ourselves with the Masters of Foxhounds Association by sending them maps of our country, which covered seven sheets of the Ordnance Survey. It was by now November and the target was to be back in business in time to parade hounds at the county show in Dumfries the following August.

The most pressing need was to find a huntsman. Tim Easby gave encouragement by assuring me that most huntsmen would give their right arm to have the opportunity of establishing a new pack and hunting our country. But we had no luck, until a friend of a friend put me in touch with Andrew Cook, who had been at the Portman and previously at the South Shropshire but was temporarily without a pack and looking to get back into hunting. He had all the attributes we were looking for in spades.

Andrew came for a look, and I gave him a road map and sent him off to recce the country. It measures fifty miles by forty miles from Newton Stewart in the west to Langholm in the east, and from Sanquhar in the

---

14 The old counties of the Stewartry of Kirkcudbright and Dumfriesshire, together with Wigtownshire, had been subsumed into the region of Dumfries and Galloway in 1975.

north to the Solway in the south. It is almost completely devoid of those enemies of hunting – plough and built-up areas – and there are only two major roads and two railway lines. In the east it resembles the Borders, with rolling hills and conventional coverts, and in the west it is much wilder, more like Ireland, with foxes found in patches of whins[15] and bogs. He must have liked what he saw as, to the committee's great relief, he agreed to come. It was now January.

We needed enough money to establish kennels and to buy essential kit, and working capital to keep us going until we had enough subscribers. I established a Phoenix Fund and three respected local landowners agreed to be the Trustees. Then I wrote to every kindred spirit in the two counties and appealed to their better natures, enclosing a vision statement for the new pack. Wouldn't it be a better place to live with a hunt at the heart of the community again? After a few days, thank goodness, the cheques started rolling in. Slowly but surely, we were heading back into business.

When the ban came in, the old Dumfriesshire hounds had been dispersed, with the Beaufort and the North Cotswold among others taking some, and there was a heated debate over whether we should try to get the old bloodlines back. Andrew was very clear that he did not want to, for the good reasons that they had a very small gene pool and a reputation for independence. Life was going to be difficult enough establishing a pack of hounds and controlling it in the field under the tight restrictions of the new law. The Committee was happy to acquiesce, although it was agreed that the hounds themselves would be owned by the Hunt, so that they could not be taken away on a change of mastership.

Instead Andrew planned to breed a 'hill hound', which is created from using a mixture of fell hound and modern English foxhound blood. The result is a big, fast, athletic type of hound that will go all day in the hills, covering huge distances. Andrew brought a strain of Modern English foxhound that he had been developing at the South Shropshire, and fused it with good bloodlines that we were given by, amongst others, the

---

15 Gorse.

Buccleuch, the College Valley and the West of Yore.

Within five years, we had our own distinctive type of hound, and Andrew's breeding has been rewarded with cups won at the various hound shows in the north, as well as by their performance in the field.

✤ CHAPTER FOUR ✤

CATTLE ARE brazenly open about their sexuality. During the month of June, the cows, flushed with spring grass, put on condition and their coats shine with bloom. Davie and I will say to each other with satisfaction, 'They're coming in.' One by one they come into season and send the others mad with sapphic desire. As they start bulling (pronounced in Scotland with a short u), they ride each other round the fields thrusting and straining, while the cow underneath has her back scuffed raw.

It is a risky time, sometimes the ones on top will get crutched and dislocate a front leg as they fall off, so that they are lame for evermore, or sometimes the one underneath will be so badly beaten up that she loses her libido and spends the rest of the summer complaining of a bad back. The young bull calves, only a couple of months old, catch the excitement in their nostrils and follow the cow in oestrus round and round the field, like schoolboys tagging along behind a sexy teacher.

This is the prelude to the year's red-letter day for the stockman, the day the bulls go out; the time when the hard work of feeding all winter and the stresses and disappointments of calving are behind us, and the herd starts to look after itself again for a few months at pasture. Midsummer, with its feverish weather, its birdsong and its lushness, is both genesis and apotheosis.

For weeks beforehand, I sit at my computer matchmaking with care. The best of the pedigree Luings will be bred pure to the Luing bulls. Their matches are made with the dynastic ambition of a medieval king marrying off his daughters, and I fondly imagine their progeny winning rosettes at the breed society sale in Castle Douglas.

The rest are split between the Angus and Simmental bulls, mixing them up to maximise the hybrid vigour. There is a need to avoid incest, as several of the bulls now have daughters in the herd. The heifers, and the cows who have had difficulty calving, have to be found suitors who are 'easy calving', and not so heavy that they will hurt them. The bulls have a genetic tendency to throw calves of a certain size and shape. Their progeny will also have a distinct gestation length. The science is in finding a bull who will beget small calves that don't stay in the womb too long, and hit the ground running to grow like beanstalks.

The bulls themselves have been kept well away from the rest of the herd, to avoid any unwanted pregnancies. We have tried to give them enough grass to bring them to peak condition, but not so much that they become fat and lazy. They are also aggressively bisexual, and care has to be taken to ensure that they are kept in groups of the same size and weight, in case the smaller ones become prey to dark predatory forces. There is the ever-present danger of all that testosterone boiling over and fights breaking out.

The bulls have an established pecking order. One of them, generally the heaviest, will be top dog and rule over an uneasy truce. But sometimes the balance of power will shift, or there will be a cocky young bull who fancies his chances. Then all hell will break loose. Watching bulls fight is majestic, like having ringside seats for Muhammad Ali battling George Foreman. The fear that one of our most valuable possessions will be killed gives it an edge, like knowing that one has bet more than one can afford on the outcome of the title fight.

When they are evenly matched they will lock heads and grind each other into the ground, every sinew straining and their hooves digging into the grass, then scrabbling and sliding before digging in again. A bull's head is like concrete and, with a tonne of force behind it, potentially lethal.

So it proved for Hammy, Drinkstone Hamilton, a gentle giant with a great red leonine mane atop his kind eyes. Poor Hammy made the mistake of getting too close to Charlie the Angus, a menacing hulk of rippling black muscle. We found him dazed and brain damaged, walking round in circles, head down in defeat, his mouth drooling and eyes staring blindly. We got him into a pen, but there was no saving him and I had to shoot him that night, my best bull, the daddy of the herd.

The day starts with the bulls being rounded up. There is an edgy excitement as we head off on the quads, our shadows long in the morning dew; working with bulls always puts one on edge. The gate is opened and one of us rides round in a circle and pushes them out of the field, the other acting as the 'kep' on the road, to stop them going the wrong way. So far so calm, they lift their heads then reluctantly walk away from their breakfast, then break into a waddling trot. As they form a bunch, the proximity of the others causes them to lurch into a swaying canter and the momentum picks up.

All is going well but then, crossing the last field before the yard, a fight breaks out. Ally the big new Simmental gives Nimrod a broadside. He swings round and they put their heads down and start pushing and heaving like a rolling maul in game of rugby. Suddenly, out of the corner of my eye, I see Davie moving in at full throttle. Seemingly oblivious to the danger, like those images of New York firemen running towards the Twin Towers, he doesn't hesitate.

'Davie, *no* … !'

There is a spinning, *Tom and Jerry* cartoon blur of man and machine and beast, then order restores itself and the cavalcade turns into the farm. Once in the handling pens, the bulls revert to sullen truculence. They need to be given a leptospirosis booster jag. Why is it always jag in Scotland and jab in England? Then they need to be split into individual pens, so that one by one they can be married up with their groups. They don't get what is going on, which makes us more frustrated, as we think they should be grateful for the treat in store for them.

'Come on, you old bastard, shift your arse … No! Don't you dare!'

The bull, rooted to the spot, snorts and shakes his head. Nose in the air, he gives me a sidelong glance. He is not pawing the ground, but show any sign of weakness now and he might turn and come for me.

'Keep moving forward. Show him who's boss. Make him afraid of you. Dinnae step back or he'll have ye.' Davie's tuition over the years is ringing in my head.

I launch myself forward, waving my stick. 'Go on! Get on with you!'

The bull turns and ambles peaceably down the race.

The rest of the day runs like silk, as we join up seven bulling groups, seven bovine piles of chips spread across the roulette table that with luck will multiply into more cattle, and eventually next year's income. We watch intently as they go out. Two of the bulls are yearlings, ones we have bred ourselves. They should be fertile, but it is vital not to over-face them in their first year by giving them too many cows to cover. In theory, a bull can handle a cow for every month of their age plus two, up to a maximum of around fifty.

For the young bull, it is like a sixteen-year-old boy being given a harem of fifteen of his mother's friends to satisfy. The red bull, Solomon, seems a little reticent about stamping his authority on them straight away, grazing on the edge. The other, Samson, a roan, finds his Delilah and takes to it straight away. He swaggers up to a cow, has a good sniff, then mounts her. The act of coitus is rapid in cattle and he slides off again.

Has he, or hasn't he? The cow walks away and her tail rises horizontally, a reflex action that tells the watching stockman that the deed is done. Result. Her number goes in the notebook and we will watch anxiously in three weeks' time to see whether she is cycling again.

And so begins the time of prurience, as we watch the bulls 'work'. Each field tells a story, a romantic comedy. The target is to have sixty per cent of the cows covered in the first three weeks. That will ensure that most of the calves will be born in April, and will have the full benefit of their mother's milk in the grassiest months of the year on which to grow. The biggest risk is that the bulls go lame, or do not work for any other reason.

One year, I had a new bull named Kojak. I had bought him second-hand off a farm near Brampton. He had everything and more that you look for in a bull. He 'filled the eye', he had real presence and a good strong neck. He had length and a good top line, so that his progeny would all produce lots of fillet steak. His scrotal circumference augured well for his fertility, and is also a trait linked to early maturing daughters.

His head was not too big nor his shoulders too wide, so that his calves should be born easily. He stood on his tiptoes with good sound feet and he moved well. He was long enough in the leg with enough 'crank' to jump. And he had a nice quiet temperament. When his heifers won the championship at the breed society sale a few months after I had bought him cheaply, I thought I was a genius.

Then, when Kojak was out with his cows, Davie said, 'There's something no right aboot that bull.'

Graham said, 'He's no jumping.' Davie said he had seen him jumping, but 'no drawing'. We wondered if he had a bad back. I rang my friend Francesca, the horse physio. 'Can you do me a favour and have a look at my bull. I'm sure if anyone can give him back his mojo, then you can.'

'Behave!'

She came and gave him a back massage, which he visibly enjoyed.

Then we turned him out again and I sat in the field and watched, and watched.

Once a cow stops walking away from the bull and stands still, their courtship sometimes has a repressed passion phase, a bit like watching *Brief Encounter* with Trevor Howard and Celia Johnson, while they stand next to each other, head to head, tail to head, head to head, whispering sweet nothings, I suppose. Then the tension builds and he jumps.

Had John Greenleaf Whittier just passed a field full of bulling cattle when he wrote 'Breathe through the heats of my desires, Thy coolness and thy balm'?

I watched Kojak jumping several times and concluded that there was nothing wrong with his back. But I was always watching from the wrong angle to see whether there was anything happening. Then he jumped again, and I stared as Kojak thrust a large, pink boomerang over the cow's rump, missing the target each time; the cow looking deeply unimpressed.

'Oh, bloody hell, he's got a wonky willy.'

The vet confirmed that 'spiral deviation of the penis', though comparatively rare, is a recognised condition in older bulls, and we had to send Kojak away and bring a substitute bull off the bench.

☙ ☙ ☙ ☙

The roe deer are at it as well, in the middle of the beach right below the kitchen window. I have seen the doe before; she is a beauty, bright red, and a picture of health, which is probably why she has come into season. I wonder if it is one of her fawns who appeared lost on the drive, still with spots on his coat, a couple of months ago. I haven't seen her suitor before. He looks an old buck.

I had read about the roes' courtship before, but never witnessed it. They are trotting round and around in circles, sometimes turning in a figure of eight and changing direction, like horses doing a dressage test; in fact, they are on the very patch of sand where we have schooled the horses many times before. The doe is in front leading him a merry dance. He is getting impatient, but she is determined not to sell her body too cheaply. She won't stand for him and, in his frustration, he butts her so that she lashes out like a filly.

On and on they go, then suddenly the buck sits down. She turns and looks at him, as if to say, 'Come on, you can't rest yet, there is work to be done.' But he looks nonchalant and picks at a bit of sea kale. She comes back over to him and he stands up and approaches her, but she turns and sets off again. He looks fed up with the whole business, as he chases after her.

It's clearly not just public schoolboys who find the fairer sex maddeningly incomprehensible at times.

The beef herd was also the product of daydreams. I had always loved cows as a child; the Ayrshires we had at home and the Jersey house cows on my maternal grandparents' farm form some of my earliest memories. When we moved to Yorkshire, I would watch a suckler herd chewing their cud contentedly each day on my way to work in Catterick Garrison, and think that I would like to own them. It was my farming mentor Michael Cowen, our first arable contractor, who had a beef herd on his own farm in Cumbria, that encouraged me to diversify into beef as a way of making best use of the parts of the estate not suitable for cereals.

We did not have the money at the time, but then tragedy struck. My mother's cancer came back and she died, too young at sixty-two and, bless her, left me a small legacy, enough to buy twenty cows and a bull. I felt that as a farmer's daughter she would have approved, and hoped that, like in the parable of the talents, they would multiply, and they have.

I knew next to nothing about beef cattle, as all my childhood memories had been of dairying and growing grain here. But being autodidactic by nature, I read everything I could and pestered my neighbours for information. Farming is perhaps the only industry in the world where your competitors are always very willing to help a new entrant find his feet. Fortunately, some of them are leading figures in the beef industry – the Kingans and the Hendersons – and Alistair Kingan and Scott Henderson had just taken over our contract farming arrangement on Michael Cowen's retirement.

I wanted a pedigree herd, so that we could grow a capital asset that might one day be something valuable to pass on. The question was, which breed? There was a scheme at the time to claim money from the Department for a strategic review, and so we used it to get the SAC's[16] beef specialist, Dr Jimmy Hyslop, to suggest how we should go about it.

It is embarrassing now to admit that prior to 2004, I had not heard of Luing cattle, as that is what he recommended. The Luing – the 'u' is silent so that it rhymes with ping – was at that time still relatively unknown; they have since become more mainstream. Jimmy recommended them because they are hardy and thrifty, as we had no usable buildings at that time and the plan was to winter them out on the stubbles, and graze the poorer fields that had been in set-aside and had now reverted to rushes.

The more I researched the Luings, the more I liked them. They are a composite breed developed by the Cadzow family on the Island of Luing, in the Inner Hebrides, in the fifties. Five-eighths Beef Shorthorn and three-eighths Highlander, they have the milkiness and the fleshing ability of the

16 Scottish Agricultural College, always known as 'the college'.

former and the hardiness of the latter. Both breeds are docile, having been used as dual-purpose house cows on small farms and crofts for centuries, and the Cadzows had been rigorous in weeding out any wild ones, so that Luing cows are generally very good-natured, unless they have just had a calf when their maternal instincts come to the fore, which is as it should be.

They are old-fashioned, hairy looking cows, and with their palette of red and roan coats they are a beautiful enhancement to the landscape, which was now of importance to our rapidly developing tourism enterprise. And I was pleased to find that their meat is some of the very best, every bit as good as the better-known Aberdeen Angus. I discovered that some other neighbours, Steven and Elaine Murray of West Preston, were Luing breeders and went to quiz them; seeing their herd grazing on the fields behind Southerness Golf Course, with Criffel in the background, clinched it. Now I had to find some.

Fortunately, the Luing Cattle Society put me in touch with a man in Yorkshire, who had a small herd to sell. The Army had prepared me for many things, but rarely in my life had I had to buy or sell anything of significance; however, my new mentors sensed this gap in my education and were quick to offer coaching.

'Never be the first to say a price. Always let the other man say what he thinks they are worth and then come down from there. And always let him think that you are happy to walk away.'

It was useful advice, and I also had my own observations of their negotiating tactics with me. These appeared to be to adopt a lugubrious demeanour, and to pretend that the commodity in question was of such an inferior quality, that they were only really buying it to do me a favour by taking it off my hands, particularly as all the talk was of prices going down again next week.[17]

---

17 I think it is a shame that Mrs May relied on the talent from the Palace of Westminster and Whitehall for the Brexit negotiations with the EU. If she had sent a Galloway cattle dealer, we might have achieved what we wanted and sooner.

I drove to Yorkshire fired up to do a deal, excited but fretting that I might not be able to afford them, and worried that there might not be another opportunity for months. Very fortunately the seller wanted to sell them quickly before they calved and, after some protracted haggling, we shook on it.

Seeing them come off the lorry a few days later was one of the most satisfying moments of my career. Davie cast a critical eye over them.

'Well, they're no spring chickens anyway!'

But I felt like a Zulu king in his kraal as I watched them graze.

Farming is the best job in the world and the worst. It allows for a hermit-like solitude, yet no other profession except the performing arts forces one to display one's incompetence for all the world to see. They say the difference between a good farmer and a bad one is a few days of rain. The hubris of boasting about a good-looking crop of wheat is followed by the nemesis of a monsoon harvest. One has the consolation of knowing that it is the only profession bar one to have survived since the Stone Age, but the insecurity of feeling that the rest of the world has found something more lucrative to do.

Gradually I became accustomed to my new role and, when people at parties asked what I did, I got used to saying that I was a farmer. I detected that farmers no longer command the place in the social pecking order I had thought. If farmers speak with a regional dialect, they are accorded a professional respect, albeit sometimes rather condescendingly. If you speak received pronunciation, then the assumption is that either you are a 'trustafarian' and farming is a euphemism for bucolic indolence, or you are the simple one of the family, unable to cut it in banking or one of the professions, left at home to mind the farm. The assumption in both cases is that you must have 'a manager', who takes all the tricky decisions. If the farming woes of the moment are in the news, there is often a pitying look, 'poor you, it must be very hard at the moment'.

But the more I experienced farming, the more I realised that farmers need skills far in excess of those in most other walks of life to survive. And the more I learnt, the more I realised how little I knew, and my respect for my farming neighbours grew. I had become used to working in a large organisation. Most of my Army career was spent either in an infantry battalion or in a large headquarters. If there was a problem, it was dealt with by a specialist with the requisite skills in finance, human resources, logistics, IT or whatever.

Running a small business means that you have to master the full range of business disciplines; however, farming requires in addition a working knowledge of plant, animal and soil sciences, surveying, various branches of civil engineering, especially road construction and drainage, building, mechanics, water divining, weather forecasting, form filling and customer relations, to mention just a few.

Buying and selling cattle is a science all of its own. And planning a crop rotation is like working out how to make a difficult bridge contract, the sequencing is all. Fortunately, the countryside is a much kinder place than the city; and other farmers, while nominally competitors, are in my experience always very happy to offer advice, more so perhaps than in any other industry. And by a stroke of good fortune, Davie had been living in one of our cottages at the time and was happy to take on the role of stockman.

His experience and practical knowledge have been invaluable, and he became to me what a good platoon sergeant is to a raw platoon commander straight out of Sandhurst, a mentor and guide, my severest critic, but unswervingly loyal and dedicated.

✢ ✢ ✢ ✢

Seeing hounds on a hunting day, one is apt to forget the centuries of painstaking breeding behind them. That foxhounds are invariably healthy with good temperaments is down to careful selection and frequent outcrossing to new bloodlines. When so many breeds of dog, even some gundogs, are now suffering from problems as a result of closed stud books and inbreeding, the wisdom of generations of masters is more and more apparent.

The breeding programme at the kennels has become one of the natural rhythms on the estate. Anxious preparations start early in the year, as stallion hounds are selected, often borrowed from other packs for a few weeks, for a few of the best bitches to be 'put to'. Then hope or disappointment as they hold or not, and finally the heart-warming sight of proud mothers feeding their whelps, like little fat piglets under their heat lamps in the whelping boxes. The kennels become a magnet for children during the summer, as they come and see the hound puppies.

Later in the summer, they go out in couples to live with local families – the 'puppy walkers' – and the previous year's puppies come back into the kennels and go out on hound exercise, coupled to steady old hounds so that they learn what is expected of them. Andrew excused us from puppy walking, on the grounds that we lived too close to the kennels, which was something of a relief in some ways, as there is nothing more destructive than hound puppies, adorable as they are.

There is no doubt that it is the puppy walkers who get the most satisfaction out of the hunt. They are the inner circle of the hunt's community and, for them, a day's hunting brings the joy of seeing hounds they have brought up as part of their families working in the field. Their formal reward comes with an invitation to lunch and tea and perhaps a prize at the annual Puppy Show at the kennels.

This has become the high spot of the estate's social calendar. I often think that if the politicians came to the Puppy Show, they might understand how hunting is a vital glue that binds rural communities together, as identified in the Burns Report.[18] But they probably would not see beyond the judges in their pinstripe suits and bowler hats, the panamas and summer frocks in the crowd, and the groaning tables of food and drink.

The first Puppy Show was a joyous affair. A rib of beef for lunch in a

18 *Report of Committee of Inquiry into Hunting with Dogs in England and Wales,* by Lord Burns, 2000.

marquee open at the sides, so that we looked across the Solway, a throng of country folk from all across the north to watch the judging in a makeshift ring by the hound lodges; then back into the tent for cakes lovingly baked by the ladies of the Hunt, stand-up comedy from judges Trevor Adams and Michael Hedley,[19] and prizes for the puppy walkers. I have a hazy memory of tea involving a barrel of Galloway Gold from the Sulwath Brewery in Castle Douglas, and late-night singing.

The next morning, I went back up to the kennels. One of the revellers had a drain cover lifted and was peering into the drains.

'Blocked drain, Jimmy?'

He looked up, and as he did so I feared that he might have had a stroke in the night. The bottom half of his face seemed to have collapsed. He gave me a guilty look and muttered something as he pointed at his mouth.

'Ah. Oh dear, I hope you find them. Have you looked in the tank? I would give them a good scrub before you pop them back in if I were you.'

You know you have been to a good party, when one of the guests has erupted with such exuberance that his false teeth have disappeared round the S-bend.

---

19 These two legendary MFHs, Trevor Adams at the Buccleuch and Michael Hedley at the
    Border, provided invaluable support in helping to get us started.

✦ CHAPTER FIVE ✦

THE TIDE is miles out and the shore is sun-dried to a post-modernist composition of blue, brown and yellow stripes. Over on the rocks, a cormorant sits with its wings hung out to dry, like the heraldic device of some dark Teutonic knight. From the riot of brambles outside my office, a blackcap is tapping. The mobile disturbs my reverie. It is a restricted number. Bugger, that usually means some emissary of the Big State intruding into our world. I hesitate, then answer it.

'Hello.'

'Is that Mr Blackett?' The voice is hard and unfriendly.

'Yes, can I help?'

'It's Bruce Tentacle here from the Department.' (Not his real name, obviously). My heart sinks.

There are some really nice people working in 'Sgurpid', as the Scottish Government Rural Payments and Inspections Division is known. Many of them are part-time farmers and farmers' wives, earning some extra cash to supplement the dwindling income from the farm – now pushed to the hours of darkness – and holding out for the promise of a gold-plated public sector pension by working 'on the dark side'. They generally share my sense of humour and can be relied upon to empathise.

But this man doesn't sound like one of them. The tone of his voice has an institutionalised edge to it that implies putting loyalty to the Big State before human considerations. It also implies that he doesn't like the cut of my jib.

'Oh. Hi Bruce, it's Jamie here. What can I do for you?'

'I'm ringing about your greening map. A check has picked up that it isn't compliant, and we need you to resubmit it before we can process your claim.'

'But I came in yesterday and went through it with your colleague. She said it was fine.' The helpful girl had rung me to say that I needed to come in and sign said map. It had been a thirty-mile round trip and an hour and

– 67 –

a half out of my day, but it had seemed worth it, as I had come away with an assurance that the subsidy payment – now five months overdue – would soon be paid. Now this. One step forward, two back.

'She wasn't authorised to say that.'

The offending map refers to last year's areas left fallow to qualify for our subsidy, under the dubious belief by the instigators of the system that strips of bare stubble from the previous year act as a haven for wildlife. The map no longer serves any practical purpose, as these fields have now been ploughed up and sown with the next crop, so they can no longer be inspected. Moreover, the areas in question were measured by an agricultural officer anyhow.

'Well, I hope it hasn't got her into any trouble, as she was very helpful.'

He sounds miffed at her collaboration. 'She shouldn't have said what she did.'

I try a different tack.

'I submitted that map last May. Why have you waited a year to tell me this?'

'Well, we are where we are.' He is sulky now, and I am pushing my luck.

'It's really not going to make any difference now, is it? I mean, we are into a whole new cropping pattern.'

As I say it, I know it is pointless, and there is little chance that I might be able to sway him. He is Binary Man, all noughts and ones; there is no two to nine in his world, no willowy sevens or corpulent eights. He is an apparatchik of the bureaucratic state, motivated by a burning desire to ensure that boxes are ticked. I imagine him as being a recent graduate of an agricultural course, probably not much older than my son, unable to get a job in farming, and now a zealot with an animus to control farmers if he can't be one himself.

'No, you still have to submit a new map.'

'What was wrong with it anyway?'

'It doesn't qualify as a map.'

I shouldn't, mustn't lose my temper, but he is getting to me.

'Don't be absurd. When is a map not a map?'

'I'll ask you not to raise your voice. I am only doing my job.'

I can feel myself getting flushed with rage and despair. I hate receiving subsidies and I feel embarrassed to be reliant on state handouts, but the corollary of growing artificially cheap food is taking the EU shilling.

'I am sorry. But this is doing my head in. I am owed nearly a hundred thousand pounds by the department, which should have been paid in December. It is now May. My overdraft is at its limit and I can't pay any bills until you pay me. The person to whom I handed it said it was fine when I submitted the map last May. Julie said it was fine yesterday and now you are telling me a map is not a map.'

'Well, if you had submitted the map correctly, you wouldn't be in this position.'

Take a deep breath and count to ten. 'OK, so please explain where I went wrong.'

'You marked areas as fallow, when they were in fact margins.'

'But they were margins that had been left fallow.' I can't believe we are having this conversation.

'Yes, but that was incorrect.' He is speaking slowly now and stressing the words. 'If you had followed the instructions correctly, you would have shown the area you allege was fallow as fallow and the other areas as margins.'

My mind is wandering now. I tell myself that right across Britain there are crops ripening or not, cattle and sheep thriving or not, farming businesses making either profits or losses, and they would go on doing so whether we had Tentacle and his forms and maps and inspections or not. We are farming despite him, not because of him, and he is a burden to be carried like liver fluke or potato blight.

'Oh, for goodness sake, this is ridiculous. What do you mean, "alleged areas", those areas were even inspected.'

'Well, we don't know that they were there, until we see them on your maps.'

'Look, there wasn't even a requirement to have the maps in the original instructions.'

I have them open in front of me and I am searching frantically for the right bit. What is it about me that I can read J.L. Carr or William Trevor, and pick up nuances and appreciate allegory, and breathe in the atmosphere from the prose. But if I sit in front of a bureaucratic instruction that is telling me what I must do and how I must do it, and the penalties for non-compliance, then the words swim on the page like a shoal of translucent fish – now you see them, now you don't – and I find it hard to extract any meaning at all.

At last. I find it. Sure enough, the requirement for maps is gold plating, added recently.

'Here it is on page twelve. So, what you are asking me to do is retrospective regulation.'

This angers him. 'No. Don't put words in my mouth.'

'OK, this isn't getting us anywhere. I'll amend the map, if that is what you want.'

'I suggest you do.'

As I put the telephone down, I feel an absurd impulse to burst into tears, and I realise that I am shaking uncontrollably with rage and stress, and impotence.

This incident was real and the conversation as I remember it. Only the name has been changed. Probably every farmer in Britain has similar stories to tell of being held captive by a global subsidy system that forces them to lose money farming, so that they rely on the largesse of the EU to keep them going; of the lunatic bureaucracy that flows down from Brussels, gathering momentum all the way to the local Area Office.

There is a deep cultural divide between farmers and agricultural officers. Sometimes it feels like being the manager of one of Stalin's collective farms, terrified that the local commissar will find fault. It is a matter of perceptions and priorities. If a sociologist showed the two groups the same piece of paper, the farmers would see RURAL PAYMENTS AND INSPECTIONS DIVISION and the civil servants would see RURAL PAYMENTS AND INSPECTIONS DIVISION.

It is in some ways similar to the relationship between soldiers in trenches and staff officers in headquarters behind the lines, of Blackadders and Darlings. Except that the Army insists that officers spend equal lengths of time in both roles during their careers. It was always drummed into us that any orders we produced would be read by some poor sod in the bottom of a trench, in the dark, with a pencil torch during a thunderstorm. This was understood, as we had all been that poor sod.

I am discovering that the same understanding does not exist in other areas of the public sector.

The foreshore falls silent in summer. The curlews and the geese are a distant memory and the few remaining oyster catchers are spread more thinly. We notice the gulls more as a result. The silence is punctuated by weird and wonderful noises from the shore, the deep *ga-ag-ag-ag* of a great black-backed being disturbed, or the herring gulls wailing and clucking, or the shrill *kyau* of its smaller cousin, the common gull. Collectively they seem able to express the full range of human emotions better than any other genus of bird. Walking along the tideline in the afternoon sun, with barely a ripple across the Solway and only the gentle lap of the tide, their happy mewing sounds complement the tender cooing of the pigeons in the woods along the shore, and complete my absolute contentment.

It is hard to comprehend that they are the same species that I see squabbling raucously over the rubbish bins in the town. Is there something about the urban condition that changes the way both birds and humans behave?

Spring and summer bring grass fever. Worry about whether the beasts have enough to eat is all consuming. The blether with neighbours is always, 'Have you any grass yet?' I agonise over when to put the nitrogen on. Too early, before there is enough warmth in the soil, and it will be wasted and leach out. Too late, and we will have lost some of the potential from our precious growing season. Then suddenly grass comes like the swallows, in fact there is no coincidence, as the swallows also seem to know to return when there is enough heat to bring the insects out of the ground along with the grass.

For a few weeks, I gaze complacently at happy cattle munching away at a thick sward that is neither too long nor too short. Then, about the middle of June, there is worry about whether it is 'getting away from them'. The grass in some fields starts to look stemmy and put on heads. Then there is nothing for it but to get the topper out and cut it, otherwise it will stop growing and the cattle don't like eating the stems, preferring the leaf blades.

There are whole books written on grassland management, another one of those farming disciplines that one never stops learning. Right now, paddock grazing is all the rage. Developed in the New Zealand dairy industry, it involves grazing small areas of grass very intensively with lots of cattle for a short time, using electric fences. You graze the sward down from 10 cm to 4 cm, then move on to the next bit and let it recover, well-fertilised by all their muck. It mimics nature, as that is what the great herds of herbivores did on the Great Plains before man either domesticated them, or hunted them close to extinction. And you have very much more grass as a result.

We are trying to do this with the young stock but it is not so easy with the suckler cows with their calves, as it would be very tricky, and possibly dangerous, handling them in large groups, and the small calves would get under the electric fences and cause chaos.

Six fields are 'shut up' for silage and they cause grass fever of a different type. The grass that needs to be conserved for the winter will provide the fat on our backs to get us through to next year. I glance anxiously at it every time I pass. It is always very hard to tell how much there is. It seems high enough, but is it thick in the bottom? Once it starts shooting, there are urgent calls to the contractors to see when they can come and cut it.

Driving everything is the weather. In a dry year, we become like Australian farmers and the chat is all, 'Have you had rain?'

'Yes, good rain.'

Or, 'No, not enough to lay the dust.'

Forecasts will be pored over anxiously, and news of any anticipated rain will be passed on, traditionally with the rider, 'As long as it knows when to stop.'

We can afford to relax in a dry time, but when the weather gets 'catchy', and the contractors need to grab every opportunity to get on, tempers get short. There is nothing worse than hearing the contractors cutting a neighbour's grass, knowing there is a week of wet weather ahead and our silage crop will be sitting there, shot, unable to grow anymore; losing quality and wasting days of growing season, sodden and needing days to dry out before it will be fit to cut. My mood is not helped by the knowledge that the disappearance of a 'barbecue summer' normally hits the price of beef.

The convention in these parts is for the dairy farmers to go first. Finally, it is our turn and Neil the contractor rings to say that they can make a start if I want to risk it, otherwise they will go elsewhere. We look at the forecasts and check the dryness of the grass crop, scanning the sky anxiously for cloud in the west.

'Och, let's knock it down.'

Ten men no longer go and mow meadows, but soon there is what looks like an armoured infantry platoon roaring around the roads. First comes the mower, or to be precise two mowers, as Dougie has them mounted fore and aft on his tractor. Later, once the grass has wilted in the sun for a day, Scott will appear with a rake, a Heath Robinson contraption that rows up the silage. Walking across the first field, I squeeze a handful of grass and it leaves a slight film of water across my palms, perfect.

All goes well, then, rain, a series of deleted expletives as the mower carries on for a minute or two, and then stops. Dougie gives me a questioning look.

'No, I think we'll have to leave it, Doug.'

The cardinal rule is that if the grass is good and dry when it is cut, then it won't matter being rained on, as long as you leave it alone. But there is an anxious time while there is silage lying and the 'showers' – the ones the forecast never told us about – move up the valley towards Dumfries. The silage in rows will have to be 'kicked out' and a day lost until we start again.

The arrival of Keith on the chopper ratchets up the tempo. This is a type of combine harvester with a grass chopper on the front, which picks the long grass up, chops it into little bits and flings it out through a chute. Taking a turn at towing one of three trailers to lead the silage to the pit, I feel like an ant in a titanic struggle to move the colony's food into the winter store. There is a palpable sense of urgency as the tractor in front pulls away and I draw level with the chopper so that he can fill me up on the move.

All the time the chopper is here, my ears are tuned to its steady roar. Any silence may mean that it has hit something – although the fields have been rolled – and a breakdown may lose us more time. For the first time this year, it has a highly sensitive metal detector that stops the blade for any objects in the grass. Embarrassingly, the first couple of stoppages are for empty shotgun cartridges. I must tell all the guns to be more careful about picking them up.

Back at the pit, Joe is on the buck rake, lovingly sculpting a huge mountain of rich, green grass from the loads being tipped at the front. Up and up he goes, so that soon his tractor is higher than the roof of the cattle shed, and I shudder as he goes backwards and forwards at ever steeper angles, rolling the grass in with his tyres. Any air trapped in the silage will cause it to spoil, and in the worst case to heat and even catch fire, and there may be scorched bits when we get to them later in the year.

At last the pit is ready to sheet, and Davie takes the lead in rolling out the black plastic sheeting to his satisfaction. He is the one who will be spending all winter unwrapping the pit and feeding the silage. At that height there is often a breeze, and on a windy day it takes three of us to stop the sheet filling like a great sail and taking off.

The team, who have been isolated on their tractors all day, now have a chance for a bit of banter as we throw the tyres on the sheet. The tyres have a fetid smell all their own of old rubber and stinking water, which splashes out as they get thrown on. A drop catches me on the lip and I spit to rid myself of it, then think that I feel my glands swelling as they combat the bacteria. The tyres seem to get heavier as we go on, and the banter subsides and the heads go down, as we push on before dark; until at last the job is done, and we sit around drinking cold beer from the can, in a harvest ritual that stretches back to the days when ten men did go to mow a meadow.

Standing on top of the pit after the second cut, looking across fields full of cows and rapidly growing calves, is one of the high points of the year. The giant loaf of silage beneath my feet will give anxiety as we eat our way through it later in the year, but for now it is like standing on a gigantic pile of gold coins.

✣ ✣ ✣ ✣

Coming back into the kitchen for breakfast, Sheri is hard at work on her part of the business, the Bed and Breakfast.

'How's it going?'

She raises her eyebrows. 'One wants boiled eggs, one wants fried, one wants poached and one wants scrambled. Can you do the scrambled?' She hands me the egg box.

It was Sheri's idea to do B&B in the House on the Shore. When we were doing our initial sums, trying to work out how we could possibly afford to live here, we had thought that perhaps we should let one wing, as had been done in the past. But we did not want anyone living on top of us if avoidable, and so Sheri nobly said that she would do B&B to help make ends meet and justify having the whole house to ourselves.

So we re-invented ourselves as Carson and Mrs Hughes, or Basil and Sybil if you must. I had been sceptical at first, but have come to appreciate the added dimension that it has brought. It helps to validate our lives here and stops us being complacent or worse, sorry for ourselves, when guests arrive from far-off walks of life and marvel at the quiet and the views and the birdsong, and it reminds us of how lucky we are.

The guests have with very few exceptions been a genuine pleasure to have to stay and we have become friends with several who have become regulars. They all seem to have a story to tell, and it has been interesting to gain a window into other people's lives. Many of them have been knowledgeable birdwatchers and we have learnt more about our own birds from talking to them.

It has not been without its moments. When we set it up, we put thought into tea trays in the rooms, breakfast menus and so on. The laundry was offering hotel-style, fluffy dressing-gowns, and we decided that these would be a nice touch. Not long after, a couple from Cheshire stayed for their silver wedding anniversary. I was just going into the drawing-room to throw a log onto the fire when I saw out of the corner of my eye the couple in their fluffy dressing gowns in intermediate foreplay on the sofa. I beat a hasty retreat; I'm sure Carson would have handled it much better. We decided that, on balance, we could dispense with the fluffy dressing-gowns after that.

I had a naïve idea that the Big State would applaud our enterprise as a business start-up. In fact, it just wanted to meddle. First the Licensing Authority telephoned.

'I am phoning, because we have reason to believe you may be selling alcohol illegally and to tell you that you must apply for a licence.'

In fact, we had decided to keep things simple and told guests to bring their own drink if they wanted it. I saw the funny side of the call, but this gave way to a quiet fury at the effrontery.

'How dare you accuse me of breaking the law. You can't possibly have any evidence, because we haven't.'

Rapid retreat and change of tone,

'Oh, I'm very sorry, I just thought you might be needing to serve drink for your hunting and shooting parties. At least you'll ken the noo, like.'

Next the fire brigade paid us a visit, when not one but two senior fire officers turned up unexpectedly. Why is it that everything gets doubled up in the public sector? They announced with Orwellian understatement that they were here on an 'advisory visit', apparently they had 'been told to target big hooses.' Proudly I showed them our hard-wired smoke alarms, our annually inspected fire extinguishers, my written risk assessments, and the fire notices in the bedrooms. But these only brought forward teeth-sucking and head-shaking.

'No, we are going to require fire doors everywhere and you will have to box in those staircases (times two), and you will need emergency lighting and sprinklers everywhere. And I think ...'

He paused for effect.

'There will have to be a steel fire escape on the exterior of the building.'

They quoted new legislation passed in the Scottish Parliament that meant that 'big hooses' had to go above and beyond the regulations required of average-sized B&Bs.

We were aghast. Sheri's chin was jutting at a dangerous angle and there was a burning flame in her eyes. That is a bad sign that could mean extreme violence, a bit like a cow pawing the ground.

'But we are only letting two bedrooms.'

'And we are not even doing it that often.'

'How come it is okay to put our own children and guests in those bedrooms, but not bed and breakfasters?'

The matter was quietly resolved when our MSP[20] spoke to the Chief Fire Officer on our behalf, and it was agreed that the regulations were not being applied with the appropriate sense of proportion.

Both these attempts by officialdom to hamstring us left a bad taste. Friends reported similar incidents. It became apparent that the Big State employs staff to search websites for any private enterprise that might yield 'jobs for the boys'. It was also alleged that the established hotels – which did have the full suite of fire escapes and the like – were miffed

---

20 The late, great and much missed Sir Alex Fergusson MSP.

by private householders muscling in on the hospitality trade, and were stirring officialdom to act. I had some sympathy for them, but it was a clear example of vested interests trying to use regulations as barriers to entry.

Ten years on and Airbnb and the like have turned nearly every house in the district into a B&B, and the Big Statists seem to have shrugged their shoulders and given up worrying about it.

✤ ✤ ✤ ✤

Geoff and Jean are here to monitor the barn owls and the swallows. Two fanatical bird lovers, I hope they will forgive me for saying that Geoff looks not unlike a barn owl with his full grey beard. And Jean has the diminutive physique of a swallow.

Despite having five owl boxes around the estate, it has not been good news on the barn-owl front since the severe winters at the beginning of the decade, when there was snow lying for weeks and we found dead barn owls, starved by their inability to find voles under the snow; pathetic objects like children's dolls found in the rubble after the Blitz.

But this time I am excited to be able to tell them that they are back, we have heard them screeching at night, and sometimes seen their ghostly shapes overhead. I have found pellets under one of the boxes. And sure enough, when we go to look, two juvenile barn owls fly out. With luck they may nest next year.

The swallows are hanging on here but only just. We have several broods this summer, including one in the garage, and they perch every night on a set of antlers on the wall. Jean rings the young birds in the nest and I wonder where they will end up. I am astonished to learn that swallows from Galloway have been found in the Eastern Transvaal. I find this humbling.

* CHAPTER SIX *

SUMMER IS also the start of the shoot cycle. Frantic preparations precede the arrival of the pheasant poults, as I know from previous experience that the only warning likely is a text to say that the game farmer is on his way. The release pen is in a three-acre patch of jungle that was once an orchard. We fight our way in and strim a narrow winding path around it for taking feed and water. The path is the only open space, and if we make it too wide or too straight, the raptors will be able to pick them off one by one. The areas that might harbour disease from the previous season have been limed to kill any pathogens. Water drinkers are filled and pellets are put in the hoppers, so that they learn to feed themselves, and don't come to rely on humans and become tame.

They take to their new surroundings straight away, and the air is filled with cheeping and the cloying smell of pheasant muck. After a few days, they run and hide under the bushes when I approach, and they are truly naturalised. It is pheasant heaven in there with plenty of insects for them to vary their diet, and there will be blackberries in a few weeks, which will turn their droppings purple. Soon there are signs of dust baths everywhere.

Pheasants go through a particularly ugly adolescent phase, as they moult and the cocks start to gain their adult plumage. Seeing them pecking about in the summer sun and pondering what lies ahead for them, I feel a twinge of guilt, as if I am the Donald Sutherland character in *The Hunger Games* viewing the new contestants. But no one can say they are not contented. And compared with the millions of chickens in broiler units around the world, who will be killed after fifty-six days without ever experiencing freedom, they are lucky.

Their odds are not bad either. They will have two hundred happy days roaming the estate between now and the end of the shooting season, and six days on which they might have to run the gauntlet of flying over the guns. About one in five of them will live to breed next spring, and some will live until they are four or five years old.

The combination of wet summers recently and 'the untouchables' means that we would have very few wild pheasants. This way it keeps a good-sized population going, but not so many that it starts to impact on all the other flora and fauna. We stopped releasing pheasants for a few years, when the school fees forced us to tighten our belts, and the woods fell strangely silent and I missed them. It is good to have them back adorning the estate, especially the cocks preening themselves in the fields, panjandrums in Chinese silk dressing gowns.

The lotus eaters are here, and they have just about cleaned us out of lotus. They do this by night, so that in the morning there is a trail of lotus skins around the house, empty bottles and cans, overflowing ashtrays, half-eaten slices of pizza and other signs of student life. They sleep by day and when Sheri and I catch glimpses of them in late afternoon and early evening, the only times of day baby-boomers ever seem to meet millennials, we learn about university.

Neither of us has been, unless you count Sheri's physio training at Guy's Hospital, or my time at Sandhurst and later an MBA, grabbed on my way out of the Army in a desperate attempt to be employable. Picking up fag ends, metaphorically as well as literally, we learn a new language from Oliver and Rosie and about twenty of their closest friends, who seem to have decided that our house is a congenial place to spend part of the summer holidays, which unbelievably stretch from early June to October.

I am indulging in a growing middle-aged crustiness here – memo to self, it's not a good look – but it feels wonderful to be parents again after months of being empty nesters.

Sick is an adjective that has replaced cool and has nothing to do with maladies. I suppose the generations above us thought that cool should correctly be applied to a state of temperature. We learn what a Beanock is, as in, 'Yeah, Chris is a Beanock.'

'Really? Is that good or bad?'

'B.N.O.C., Dad, stands for big name on campus.'

'Ah, I'm glad you have cleared that up.'

'Whatever.'

They intersperse their sentences with the word 'like'.

'So, I was like coming back from the library, when ...'

'Hang on, darling, I don't quite understand. Were you actually coming back from the library, or were you on some parallel journey that was similar to the one back from the library?'

Withering look. 'Funneee, Dad.'

If you ask one of them a question, they start the responding sentence with the word 'so', as if patiently teaching a retarded child.

Their dress sense appears post-modernist. Gone are the generational statements of drainpipes or flares, replaced by an anonymous blur of hoodies and trainers. I have yet to meet a young fogey of the children's generation in cords and brogues, which speaks well of their self-confidence. Differentiation among young males now seems to be achieved with their hair.

Geordie is a surf dude and has a pre-Raphaelite 'mun' growing out of the back of his head. The others have a variety of hair styles with no discernible trend. Their cheeks display every pogno-option from clean shaven to Old Testament prophet. I notice that moustaches are definitely out; perhaps Freddie Mercury saw to that. Girls on the other hand have uniformly flickable 'Kate' flowing locks.

They seem permanently linked through their iPhones to Phoebe in Thailand and Archie surfing in Cornwall, and I feel a pang of envy when I think of the school friends I lost touch with before the digital age. Their musical tastes are anodyne: Ed Sheeran and Newton Faulkner, hardly the stuff of the Clash and the Sex Pistols. Far from being like my dad – 'Turn that rubbish off!' – I like what they listen to.

The other striking thing about them is how left-wing they are compared to their 'Thatcher's children' parents, and their sympathies with Corbynism. I do not think any of them are die-hard Corbynistas, but they certainly seem to think that 'he has a point', and he seems to have taken over from Che Guevara as a rather unlikely hero of the young, in a string vest.

My friend, 'The New Statesman', rang me a couple of years ago with a wizard wheeze. 'Pay three quid to be a member of the Labour Party and you can vote in the leadership election. I've voted for Corbyn, that'll fix them!' And he gave one of his great gurgling chuckles normally reserved for filthy jokes and extreme *schadenfreude*. It seemed on the face of it a good investment, better than buying the Conservative Association raffle tickets sitting unopened in their envelope on the kitchen table. I started Googling the Labour Party, then something inside me said, 'Be careful what you wish for.'

As I write in 2018, the Left seems hopelessly split, but after Jezza nearly pulled off the election surprise of the century, and caused Theresa May to throw away the majority she needed for negotiating Brexit, it doesn't seem to have gone quite according to plan. In fact, it could still be as big a cock-up as the Germans putting Lenin on a train to St Petersburg to undermine the Russian war effort.

You have to hand it to Corbyn. He has connected brilliantly with the urban classes disillusioned with the old politics and left behind by globalisation. If I had lived in the Grenfell Tower, I have no doubt that I would be a Corbynista.

He acts as a powerful conscience for the nation and is good at pointing out what is wrong. It is his last-century remedies that I find chilling. I had read with silent disbelief that Corbyn and John McDonnell had been sworn in as privy councillors, without making the customary gesture of loyalty to the Crown by kissing hands. My understanding of the British constitution is that opposition front-bench MPs are given this honour, so that they can be 'privy' to certain state secrets that might not be discussed on the floor of the House of Commons, in order to enable them to do their job of scrutinising British strategy.

I had always assumed that before this happened they would be positively vetted by the security services, in the same way as servicemen and civil servants are, so that they are not a risk to national security, or to agents in the field. I remember my own vetting. A retired police officer quizzed several of my friends about my political allegiances, my finances, my drinking habits, my sex life – pretty well everything about me, in fact – and then gave me a grilling.

'Any links with Irish republicans? No, good. What about your sex life? Girlfriends?' Nod of approval, little dry cough, 'Any kinky stuff, threesomes that sort of thing? No?' Tick.

I would love to have been a fly on the wall if Corbyn and McDonnell had the same interviews.

'Have you ever had any links with potential British enemies, terrorist organisations, that sort of thing?'

'My friendship with the IRA, the PLO, Hezbollah and Hamas is on record and I have also made my support for Fidel Castro and Colonel Gaddafi known. I think that's about it, unless you count my sympathising with the Argentine Military Junta in the Falklands War and the excellent capitalist dictator Vladimir Putin in the new Cold War.'

To my generation, brought up reading *1984* and *Animal Farm*, learning at school about Stalin's show trials and famines and the Gulag, remembering the chaos of the seventies, and soldiering in the last decade of the Cold War, it seems surreal.

It feels especially odd in this house, where I first learnt about communism from my grandfather and his friend Charles. It seemed an unlikely friendship, Gaffer, the archetypal patrician and Charles (I'm sure he was probably Charlie on the shop floor), a retired trade-union official. They had become firm friends in the shadowy world of counter-extremism as fellow Directors of Common Cause, an organisation set up after the war to counter communist infiltration of the trades unions.

Their stories seemed to come straight out of a John le Carré novel, of running multiple candidates in leadership ballots who happened to share the same name as the Marxist runner, or the radical move for those days of putting together a freelance, non-union television crew to broadcast a documentary about communist infiltration.

I must have been ten or eleven when Charles gave me my first lesson in political theory.

'You see, Jamie, I am not a capitalist like your grandfather. I am a labour man and I came up through the ranks of the trade union movement thinking that socialism was the best way of improving the lot of my people, the workers. Many of my colleagues became communists, but I believe passionately that communism is the one thing you should never support. Do you know why?'

I shook my head.

'It's because if you vote Conservative or Labour, you can change your mind after five years and vote for a change of government. But if you vote in Communism, it is the last vote you will ever make.'

✤ ✤ ✤ ✤

'Come and look. I think it's an egret!'

Sheri is beckoning me in a high state of excitement and sure enough, there, on the beach below the house, is an egret. I have seen them often enough before on my travels, feeding in the paddy fields and duck farms of Hong Kong's New Territories, or accompanying the buffalo on their stately procession to drink on the shores of Lake Kariba. Recently, we had been absorbed watching them feeding their young in their treetop nests in a Cuban swamp, but never here, outside our kitchen window.

The egret pokes about in the shallows in the heron's usual spot, where the oncoming tide has created a pool in the delta of the burn, and it looks unconcerned and accustomed to its new surroundings. It is alone and I wonder how the poor thing has been blown here away from its own kin. Further research reveals that they are moving north across the UK and are now quite common in the south of England. Who knew? Perhaps this one is here on reconnaissance duties.

Is it evidence of global warming? Maybe, but I get a strong sense that it has been here before, when the fossilised coral on the rocks was bright with colour and patrolled by zebra fish and sharks. Perhaps, when the Romans were growing vines along the Wall across the water to our east, egrets were a common sight on the Solway. What goes around comes around and I am pleased to see him (or her?) anyway.

✢ ✢ ✢ ✢

The biggest event of the year here is the harvest. I was pleased to read the other day that in financial terms it is still the biggest annual event on the planet, despite some people believing that farming no longer matters. Although it lasts from mid-July through sometimes until October or later, it casts light or shade onto all the other months of the year. Its twin factors, price and yield, follow parabolas of optimism, doubt, uncertainty, anxiety, hubris, triumph, dismay, self-congratulation and self-delusion in my mind through the year.

The farming press makes helpful predictions based on imperfect information about supply and demand in global markets. News that Australian farmers are suffering another drought, or Canadian farmers are pessimistic about 'winter kill' of wheat by frost on the prairies, brings sympathy with our fellow farmers, but also – and I am embarrassed to admit this, but it is true – a little *schadenfreude*. A little bit of arable farmer in me thinks maybe that will sharpen up the price of wheat a bit.

Conversely, a little bit of livestock farmer in me views it pessimistically, thinking that cattle feed will be a 'whoor of a price this back end'. The trick, I have learnt in time, is to try to be both a barley baron and a cattle man, so that the one cancels the other out: 'up corn down horn and up horn, down corn'.

The other trick is to hedge one's bets through the year by selling forward. Growing corn buys one a seat in the great casino that is the global grain market. The world price of wheat is fixed by the Chicago Board of Trade. Information about actual and projected supply and demand is processed by some of the world's quickest minds and the price finds its level by their decisions to buy or sell, not just the physical commodity, but also the much larger derivatives, the futures and options sought by farmers, flour mills and compounders, and gamblers. When the price is heading in an unhelpful direction, farmers tend to blame the men in red braces, forgetting that it is also the commodity dealers who send it in the opposite direction.

Underpinning this never-ending conversation in my head is a shaky understanding of economics. Farmers keep going on growing food, despite ample evidence that they are often working for less than the minimum wage, because they hold as an article of faith the theories of the Reverend Thomas Malthus,[21] known in some quarters as Malthus the Bastard. Malthus argued that, 'The power of population is indefinitely greater than the power in the earth to produce subsistence for man.' In other words, the world's population will grow to the point where eventually we will all run out of food.

Over two centuries later, his thinking still influences morale-boosting articles in the farming press that start, 'With an extra two billion mouths to feed by 2050, food prices are predicted to rise ...' This optimistic theory, together with Mark Twain's observation that you should 'buy land, they ain't making it any more', have underpinned the price of agricultural land, which sometimes seems to behave with the irrational exuberance of shares in internet businesses that have never turned a profit, and for the same reasons: triumph of hope over experience, and the gleam of distant rewards on the horizon. Malthus is also a popular theorist with farmers, as he supported protectionism on the grounds of food security. But lately there has been talk of food surpluses again and doubts have been cast about demand outstripping supply.

Wanting to know more, I seek out Matt Ridley for an expert and unbiased view. Matt is a rare bird, an elected hereditary peer, landowner, farmer and pillar of the establishment on the one hand but, on the other hand, one who fully justifies an hereditary element in the House of Lords by cutting the mustard as a columnist for *The Times*, bestselling author, leading academic in the field of biology, and especially conservationist. My

---

21 *An Essay on the Principle of Population*, 1798.

guess is that he contributes more practical knowledge to the scrutiny of legislation than most of the passed-over politicians in the place. I find him at Blagdon, his family home in Northumberland.

'Can we walk and talk?' he asks, pulling on some boots and whistling for his dogs. He is eager to show me the wildflower meadow he has planted on a former open-cast coalmine. He is a passionate observer of nature, a latter-day Gilbert White, and I struggle to follow his train of thought as he leaps to a description of how the buffish mining bee is parasitised by the nomad cuckoo bee. On our walk, we hear a curlew, and see a peewit[22] putting on a frantic diversionary act near her nest.

'It's that corbie[23] over there. We need more Larsen traps.'

A keen shooting man, he is dismissive of the *faux* conservation arguments circling around field sports.

'Conservationists should wear boots, not suits,' he says, poking around in the sward to find some yellow rattle.

He is another farmer who has also picked up his pen to supplement his income from the land.

'Did estates like this ever make money, do you think?' he grins, with raised eyebrows.

I ask him what he thinks the future holds for food production. I know that Matt has been quoted recently as a counter-Malthusian. Are farmers going to reap the rewards from a rising population?

'No. Malthus is the dog that never barks. We have doubled the population of the world in my lifetime and trebled food production on the same acreage.'

But can we keep doing that?

'Realistically we are going to need fifty per cent more food by 2050 and we are roughly on course. When Africa gets the same level of fertiliser as Asia, there will be a big increase in production.'

But, I persist, surely our crop yields are flat-lining?

---

22 Lapwing.

23 Carrion crow.

'They are only flat-lining because in recent years it hasn't been worth putting as much fertiliser on due to the price. Also, we haven't been embracing new technologies. We need GM.' His eyes gleam with passion. 'Genetic modification gets us off chemicals. This is the mistake the environmental lobby in Europe is making. We cannot do without high-yield agriculture. There is a choice to be made over land sharing or land sparing. I believe land sparing for nature is the way to go; growing an acre of food intensively there, allows us to re-wild an acre over there.'

I nod thoughtfully, absorbing these big ideas, as he leaps sideways into a counterintuitive view of global warming.

'The really exciting thing is the extra CO_2 in the atmosphere. Global warming brings parts of Canada and Russia back into play agriculturally. But more importantly, CO_2 has a fertilisation effect, and with more CO_2 you need less water. It is the reason they pump CO_2 into Dutch greenhouses to produce more tomatoes. Satellite data shows the planet greening as a result. The Leaf Area Index is fourteen per cent more than thirty years ago. That is a green continent the size of North America. I think we are ignoring the beneficial effects of climate change. I am a 'lukewarmer', I believe it is happening, but not at a rate that we need to get so worried about. Sea levels rising at one foot per century we can handle. It is sucking all the oxygen out of more important environmental issues and leading us to make bad decisions, like putting cladding on the Grenfell Tower, for example.'

Matt's advice to the government's Brexit Committee is that British farmers cannot rely on rising commodity prices to bail them out if subsidies are removed. I guess we are going to have to keep muddling on. So, Malthus is an old fraud after all. Bastard.

But then I wonder about everything else that farmers produce. In Malthus's day, all our fuel and fibre for clothing was grown on the land. He could not have known that the petrochemical industry would largely replace that.

Tentatively, I ask Matt what would happen if we got rid of plastics and man-made fibres and embraced biofuels.

'When we produced all our own fuel and fibre on the land, every square inch was used, with pigs in woods and so on. No, I don't think we could do it now and if we did, we would have to destroy all the wildlife to do it. We would have to farm right to the edges.'

Maybe that is where the argument will go in the twenty-first century and farmers will see the greens – genuine lime greens as opposed to watermelons[24] – as our friends, while we campaign together to rid the world of plastic, and try to stay in business by growing non-food crops.

✟ ✟ ✟ ✟

Living on the shore here, I feel connected to the earliest millennia on earth, as the planet's history is laid bare on the fossil beds in front of the house. The fossils reveal that we were once on a coral reef close to the equator and looking along the shore where the woods come down to the sea, it does look like a jungle fringe on a sunny day. It transpires that Scotland and England were once on different continents, but please don't tell Nicola Sturgeon, and the Solway that divides us from Silloth only nine miles away is what remains of the Iapetus Ocean.

You can see from the rock formations where the two continents collided and there are still occasional earth tremors centred on Carlisle. One caused a great crack in my parents' bedroom ceiling years ago, which caused lots of ribald comments. It is strangely comforting to know that I am only a microscopic piece of life in an infinite progression, rather like looking at the stars, and I might as well try to make the best of it, before sliding back into the mud and becoming a fossil like the ones on the beach.

The other thing about shore living is the litter. I don't remember there being much when I was paddling in the rock pools five decades ago, but perhaps there was. Now every tide brings fresh flotsam and jetsam. Plastic

---

24 This distinction was explained to me by a friend who is a Green Party candidate. Limes are green all the way through, watermelons are green on the outside and red on the inside. Unfortunately, the latter predominate.

is one of the great evils of our age and David Attenborough deserves a Nobel Prize for changing public attitudes through his *Blue Planet* series.

On my office wall is a geological map of the estate with all the different layers – Devonian, Pleistocene and so on. I am convinced that in centuries to come there will be a plastic layer. It is shocking when you consider how little previous generations have left behind. Whenever we have hosted archaeological digs here, they have uncovered objects made from natural materials, such as clay pipes, metal belt buckles and glass bottles, but not very much, as every object they used was capable of being burnt, recycled, decomposed or returned to natural compounds. Tiny bits of plastic are now mixed inalienably with the crushed shells and small stones in the shingle. They will be there forever.

It is worst after the winter floods. There is sometimes evidence of a lot of safe sex being practised in the Solway towns. And on my litter-picking patrols, I collect bone-shaped strips of thin plastic. Ridding our seas of these is going to be a challenge for the advertising agencies. I am sorry to draw attention to this, but we are going to have to address it as, after all, these products are always being advertised on prime-time television.

Henceforth, instead of seeing girls diving into water, we are going to need to see ads of girls walking past swimming pools, saying, 'No, I am not swimming this weekend, I want to save the whales.'

✦ CHAPTER SEVEN ✦

ANDREW COOK arrived at the Kennels accompanied not only by horses and hounds, but also by a menagerie of snappy terriers, a lurcher, several sheep and two miniature goats. The latter two species were 'to help make the young hounds steady with sheep and deer'. By 'rating' (disciplining) any hound who showed an interest in either Larry the Lamb, an enormous wedder,[25] or the two goats who had the run of the yard, Andrew trained them so that they could be taken through fields of sheep with confidence that they would not chase them.

The importance of having hounds that are trustworthy with sheep cannot be overstated. We were promoting ourselves to farmers as a service to help them control foxes, and any lapse would have been round the two counties in minutes and had us grounded. There is often an assumption that foxhounds chase foxes, because that is what they are bred to do. In fact, like any other canine, young hounds will chase anything that gets up in front of them, until it is schooled out of them. A huntsman's skill is in 'entering' the young hounds to fox and fox only. It is an extraordinary achievement.

My own attempts at dog training have been less than successful by comparison. They reached their nadir with a black Labrador bitch named Beetle. We were still living in the smallholding we had bought at the foot of Wensleydale in Yorkshire, with an old barn in the middle of it that, with Sheri's gift for doing up houses, we had converted into a happy home. The surrounding fields were covered in our grazing tenant's sheep.

When Beetle was still a puppy, I went through the textbook training and took her out on a choke lead through the fields, giving it a yank every time she showed any interest in them, and saying 'No' in my best Barbara Wodehouse voice. We scolded her and grabbed her by the scruff of the neck and shook her when she showed signs of chasing them. Things

---

25 Castrated male sheep.

proceeded smoothly, and Beetle seemed to have got the message, so that she and our terrier, Squiggle, roamed about outside without any problem. Then one day Sheri came rushing back to the house screaming, 'Quickly, run, Beetle has got a sheep by the throat.'

I ran in panic and, seizing her by the jaws, prised her off the ewe and pulled her away. But she was mad with blood in her mouth and nose, and in a frenzy she escaped me and locked on again. We battled once more and eventually I managed to wrestle her off and, shaking with fright and shock, manhandled her back to the house. Our beloved pet, the apple of my children's eyes, had turned into a wolf.

The sheep was beyond salvation, so I put her out of her misery as soon as I had locked Beetle away. In shame and sorrow, I got my chequebook out and went to see its owner, Frank Thornton, another important farming mentor in my life. He was very nice about it, saying, 'Don't worry, there was one in there that looked a bit boogered, that's probably how the dog got it.'

But we both knew what had to be done. You can't have a dog that isn't safe with sheep in sheep country.

I was in deep depression, and the idea of needing to have her destroyed and of telling the children was more than I could bear. Then I thought some more. I remembered years ago one of my father's yellow Labradors, Bunter, had done the same thing as a youngster. With the farmer's help, we had put a muzzle on him and tied him in a loose box with a couple of tups. They had butted him repeatedly until he was battered and bruised, so that he was always scared of sheep thereafter and we had no more problems. Maybe we could try something similar? It was worth a try to save her. I had read somewhere about shock collars and thought that might have the same effect, in a less brutal way than the traditional method, so I sent off for one.

The shock collar works on the Pavlovian principle. It modifies a dog's behaviour, so that it associates doing something wrong with pain and doesn't do it again. First, the dog gets used to wearing a placebo collar for a few days, so that it doesn't suspect anything. Then you put the real one on and, without letting her realise it is you doing it, you gently turn the electric charge up by remote control until the dog gets a small shock, that gives you your level and you are ready to go.

Then I took her for a walk out in the fields. Beetle immediately saw the sheep and shot off in pursuit. I waited a couple of seconds, then gave her a zap. She gave a little yelp and instantly turned and started running back to me for reassurance. Then she paused as if to say, 'It can't be those daft sheep doing that to me, can it?' and started back towards them. I gave her another zap and that confirmed it in her mind, 'Sheep have developed supernatural powers, I won't ever go near them again.'

She ran back to me and didn't leave my side as we continued our walk past the sheep. She never gave us cause for concern with sheep after that. Nor did she show any ill effects from having had a mild shock. And she never turned into a wolf again and reverted to being a loving pet.

This all came back to me recently, when a spate of dog attacks on livestock has been in the farming press. The Scottish Government is looking at taking action to beef up the law. However, at the same time, under pressure from the animal welfare charities, they are also taking steps to ban shock collars and they have already been banned in Wales.

I can only write about my experiences, but they have led me to an opposite view. Clearly, in the wrong hands, shock collars could be abused to cause animal suffering. But so could bleach, electric irons, kitchen knives, in fact almost any household item you can think of. And I am sure that more use of shock collars could help to prevent the appalling sheep losses suffered on farms every year, and the heartbreak of family pets being destroyed. The Big State should think carefully before coming between a man and his dog.

Dusk. Walking round the cattle sheds in the gloaming, gloating over the fat bulls putting on their final bit of finish before going away, I almost collide with a badger in the passage. We both stop and stare, as if to say to one another, 'You are not supposed to be here.' Then he insolently turns and waddles off slowly, letting me know that he's thinking, okay Jimmy, I am off the noo, but I'll be back.

This one is a scraggy looking specimen with a yellowish hyena-like tinge to his fur. I have a countryman's love–hate relationship with the badger. I love seeing them trundling along at night, for they can be beautiful creatures, and I am pleased that the estate provides a home for several colonies, but as a conservationist I am in no doubt that we have far too many of them to be good for our biodiversity.

Kenneth Grahame had the right idea when he portrayed the stoats and weasels in the wild wood in *The Wind in the Willows*, but then he made the classic error of characterising – anthropomorphising – Badger as a wise and kindly old man, ignoring the fact that he would have scoffed Mole, Ratty and Mr Toad given half a chance.

Beatrix Potter was a proper countrywoman and her portrayal of Tommy Brock is more realistic. She does not pay him the compliment of giving him his own story, instead he comes into *The Tale of Mr Tod* as the thief of Flopsy Bunny's baby rabbits – 'seven of them and all of them twins'. Potter calls him 'very disagreeable ... not nice in his habits. He ate wasp nests and frogs and worms; and he waddled about by moonlight, digging things up.'

The omnivorous badger is the most deadly meso-predator of them all. Nothing except the car kills them, which in practice on our slow estate roads means nothing, and they will eat almost anything. I remember as a child, hearing gloomy prognostications when they became protected in 1973, and much of what was predicted then has come to pass.

The population has exploded and as badgers have increased, so more vulnerable species that were once far more common here – hares, hedgehogs, bumblebees, grass snakes and ground-nesting birds like the lapwing and the corncrake – have declined in a kind of zero-sum game. I have not seen a hedgehog here for years; we used to see their skins like chestnut husks where the badgers had eaten them, but it is a long time since I have seen even one of those. The hedgehog's trick of 'knowing one big thing' and curling up into a ball is effective against foxes, but not against the invincible badger, who will chew through chicken wire or stick his snout into a wasp's nest without taking any harm.

Our opponents would blame 'modern farming practices' and in many parts of the countryside, I would agree with them. But we have farmed here in a much more wildlife friendly way for the last twenty years. We do not cut silage until the hares and grassland birds have had a chance to rear their young, we spray much less and with less-toxic chemicals, we have more winter stubbles and many more hedges. We have woodlands planted with native species of hardwoods, where before they were mainly sitka spruce. We grow fifty acres of wildflowers.

There is certainly no shortage of slugs, the hedgehog's favourite food, as the hostas testify every summer. All things being equal, we should have seen lots of species multiply, but we have not, and it must be folly to assume that the addition of tens, if not hundreds, of extra badgers in the parish has not taken its toll.

I like to think that I do my best to conserve as many species of wildlife here as possible; in fact, it is what motivates me most as a landowner and the thing that gives me most pleasure, but I no longer have the right to exercise 'dominion' over the animal kingdom in the way that my predecessors could. Sometimes it feels like being the police chief in a large crime-ridden city, where the biggest mafia bosses are in league with corrupt politicians, and there is nothing that can be done about 'the untouchables'.

If Beatrix Potter was writing in the Lake District today, she would be unable to draw Mrs Tiggy-Winkle (or for that matter, Squirrel Nutkin), and it is hard to find Kenneth Grahame's Ratty now that the mink has rampaged up and down our rivers, released from fur farms by animal rights fanatics – but at least we can still try to control them. How many more species do we have to lose before we reform our wildlife laws to bring the meso-predators back into balance? Something that Brexit would allow us to do once more, when we are free of European Wildlife Directives.

It is the tragedy of the badger and his victims that he has been 'weaponised' by the Left. He is the ideal species for them to give iconic status. He is nocturnal and unlike the fox never goes near the cities, so he can be portrayed, completely disingenuously, as rare.

He has a sad history of persecution, portrayed in John Clare's famous poem about badger baiting:

> *He falls as dead and kicked by boys and men,*
> *Then starts and grins and drives the crowd again;*
> *Till kicked and torn and beaten out he lies*
> *And leaves his hold and crackles, groans, and dies.*

The Big State correctly took action against such vile abuse, but then, as it so often does, overdid things by giving badgers full protection without considering the unintended consequences for smaller fauna, throwing the baby out with the bath water.

Best of all for the coalition of animal rights campaigners and Big Statists, the badger fits the bill as 'our enemy's enemy is our friend'. Legislating on badgers was another way of harming shooting and getting at foxhunting. As Beatrix Potter correctly identified, 'as he slept in the daytime, he always went to bed in his boots. And the bed which he went to bed in, was generally Mr Tod's.' By making it an offence to tamper with a badger sett, it gave them extra ammunition to use against hunts.

Frequently a fox will go to ground in a hole that on closer examination turns out to be a badger sett. The protocol is then for the terrier man to announce that 'it looks a bit stripy' and withdraw, rather than to use terriers to bolt the fox out and shoot it. A few more foxes living to fight another day is no great problem in itself. What is invidious is that hunt staff are vulnerable to accusations of tampering with badger setts.

The setts themselves are some of the most robust constructions in the countryside. I remember years ago, there was one on the edge of a wheat field. Every year when the field was ploughed, the plough filled in some of the holes, and within twenty-four hours the badgers had cleared them again. Ploughing to a depth of less than a foot would hardly damage the badgers, who sleep several yards below the surface. Yet now if one wanted to plough that same field, one would need to fill in reams of paperwork and make the case to the relevant civil servants for relocating the sett, a highly complicated procedure – which presumably inconveniences the badgers even more – or risk a hefty fine.

A couple of years ago, two policemen arrived at my door. Someone had reported activity at a badger sett down in some woods on the shoreline. I knew just the place. I scratched my head, 'No, I can't think why anyone would be there, and it certainly wasn't us.' The police accepted my answer and went on their way. A few days later, the story came out. A young local girl had been walking her terrier along the shore when it disappeared down a hole, as terriers are apt to do, and her attempts to get the dog out, thankfully successfully, had been witnessed by a fifth columnist who had rung the police, and they had then spent several hours, and no doubt reams of paperwork, investigating it.

✥ ✥ ✥ ✥

There are few vicissitudes of modern life that cannot be put into perspective by a few days on the river bank. Being part of the river, absorbed like the heron with the all-consuming business of catching fish, hypnotised by the sound of the water and in communion with the osprey circling overhead, seems to wash away life's cares.

I have always loved fishing. Early summer holidays were spent with my grandparents on the River Borgie in Sutherland. My grandfather Gaffer had his passion for fishing passed onto him by his own grandfather, who lived on the River Barrow in County Carlow, then one of the best salmon rivers in Ireland. The Borgie had come up for sale during the dark days of the war and Gaffer had asked his commanding officer for leave to go and look at the river with the intention of buying it. Brigadier Holdsworth had agreed on condition that he could come and fish, which he did annually for many years!

The Borgie is a spate river and was little more than a rocky stream when he bought it. It had been part of the Altnaharra Estate, which contains the much larger River Naver, and so there had previously been little incentive to treat it as anything other than somewhere to go when the water was right. But over the next thirty years, Gaffer painstakingly laid out the Borgie as a proper salmon river with the help of his right-hand man, Donald Davidson MM, who had been a sniper in the Lovat Scouts in the war and was employed as water bailiff.

They put in a hatchery and built weirs and created sixty-four named pools. Diggers moved boulders and created holes for salmon to lie in, and oxygen-rich glides. Things could be done easily in those days, if you had the determination. The whole river was in his ownership, so there were no differences of opinion with other riparian owners, and the Big State had not learnt to insinuate itself between a landowner and his river.

Today SEPA and SNH[26] would be all over him like a rash and the paperwork would keep several paper mills turning. Probably some of his improvements would not be allowed now. His passion has had a lasting benefit and the Borgie has been one of the few rivers in Scotland to be very prolific in recent years, although it is sadly no longer owned by my family. A friend of mine was staying recently in a fishing party on the Borgie, and they had toasted all the former owners of the river for looking after it so well, and creating the fun they were having.

Gaffer and my grandmother, Kitty, did up the Old Manse, which they used for holidays, before living there full-time during the summer months in retirement. Their grandchildren all have indelible memories of picnics by the Falls Pool, and on the white sands of some of the loveliest beaches in the whole of Britain. I remember one April standing on the hill above the house, watching skein after skein of geese passing high overhead on their way from the fields at Arbigland – or so I liked to imagine – to their summer breeding grounds in the Arctic Circle.

The Manse was warmed by peat fires, which gave off a wonderful

---

26 Scottish Environmental Agency and Scottish Natural Heritage. The Environment Agency and English Nature perform similar functions in England with equally mixed results.

smell. It is part of a small crofting community and it seemed like going back in time to go up there and see stooks of oats in the fields in the early seventies. With hindsight, it seems very unorthodox to have been put by the side of the road by Granny with the task of stopping the grocer's van. As a four-year-old, it seemed the greatest responsibility I had ever been charged with, but I suspect the van was going to stop anyway.

These days the Scottish Government sometimes likes to portray the owners of rivers as being at loggerheads with communities, but I never remember any disagreement; although there was a fear back in the seventies that the Scottish Nationalist Party would one day be able to enact their previous manifesto commitment to nationalise the rivers, and allow them to be exploited by everyone and cared for by no one, as happens in some other countries.

The bottom stretch of the river was, and still is, public water and my grandfather was always happy to let locals fish higher up, if there were not paying rods staying. And the community was glad of the income that the river created in the strath, especially for the Borgie Lodge Hotel.

My other grandparents lived in the Gade Valley in Hertfordshire and joined a fishing syndicate on the river; largely, I see in retrospect, for my benefit. Other syndicate members included the comedian Eric Morecambe and the wildlife artist Gordon Beningfield, whose books and paintings capture the beauty of that golden corner of England. Sadly, he died before his time and lies next to my grandparents in the little churchyard at Great Gaddesden.

It was a huge treat for a twelve-year-old to be able to sneak along the river bank of that lovely chalk stream, the River Gade, disturbing the coot and once catching a halcyon glimpse of a kingfisher. Looking back, I was probably allowed to break all the rules of dry fly fishing, but catching six trout one glorious summer evening was one of the high spots of my childhood and I was hooked.

Like many people, I have cherished a hope that one day I will spend a happy retirement on the river bank, like one of those old buffers one sees from train windows, casting across a river. But all is not well with the state of salmon fishing in Scotland. Some blame disease spreading from the salmon farms up the west coast, while others say that Russian trawlers are hoovering up the salmon out to sea. Overfishing by estuary netsmen is also blamed on some rivers. Another theory is that global warming is pushing the pelagic fish northwards, so that they compete for food with salmon. Predation by seals, cormorants and other 'untouchables' is another likely factor. Others say that there have been these crashes before and it is part of the natural cycle of rivers, changing from spring runs to autumn runs and back again. Or it may simply be that the abnormally high rainfall in recent years has caused spates to destroy salmon eggs and parr.

It is one of the wonderful mysteries of the *Salmo salar* that no one knows for sure; every river is completely different, and all these factors will affect them to varying degrees. What is certain is that the salmon are disappearing fast from some rivers, to the extent that 'catch and release' is becoming the norm, with all the ethical questions that entails, and one owner lamented to me recently that rather than charging high weekly rents for the fishing, he may have to consider throwing it in for free with the holiday cottages.

At Arbigland, we do not have any freshwater salmon fishing, but we used to have the netting rights in the Nith estuary until we voluntarily gave them up. The stake nets were taken off in the 1890s, but *haaf* netting was still going on here in my boyhood. A haaf net, which is something the Vikings bequeathed the Solway, looks like a football goal and the idea is to stand holding the net until a fish swims into it, when you heave it up and whack the fish on the head with your priest and stick it in your bag.

It was a considerable perk for local farmworkers to be able to have a season ticket for a nominal fee and one fish for the 'big hoose'. The doyen of the haaf netters was the late Gordon Paterson, a bachelor of indeterminate age, who would make his annual visit to pay his dues to my father. The conversation was always the same.

'How are you, Gordon? Have you got yourself a wife yet?'

'No, captain, I'm still taking free samples!'

'And how has the fishing been?'

Then a cloud would pass over Gordon's rubicund features and he would adopt a doleful tone, as if discussing a death in the family: 'Very bad, captain, only just this one I have brought you.'

As a teenager, I would sometimes go out with Chris Rourke, our keeper, and Gordon and the others. I have treasured memories of a hike across the mud in our waders to catch the tide, disturbing the plover and the dunlin on the foreshore, a last smoke before entering the water and forming a line with our nets. Standing up to our waists in numbing seawater – this was before the days of neoprene – as the channel flooded, blethering all the while.

Then the excitement as salmon came like torpedoes into the nets and the splashing and the laughter as we caught hold of them. Finally, a tired trudge back with our haul and a well-deserved pint in The Steamboat, with Gordon holding court through clouds of blue smoke from his special seat in the snug bar, his personal pint mug in hand.

Now the shortage of salmon is even threatening the haaf netting, in those places on the Solway where it still goes on.

⚜ CHAPTER EIGHT ⚜

IT WAS John who first noticed that something was amiss.

'The birds seem very jumpy. I think we might have a hawk.'

Then pheasant corpses were found. Looking in the pen, I see that the birds are reluctant to show themselves on the feed rides. Scratching around, I find a feather that certainly never belonged to a pheasant; more like a Wyandotte bantam's or a Maran hen's, it is barred grey and white, a beautiful thing, exquisitely worked like the top of a *mille-feuille* pastry in an expensive confectioner's window.

I run through various members of the hawk family in my mind. Certainly not a buzzard, it could be from a peregrine or perhaps one of the others. Then, driving away, I see it sitting motionless on a branch. As it turns its head imperiously to look at me, there is no mistaking that cold yellow eye, the psychopathic look of a goshawk. It makes me shiver. One cannot fail to be awed by the goshawk's ruthless perfection, every feather honed to deadly fitness, like the muscles on a contract killer in a Bond movie.

I have a cold fear that we may sustain heavy losses. Goshawks are the swift, silent killers of the forest; the poults will not stand a chance. I can only hope that they have learnt some hawk sense from witnessing this one swooping down and seizing a terrified poult to carry off in its talons. I have become protective of our birds, and I understand the impulse of a young keeper wanting to shoot a raptor threatening the lives of birds he thinks of as his babies, and by extension his livelihood. But even if it was legal to do so, and it certainly isn't, I couldn't bring myself to shoot the bird with its savage beauty.

In fact, perversely, seeing it has made my day. But we cannot go on subsidising its lunch either. I can't blame it for wanting to try; if we have been foolish enough to introduce a few hundred not-yet-fully naturalised pheasant poults in his territory, we should not be surprised that he has identified them as soft targets. There is no point in getting mad, so we have to get even and outsmart it. It's time for Operation Disney.

Driving into Dumfries, I buy a clutch of helium balloons. Silver on one side with large heads on the other side, the idea is that these strange new 'über birds' will scare the hawks away. The critical success factor is that the balloons should have eyes, the bigger the better. And so that evening, in the silent hour between sundown and darkness, as the bats circle overhead, I deploy Minnie Mouse, Buzz Lightyear and Mr Potato Head to watch over them, until they are big enough and savvy enough to look after themselves.

Raptors are the shock troops of the proxy war being waged in the countryside between, in the red corner, the Axis of Spite comprising the animal rights lobby, certain sections of the media, and the watermelons in political parties mostly on the Left, and in the blue corner, the landowners, shoot tenants, keepers and shooting folk. It is to the class war what Vietnam was to the Cold War. As with the class war, there are some historical justifications in the red corner. Just as landowners once had it all their own way, before the various reform bills ushered in universal suffrage and so on, so they also let rip through the top end of the bird world.

I collect bird books and one of my favourites is *Bird Life Throughout the Year* by John H. Salter, first published in 1917. It is sobering to learn about the birds that were numerous in the early part of the twentieth century and have now disappeared. And profoundly shocking to read his description of the Edwardian gamekeepers' vermin control:

> Who does not know the 'gamekeeper's museum'? There are whole regiments of stoats and weasels with their thin, dried-up bodies, rows of cats' tails and bunches of rats' tails, hedgehogs' heads … Here upon the rails are the recognisable remains of sixty owls … There is something pitiable in seeing an owl, with its soft and downy plumage … becomes a mere scarecrow, a thing of shreds and patches. It is the pole-trap which has wrought this fatal hazard.

It helps one to understand why landowners are still facing such hostility from the authorities and the Axis, and why it may be some time before we are trusted to maintain a balance in the avian world again, frustrating as that is. Salter, incidentally, though he deplored indiscriminate vermin control, was not a rabid animal rights fanatic. He wrote in the same chapter:

> Upon weasels and stoats one need waste no sentiment … the sparrow hawk deserves no mercy … From what has been said, it might be inferred that game-preserving fosters the favoured few at the expense of dealing death and destruction all around. This is far from being the case; with more justice it may be likened to the arm of the law which descends with crushing force on the evil-doer, while promoting the happiness and security of the general public. Myriads of small birds, such as the various warblers, breed in safety in the game-coverts, protected from intruders and from the attacks of their natural enemies.

Quite so. It is a tragedy for the avian world that the balanced view of conservation articulated by Salter, and promoted in the mid-twentieth century by ornithological knights who were also keen shooting men, like Sir Arthur Duncan and Sir Peter Scott,[27] has been starved of oxygen in the media and hijacked by the animal rights lobby.

Then, of course, there is the incontrovertible evidence that farmers in the fifties and sixties poisoned millions of birds by spraying their fields with chemicals. And the raptors at the top of the food chain suffered most. Reading Rachel Carson's book *Silent Spring*, I am struck by how often it was the horrified farmers who were first to report it. And, also, how

---

27 Sir Peter Scott was a founder of the World Wildlife Fund (WWF) and the founder of the Wildfowl and Wetlands Trust (WWT). Sir Arthur Duncan was Chairman of the Nature Conservancy.

frequently the farmers were victims themselves; Carson writes about them suffering from poisoning through using arsenic dusts on crops, and of dreadful effects on the nervous system from organo-phosphates.

Nor can you blame the farmers for embracing the new technology, which promised to do away with the backbreaking hoeing of weeds portrayed in books like *The Worm Forgives the Plough*. It was Big Business that produced the chemicals and the Big State that allowed their use. Yet the enduring impression is that the fault lies squarely with farmers, and this makes it fine to persecute the grandsons of the men who used the poisonous sprays all those years ago.

One effect of the inadvertent but wholesale destruction of raptors by agricultural chemicals is possibly that my generation grew up with an artificially large population of small birds like sparrows, and perhaps sometimes we are too quick to get upset when we see the avian predators killing songbirds. But I don't think there is ever going to be some primordial, Garden of Eden balance; there are too many distortions, too many verminous rubbish tips and cats and red kite feeding stations. And the songbirds are now in danger. It can't be any accident that as sparrow hawks have proliferated, sparrows have become nearly extinct in some places.

I must have been well into my twenties before I had seen a buzzard or a kite. Now they are some of the commonest birds in the countryside and I am grateful for the added vertical dimension they have added to my world. I would miss hearing the buzzard mewing in springtime, as he soars carelessly on the thermals. Growing up, I saw kestrels and sparrow hawks, but seldom anything larger. Now the reverse is true. I see the big hawks on a daily basis, but the kestrels seem to have disappeared. I don't have any scientific evidence to back it up, but it seems more than sheer coincidence that the graceful 'windhover' should have become practically extinct when the big raptors moved into the neighbourhood.

It's possible that the harsh weather of 2010/11 played a part, but it seems more likely that the bigger hawks have been intolerant of smaller raptors and ethnically cleansed them. I am fairly certain that it isn't our usual scapegoat 'modern farming practices', as in this parish, farming is if anything less intensive and certainly less toxic than at any time since the war. And kestrels eat the same things as owls, buzzards and kites, so if we were doing bad things to the voles, they would also have disappeared. It is a mystery and one that the bird charities ought to be investigating.

My own exposure to the proxy war gave me a rude shock. About halfway through the noughties, my mobile rang. Number withheld, which usually means Big State or Big Business. Sure enough, it was one of the agricultural officers from the Department. I had dealt with him before, a very nice man, an old-school civil servant, who was scrupulously fair-minded and decent. He sounded embarrassed on the other end of the telephone as we exchanged greetings.

'Look, there's no easy way of putting this. I'm afraid there has been an allegation made against you. As it potentially affects your single farm payment, the Department is involved and I am on my way to see you with the police.'

I felt physically sick and my whole body tingled, as if there was an electric current passing through it. 'What do you mean? What sort of allegation?'

He hesitated, 'I think we had better wait until we meet to discuss it. Where will we get you?'

It was one of the most terrifying days of my life, worse than going in front of the headmaster to be beaten at school. The words 'single farm payment' implied that whatever I was supposed to have done could cause the Department to 'withhold' the payment of the subsidy indefinitely, money which is the lifeblood of our business, and without which we would rapidly go under. After all our efforts, it seemed heartbreaking that we might be defeated by some unspecified crime.

When the police wildlife officer arrived, he explained the situation. It transpired that there had been an anonymous tip-off that there was some 'bird poison' in one of our sheds and, sure enough, when they went to look there was a tub of an illegal product 'licensed for sale in Ireland' – so much for EU common standards – and it did indeed say BIRD POISON in large letters on it. The shed was derelict and in fact had not been used for years. As the wildlife officer was quick to agree, whoever 'happened to see it through a window' would have had to fight their way through a dense jungle of briars and nettles to get there. And the fact that we were advertising birdwatching holidays in our cottages on our website, did suggest that we were not seeking to eradicate birds. On the other hand, he had a duty to investigate it and he did so in a penetratingly sharp interview, 'under caution'.

I was fortunate that the attempt to smear me had been a crude one. Had they also planted a dead raptor, I might have faced years of litigation and adverse publicity as I cleared my name, and it could have been ruinous.

I was also very fortunate that the wildlife officer was not the same one who investigated the Grove and Rufford Hunt for an alleged breach of the Hunting Act in 2017. The hunt's conviction was recently overturned on appeal, after it was discovered that the court had not been given the evidence of sections of film, which clearly showed the accused trying to prevent hounds hunting a fox.

Then it was said in court that a Twitter account in the investigating officer's name had tweeted, using numerous expletives, against people involved in field sports. The tweets described the magazine *Shooting Times* as being 'a right-wing publication written by six-fingered, harrier-killing cousin f***ers'.

The wildlife officer, the one who interviewed me not the one with an unprofessional bias, accepted the balance of probabilities was that I had been framed. He said it would be up to the Procurator Fiscal, but he didn't think that I would hear any more about it and closed his notebook.

'I guess in your position, it's hard to avoid making a few enemies. Is there anyone who might want to have a go at you, former tenants or employees, neighbours?'

It was an uncomfortable question. Off the top of my head, I couldn't think of anyone who would want to do that, but later I began to wonder and it gnawed at me. That day was for me the end of innocence, when I first became aware of dark forces in the countryside, of fifth columnists for the Axis who are viscerally opposed to us. Motivated by class hatred and cloaked in the Marxist excuse that 'ends justify means', they will stop at nothing to avenge the sins of the forefathers by attacking their successors.

In medieval times, if you wanted to ruin a man you accused him of witchcraft; under the Tudors and Stuarts, you accused him of heresy. In Victorian times, you accused him of homosexuality; in twenty-first-century rural Scotland, it seems you plant a dead buzzard on him.

I have agonised over whether to include this episode, but it happened, and I think it is a striking example of 'rural life in an urban age'. It happens increasingly frequently, and I think it is best to shine a light on it. I know of an estate with a wind farm that, inevitably, polarised views in the local community, whilst transforming the fortunes of a marginal upland estate. A dead hawk was found at the bottom of one of the turbines, as if it had flown into one of the blades and perished. Remarkably, there wasn't a mark on it. Fortunately, the laird insisted on a post-mortem, and it was established that the deceased bird had spent some time in a deep freeze before mysteriously turning up at the wind farm.

There are stories of the Royal Society for the Protection of Birds sending undercover agents onto estates without the landowner's permission, and of trying to act as judge and jury in cases of wildlife crime. This has caused deep mistrust between farmers and the charity and, although in all fairness it has probably deterred some hotheads from killing raptors, it has also set back the cause of conservation many years.

Certainly it has made any sort of debate on achieving a balance of wildlife in the countryside almost impossible. Whilst I would not deny that there are still some Neanderthal attitudes in the shooting fraternity, where 'the only good buzzard is a dead buzzard', attitudes have changed markedly since the Edwardian times I quoted earlier. Most of the landowners I know want to see raptors on their land, but would like to move beyond the current situation to a more scientific approach to controlling their numbers. There is no doubt in our minds that if numbers of feathered meso-predators like the buzzards and kites are allowed to grow unchecked, it will have an adverse effect on the more vulnerable species.

In theory, there is nothing to stop a landowner applying for a licence to control them, but the bureaucracy, the unlikelihood of a licence being granted and the danger that it might attract unwelcome attention, mean that in reality no one ever does.

Matt Ridley summarises, 'There are three issues that prevent us managing the countryside properly: first, misplaced compassion; secondly, the theory that there is some magical Garden of Eden that we can get back to, ignoring the fact that we are here and affecting the balance; and thirdly, a bias against good news.'

The last point has a depressing ring of truth to it. If a raptor goes missing, it is all over the media, while the steady rise in nesting pairs of hen harriers and other formerly rare species on Scottish estates goes largely unreported.

✤ ✤ ✤ ✤

It would be fair to say that I am not the Scottish National Party's biggest fan, although that does not stop cordial relations with many of their councillors and MSPs that I know. Individually, they can be very likeable, it's collectively that somehow they turn into something out of one of Orwell's novels. The worst manifestation of this is their policy of forcing every child in Scotland to have a 'state guardian', known as a Named Person. This is anathema to most parents, who rightly fear the sinister state coming between them and their children, not least because of the risk of the role attracting paedophiles.

Their fears were exacerbated when an official explanation written for children, bizarrely, stated that children should think of all the adults in their lives as gardeners and the Named Person as 'head gardener'. I was going to make a cheap quip here about wondering how many children still live in houses where there are head gardeners. But it feels wrong to make light of something so obnoxious.

The SNP politician seems very nice. We have had a constructive chat and, though we have agreed to differ on some things (hunting), she is keen to help with other issues. Emboldened, I ask her, 'There is one thing I am still really confused about. Where are you going with this Named Person policy. Surely that was the sort of thing they did in East Germany?'

She looks a little ashamed. 'Aye, my mum gives me a hard time about that.' And then she remembers herself, 'But it is absolutely right that we protect children.'

It is amazing how often mothers really do know best.

✢ ✢ ✢ ✢

Every year I strive to move the estate closer to a Utopian state I can see in my mind's eye. Everything would be 'fit for purpose', gates would swing, roads would be free of potholes, roofs would not leak, fields would be perfectly drained and stock-proof, and the soil would be bursting with fertility. Management accountants would call it a 'balanced scorecard' and I score myself harshly and vow to do better each year, until poverty forces me to limit my plans and to 'shoot the wolf closest to the sledge'.

In the early days we would complete a job and, standing back and admiring a new fence with Davie and Graham, we would say, 'Well, that will be Oliver's problem to replace that next time.' Barely a decade later, it is bitterly disappointing to be back at some of those fences again.

'Shite,' growls Davie, pulling at a rotten stob.[28] 'Look at it.'

When anyone whinges about EU regulations, I think of creosote. A wonder product made from tar, creosote adds years of life to timber. Stobs used to be saturated in the stuff. I keep coming across ones that must be as old as I am and still in good condition.

Unfortunately, there is a theoretical link between creosote and cancer, if you expose yourself to very high doses of it. The EU has applied its 'precautionary principle' and so modern fencing materials come coated in inferior products that do not last. This is very good news for timber merchants and fencing contractors, but bad for trees, farmers and the

---

28 Small fence post of about four inches in diameter.

environment. Norway, which as everyone now knows is outside the EU but able to trade with it, has not banned creosote and so my friend the Jolly Green Giant[29] has set himself up as an importer of Norwegian fence posts. This would have been a case of coals to Newcastle, before the EU wrapped fencing in red tape.

I will know if Brexit has been 'a good thing', if stobs start to look black again. But I have a horrible feeling that the 'Green Blob' will prevent any deregulation like this.

✛ ✛ ✛ ✛

Continuous professional development, that's what I tell Sheri, when I disappear off for a day's shooting. And it's true, I do gain many of my farming ideas from observing other people's systems and chatting to other farmers in the shooting field. Today at tea after shooting, Al asks us all if we would like to see the new dairy. We are all there like a shot, marvelling at the robots.

'You see there, that cow wants to be milked, so she comes up to the barrier and the computer works out from the chip hanging from her neck who she is and when she was last milked.'

The barrier opens and she goes and stands by the robot. An arm comes out and washes her teats and then, as if by magic, the cups are guided on to her teats.

'The computer memorises the shape of her tits so that it gets it right.' Astonishing. There is a whoosh as some cake rattles down into a bucket in front to her. 'You see there she is being given the exact amount, tailored to her needs. And there on the screen is an analysis of her milk yield.'

The dairy is a state-of-the-art vision of innovation, a far cry from the byres and later the herring-bone parlours I remember at home as a child. The cows seem more in control and look content as they lie in their

---

29 Neil Gourlay, so called because he is 6'4" and was once named Green Farmer of the Year.

cubicles, or walk under the back scratchers. But it makes me uneasy all the same.

Every time I go into town, I interact with fewer humans. The cheery checkout girls in the supermarket no longer smile and call me 'dear', as they are now robots, who only say, 'Please place your items in the bagging area.'

Likewise, the bank seems to have fewer employees every time I go into it, and the garages no longer have cashiers, let alone pump attendants. There is no eye contact, no banal exchanges about the weather and definitely no flirting with the computers, and the world seems a lonelier place in consequence. The cost of people is rocketing, as employers grapple with the new workplace pensions and other costs being loaded onto them. Big Business seems to have cottoned on to this trend and brought in the robots. The rest of us scratch our heads and wonder how we are going to manage.

We should be thinking about doing the same. There are already friends with robots to mow their lawns. But I am not sure that I want to be sitting alone in the countryside, surrounded by 'bots, old-aged pensioners and workless, unhappy young people. The economists say that this is an irrational fear, that technology has always created more jobs than it destroys, and that has been true of the country as a whole, but not here where we have lost twenty jobs on the estate since the seventies, and forty since the thirties. And what if the experience of the mechanical age turns out not to be true in the digital one?

It seems even more perverse when the Left threatens to eradicate hunt staff and gamekeepers, jobs in the countryside that could not be done by robots.

✤ CHAPTER NINE ✤

I AM turning the tack room upside down searching for Chester's passport, as the lorry can't move him without one. Chester is a horse and looking for his passport is a drain on my time that would have been unimaginable before 2003.

I remember it well. I kept receiving menacing literature through the post telling me that I had until 30 June to apply for horse passports for our two nags, or risk a £5,000 fine or six months' imprisonment. Unsurprisingly, one of the senders of this unwanted mail was a local veterinary practice that had spotted a nice new income stream in issuing the passports at twenty-five quid a time.

The other correspondent was more unexpected: the local branch of the Pony Club to which my daughter belonged. The Pony Club is an outstanding institution that instils all the right qualities in the young without any public subsidy, as well as allowing women of a certain age and class to indulge their authoritarian tendencies in a benign way. It even provides teenagers in remote rural areas with valuable opportunities for sexual advancement at its summer camps.

However, on the whole, I would rather it stayed out of politics. I certainly didn't want it to act as an agent of the European Union and its useful idiots in Whitehall. If the Pony Club was to act at all, having rightly opposed the introduction of horse passports in DEFRA's perfunctory public consultation exercise, it should have mobilised its forces to blockade parliament with small girls on Thelwell ponies, until this gratuitous legislation was repealed.

The root cause of this irritant was the Orwellian-sounding European Commission Decision 2000/68/EC, which was nodded through by our own compliant legislators. I see from Hansard that there was a spirited opposition by the few Tory MPs who understood the full stupidity of what was being proposed. But the sad fact is that MPs either (Lab) secretly delight in making life difficult for the horsey classes (irrespective of their genuine classlessness), or (Con) are too busy these days to be Pony Club dads themselves and therefore become detached from what passes as reality for us backwoodsmen.

It all stemmed from the Continental habit of eating horses. Now, I admit there were fleeting moments when I could cheerfully have spit-roasted Nutty, my daughter's truculent Shetland pony, when she refused to be caught or stood on my foot, for example. But like ninety-nine per cent of my fellow countrymen, I would have drawn the line at eating her. I therefore didn't see the need for a passport detailing all her vaccinations, in case she entered the human food chain. If by some quirk of fate she had headed for the *charcuterie*, then a simple declaration that she was free of antibiotics should have been sufficient.

I was glum at the thought of all the extra civil servants employed to oversee the accompanying web of state control, such as the National Equine Database. Don't get me wrong, I'm all for horse passports in the right context – breed societies and regulatory bodies like the Jockey Club have administered them for years – where there is a useful purpose like disease prevention. But I failed to see why I should have to pay this involuntary tax by any other name. And the idea of the dead hand of DEFRA meddling with a strand of our national life that stretches from Romany horse dealers at Appleby Fair to Royal Ascot, was frankly risible.

Every year I find that, by the time I have licensed my car, my shotguns and my television, and filled in tax returns, VAT returns, PAYE and the ever-more complex agricultural returns and census forms, I have less and less time to go out and generate taxable income to pay the salaries of all the civil servants who process them. Recording the nation's horses on bits of paper, so that the gee-gee-eaters could consume them, seemed a further distraction from making the economy go round.

The government failed to persuade anyone of the merits of this gratuitous red tape, except those who might benefit by being issuing authorities, which is why, once the deadline had passed, only half the horses in the country were registered. What did they do? Instead of acknowledging that this was a silly idea in the first place – which they were told by virtually every organisation they consulted – they resorted to bullying.

DEFRA sent out press releases telling us that horse movement was impossible without the paperwork. Not surprisingly, this was not something they told us when the legislation was being passed. Hence my prayers to St Anthony for the recovery of the passport, as I turn the tack room upside down; it's a bit of bureaucratic harassment by the state that we could all do without. Will it be thrown on the post-Brexit bonfire of regulations? I have my doubts.

Cattle passports, on the other hand, though the proven cause of grey hair and baldness, I can accept as a necessary evil. They were introduced to ensure traceability of cattle after the BSE crisis. In theory, this should work to our advantage, differentiating our beef from imports, as the consumer should be able to read which farm a steak comes from and the breed of the animal. But supermarkets have been curiously reluctant to do this.

The Department can turn up at any time to inspect all our cattle and their passports. These inspections are anticipated with the same eagerness with which Gogol's villagers awaited the Government Inspector. The penalties for maladministration are severe. A friend of ours had a crisis when his wife, who normally did the passports, went into hospital. He had a dead calf and sent the wrong passport back. The mistake was picked up on an inspection and he was fined £20,000.[30] Criminals are treated less harshly for mugging old ladies.

About once a year, I get in a panic because I find a bull calf that was registered as a heifer in the heat of calving or vice versa, or worse, mislay a passport. This causes the team great amusement and they sing, 'Jimmy's gan in the jile, he's gan to be in a while.'[31]

Imagine then the frustration in the beef industry when in 2013 burgers in Tesco, Asda and others were found to contain, wait for it, horsemeat. As

---

30 Later reduced by two-thirds on appeal.

31 Jail is pronounced jile locally, so this is perhaps the only part of the country where this rhymes.

Swift wrote, 'Laws are like cobwebs, which may catch small flies, but let wasps and hornets break through.'

✤ ✤ ✤ ✤

Those febrile months of the Independence campaign in 2014 changed the way we think about ourselves and the divisions may take generations to heal. Flagpoles have gone up in gardens where they never were before. The Saltire was once flown proudly alongside the Union Jack, as Scots proclaimed pride in being both Scottish and British. All that has changed, and it has become more like the Irish Tricolour that I remember being displayed everywhere in nationalist areas of Northern Ireland. Conversely, unionists now don't do flags, as it's easier not to draw attention.

Scotland is divided. It is like living with an unhappy marriage in the family, where one is forced to take sides and deal with each toxic twist and turn. It is the tragic legacy of the Blair government's cynical strategy of devolution, a crude attempt to gerrymander the UK into one big Labour pocket borough, and to hell with the West Lothian question.[32] It opened up deep wounds and released poison into the nation's bloodstream.

I have no doubt that if I had grown up in a sink estate in Glasgow, if my parents had lost their jobs in the shipyards under an uncaring Tory government, and my ancestors had been booted out of the Highlands during the Clearances and butchered at Culloden, then I would be in the vanguard of nationalism. The SNP has brilliantly exploited a deep-seated hatred of the English, aided by a Tory stupidity and complacency about Scotland, and its tendency to conflate British interests with English ones.

My memories of that period will take a long time to fade. For months beforehand, I had a sinking feeling that the Union would be lost. I remember coming across an old soldier at an event in Edinburgh. There

---

32   The West Lothian question is attributed to the then Labour MP for West Lothian, Tam Dalyell, who raised it in 1977 when Jim Callaghan's Labour government proposed a devolved assembly in Edinburgh. An anti-devolutionist, Dalyell argued it would be unfair for Scottish MPs to have equal rights to vote on English-only legislation.

was no mistaking his regiment with his Black Watch glengarry, tie and blazer badge; and his medals, gleaming proudly on his chest, told a story of long service and good conduct for his country.

I did not ask him which way he was going to vote, as I have a British reserve about such matters and, in any case, I thought that those of us who had served in the British Army, and seen at first-hand what can be achieved in the world by British institutions, would be natural unionists. But he told me anyway.

'Aye, I was Black Watch man and boy. It's a crying shame what they have done to the regiment. I am going to vote Yes. The SNP have promised to bring back the Black Watch if they win.'

I stared at him with incredulity. The SNP's defence policy involved booting Britain's independent nuclear deterrent out of Faslane, and creating a Scottish Army that would in all probability be little better than a Home Guard never to be deployed outside Scotland. Disgracefully, Scottish soldiers serving outside Scotland were being denied a vote in the referendum. Yet the SNP, opportunistically but in my view rightly, had said that they would restore the old Scottish regiments. I thought at the time that it was a mistake for the Ministry of Defence to axe famous old county regiments, with their distinctive uniforms and unique traditions, and form generic infantry regiments like the Royal Regiment of Scotland, cutting vital recruiting links with those counties in the process – and here it was coming back to bite them.

People give their loyalty to the British state partly via institutions like family regiments, and at the click of a Whitehall bureaucrat's mouse, the United Kingdom had lost the support of my new friend here. I was struck by the irony: the Black Watch was the one Highland Regiment that had fought for the Hanoverians at Culloden, and here was one of them opting for the modern equivalent of the Jacobites.

A few days later, I gave a lift to a local teenager I had seen walking back from the bus stop in the rain. Sixteen-year-olds were being allowed to vote in the referendum, in what many saw as another blatant skewing of the rules to the nationalist cause.

'So, are you going to use your vote next week?'

His face lit up. 'Aye, I am.'

He paused, unsure whether to go on, then gave a look of resolve. 'I am going to vote Yes. I think we can be independent again. I did a' that aboot the wars of independence in school.'

I sighed inwardly. Years of partial history being served up by the education system and half-truths in Hollywood movies had prepared the way for the nationalists to seduce the Braveheart generation.

'We were never conquered, you know. And they weren't strictly speaking wars of independence, more of a fight between Norman rivals for the throne with the English sticking their oar in. We are part of the United Kingdom, because a Scottish king inherited the English throne in 1603. So, if anything, it is the other way around.'

He gave me a sideways look, not sure enough of his history to argue the toss and thinking, well, he would say that, wouldn't he?

'It's true, you should Google it.'

Then there was the Friday when my copy of *The Scottish Farmer* was delivered with a picture on the front cover of four of the most influential men in Scottish farming, holding placards and urging farmers to vote Yes. All four were former leaders of the NFU, some of the biggest farmers in Scotland, and key opinion formers in their own communities, and one was shortly to become a Lord Lieutenant. Uneducated have-nots these were not.

Their reasons, I was forced to admit with a sense of foreboding, did have some logic. The thrust of their argument was that Scottish agriculture was neglected by the UK government, Scottish farmers received much less in subsidy per acre than their English counterparts and a recent adjusting payment from Europe had not, as had been assumed, been given to Scotland, but had been distributed across the UK.

It's the old P.G. Wodehouse thing, 'It has never been hard to tell the difference between a Scotsman with a grievance and a ray of sunshine.' It was a highly complex issue and not entirely straightforward. But the perception was what mattered, and it was toxic. They also argued that if we stayed in the UK, we would in all likelihood be dragged out of the EU on the back of an English vote. (That much has so far been proved true.)

I groaned. Seventy per cent of Scotch beef goes to England and leaving the UK would mean leaving the EU anyway, as well as divorcing us from our main market and leaving us repaying loans in sterling from a position of weakness – saddled, as we would be, with a massively devalued new Scottish currency. But they had a point. Whitehall had underestimated the anger that the failure to resolve, or at least explain, the subsidy imbalance was causing.

That weekend, I attended the annual Dowding Memorial Service in Moffat. Hugh Dowding, the Air Marshall responsible for winning the Battle of Britain, had been born there. A senior RAF officer spoke movingly about how the Battle of Britain might well have been lost without Dowding's leadership, and with it the springboard for the reconquest of Europe four years later. Then, preceded by that iconic roar of defiance, a lone Spitfire flew over; a beautiful plane, it seemed a very potent symbol of Britishness that weekend and the 'sound of freedom' filled the Annan Valley.

I fell to thinking what might have happened if Scotland had broken away from the Union when Ireland did. Would she have joined England in the fight against Nazism, or stayed on the sidelines, like the Irish? Would some Scottish De Valera have sent condolences on the death of Hitler?

Another Hugh,[33] Hugh MacDiarmid, the laureate of Scottish nationalism, was born over the hills from Moffat, at Langholm.

While Dowding was busy saving the free world, MacDiarmid wrote poems:[34]

---

33 In fact, MacDiarmid was a *nom de plume*. His real name was Christopher Murray Grieve. He was a founding member of the National Party of Scotland (forerunner of the modern SNP) and stood as an SNP candidate in 1945 and 1950, before defecting to the Communist Party.

34 *The Revolutionary Art of the Future: Rediscovered Poems* by Hugh MacDiarmid, Carcanet Press, 2003.

On the Imminent Destruction of London, June 1940:

Now when London is threatened
With devastation from the air
I realise, horror atrophying in me,
That I hardly care.

In another, *The German Bombers*, he wrote:

The leprous swine in London town
And their Anglo-Scots accomplices
Are, as they have always been,
Scotland's only enemies.

MacDiarmid is honoured with a large road sign on the A7 proclaiming his birthplace. Strangely, Thomas Telford, arguably Britain's greatest engineer, born nearby, is not so honoured and neither is Dowding. But then they achieved greatness south of the border, which is a cardinal sin in the eyes of the Nats. In fact, it is a central plank of their philosophy that greatness outside Scotland doesn't count. Otherwise a casual observer might consider the surnames of British Prime Ministers – Bute, Aberdeen, Gladstone, Rosebery, Balfour, Campbell-Bannerman, Bonar Law, Ramsay MacDonald, Macmillan, Douglas-Home, Blair, Brown, Cameron – and conclude that Scots had done rather well out of the Union.

I did what I could for the No campaign. We put placards up along the major routes, in fields with bulls in them as a deterrent to vandalism, but that did not stop them. We left the graffiti up as a powerful message to floating voters.

Friends rang to share their dismay at what was happening. An eighteen-year-old girl we knew had her car vandalised for displaying 'Better Together' stickers. Several people had their computers hacked by 'cybernats' and their emails disabled. Any unionist bold enough to tweet brought down a torrent of vitriol on themselves.

On the final Sunday, we went to Church. The minister led the congregation in a prayer 'for us not to be afraid of taking bold decisions'. We came out feeling cross and dispirited.

In the event, half of the Central Belt voted to go off and create a socialist nirvana in the city states of Glasgow and Dundee. The rest of Scotland, especially rural Scotland, voted strongly to stay in the UK. Fully two-thirds of people in Dumfries and Galloway voted for the Union, a greater proportion than the Yes vote in Glasgow.

✢ ✢ ✢ ✢

What is so discombobulating about the simmering independence argument is having to choose one's nationality. It is so much easier just to be British, as I am neither wholly Scottish nor wholly English, and my granny was as Welsh as it is possible to be.[35] Apparently Alex Salmond chose the timing of the referendum to be in the year of the seven-hundredth anniversary of the Battle of Bannockburn. The genealogical power of the internet reveals that as a direct descendent of both commanders (like millions of others), I share a thumb-sized test tube of DNA with Edward II, the Angevin-Castilian King of England, and the Scottish King Robert the Bruce, aka Robert de Brus, one of the Normandy de Bruses. Making me choose sides is as pointless as making my thumbs wrestle against each other. And the emphasis some Nats put on the purity of Scottish blood is eerily reminiscent of the German obsession with *Das Volk*. Or as J.K. Rowling wrote during the campaign, 'When people try to make this debate about the purity of your lineage, things start getting a little Death Eaterish[36] for my taste.'

In fact, most people in Galloway are no more related to Scots north

---

35 But for Edward I, her family the Williams-Wynns would be on the throne of Wales.

36 For non-Harry Potter fans, Death Eaters are fictional followers of Lord Voldemort, who seek to purify the wizarding community by eliminating the Muggle-borns (wizards or witches born to non-magical parents).

of the Clyde than they are to people in Kent.[37] And whilst vehemently Scottish when we play England at Murrayfield or Hampden Park, a recent gene-mapping exercise showed that Gallovidians are almost identical to people in the northern counties of England, which figures, as the Novantae and Selgovae tribes encountered by the Romans, and later the Brythonic-speaking Celtic kingdom of Rheged, covered both regions. Analyse Gallovidian DNA and you will find evidence of occupation by Irish Gaels, Norwegian and Danish Vikings and Northumbrian Angles (of Baltic extraction).

Galloway only ended up being part of modern Scotland, because the Scottish King Alexander II behaved towards Galloway in the manner that the English kings had done – ultimately without success – towards Scotland. Unlike her close neighbour the Isle of Man, she had no sea defences to prevent Alexander subjugating Galloway in the 1230s, in a brutal repression known euphemistically as 'the pacification'. Though as late as 1384, Archibald the Grim, Lord of Galloway, successfully argued that laws passed in Scotland had no validity in Galloway.

Strangely what we now identify as Scottish culture only really permeated the southern regions of Scotland after the Act of Union. In his book, *The Reivers*, Alistair Moffat writes, 'Borderers [of the sixteenth century] ... would not have been seen dead wearing tartan.' Ironically, it was a Borderer, Sir Walter Scott, who did more than most to promote tartan and develop the distinctive Scottish culture that we recognise today. And this culture has been cemented over the last three centuries through Scottish regiments, football leagues, newspapers and so on.

Perhaps, given our very different voting habits, and a growing dissatisfaction with the authoritarianism of Holyrood, it is time for Galloway to reassert our identity. If the Union Kingdom is to be restructured via an 'indyref2', we should be allowed the option of remaining in the UK as an autonomous province, like our near neighbours Ulster and Man. After all

---

37 If you doubt this try introducing a Gallovidian to a Doric speaking Aberdonian and see whether they understand each other.

that she has said recently about Brexit, I am sure Nicola Sturgeon would agree, there is no question of us being dragged out of the Union against our democratic wishes.

This is not as fanciful as it sounds. I have heard it said privately in political circles that any future referendum would need to have a double safety lock to allow regions unhappy about secession to vote themselves back into the Union in a second referendum. And a devolved Southern Scotland would be a viable entity not much smaller than Wales. But it is a taboo subject, as unionists will not deviate from the script that there is not going to be another referendum, and nationalists dare not contemplate breaking up Scotland, in case the old Norse kingdoms of Shetland and Orkney go off with what remains of the oil.

So, if we ever did end up in an independent Scotland against the wishes of the people of Dumfries and Galloway, I would take off into the hills of Galloway and foment the resistance like my illustrious ancestor The Bruce, or de Brus.

Autumn

+ CHAPTER TEN +

THE BACK end, that's what country people call it; rarely autumn and certainly never 'the fall'. It's a sort of code, letting others know that you are genuinely rural; like saying loo rather than toilet, so that 'people like us' know that you are one of them. It was drummed into me at school and in the Army that you shouldn't use three words where one will do, but there is something nicely rounded and unhurried about rural circumlocutions.

In case some twenty-second-century scriptwriter is reading this book in the hope of finding material to write dialogue for a period drama set in a Scottish country house around 2018, I had better give some flavour of dinner-party conversation of the time. The sexes will talk together in groups in the drawing-room before dinner. The men will talk farming, shooting and politics, while the women will talk herbaceous borders, curtain material and children – I generalise to provoke and I am risking hate-mail from the sisterhood here – that much is unchanged from Jane Austen novels.

The host wanders around urbanely, open-necked shirt, sleeveless jersey, or perhaps one of those natty Nehru jackets, hosed in tartan. He clutches a bottle of champagne, or possibly more recently cava or prosecco, with which he plies his guests' glasses. After the first glass, every other guest will utter a tight-lipped, 'No, thank you, I'm driving.' Whereupon he disappears off to find some elderflower cordial. Dinner will proceed with one half of the party, mostly the male half, if I'm honest, getting progressively more animated and florid, and the other half looking glum, and then glancing at their watches and giving their spouses 'the look'.

If anything characterises the neo-puritanism of Sturgeon's Scotland, then it is this. In fact, I can confidently predict that long after anyone has ever heard of Nicola Sturgeon, people will still respond to a proffered bottle by grimacing and muttering, 'I had better not ... that bloody woman,' an historically based social convention, rather like the way that Jacobites once passed their wine glass over their water glass, to toast the king across the water.

It has been the SNP government's mission to dry Scotland out. The permitted level of alcohol in the bloodstream was reduced from 80 mg to 50 mg, barely one drink, in December 2014, 'to bring us into line with the rest of Europe' (but pointedly not the part of Europe south of Gretna); a slap in the face for the wartime generation, who made so many sacrifices to ensure that we could be different.

A cynic might argue that if England had reduced the limit, Scotland would have followed a policy of differentiation and kept it the same. Or that a minority government was seizing any opportunity to push legislation through on which they could be guaranteed of cross-party support, since no politician would dare recommend maintaining the status quo, as that would lay them open to being branded *in favour* of killing innocent people through drink-driving.

I hasten to assure readers that I am not defending drink-driving, far from it; like all parents I worry about my children. I possibly owe my life to the wisdom of the Army Board, who decreed that there was zero tolerance and instant dismissal for any young officer caught drink-driving, which inculcated a good habit that has stayed with me.

But it would be remiss of me, in providing this snapshot of rustic life, to miss out something that has been a rural preoccupation of late. Ours is the first generation to be unable to drink at social occasions and perhaps the last, since driverless cars may soon perform the same service as once did chauffeurs, and before them coachmen. Conversation now includes speculation on whether you can be prosecuted for being inebriated in a car driven by a robot and on how driverless cars will cope with Dumfries and Galloway's potholes.

One unexpected side effect is that it has revived the sleepover party in country houses, not seen since before the invention of the motor car, as hosts have remembered why they have so many bedrooms and now often offer a bed after dinner parties. It doesn't seem to have precipitated Edwardian levels of adultery, but perhaps it is too early to tell.

It was not always like this. In my youth, there were quite a few local characters one would not have wanted to meet coming the other way on a twisty road. Although it has to be said that I don't remember any accidents, and their aged Volvos always seemed to find their way home along the back roads unscathed. Memories of shooting with my father's friends, as a young man in Dumfriesshire, always seem to include Herculean drinking bouts afterwards. It was in what I think of as the 'Age of the Captains', as they had nearly all left the Army as captains, normally in one of the smarter cavalry regiments, and kept their rank. So that locals would refer to Captain Eddie, Tony, Ronnie or whoever, and add the vernacular term of approbation, 'He's some man!'

Larger than life characters with 'Dumfriesshire complexions' and huge appetites for life, they had spent their youth enduring the austerity of the war and its aftermath, and made up for lost time in the last decades of the twentieth century, shooting, fishing and racing, or disappearing to their London clubs 'to get their hair cut'. (This was in the days when most estates were run by factors.) They stood out like ageing Regency roués, left high and dry by the priggishness of the Victorian age. The introduction of the breathalyser hit them in early middle age.

In my mind's eye, I can see them all sitting around the table in the fishing hut by Hoddom Bridge after a day's shooting. A whisky bottle is on the ebb and Captain Eddie is chain-smoking his untipped Player's Navy Cut that he pulls from a tin, which he taps ruminatively with each cigarette before lighting it.

'I hear *so-and-so* has been excused driving.'

The assembled company shake their heads in commiseration.

'Hard times for the gentry,' says Captain Ronnie.

'Did I tell you about the time I got caught?' asks Captain Sam. 'I was driving back after shooting one day, a little refreshed, when I saw a blue light in my wing mirror. So I pulled over and racked my brains. When the rozzer approached, I said, "I wouldn't come too close, constable, my dog has just farted." Then I got a queezy feeling inside, as I remembered to my horror that my dog was on heat that morning and I had left her at home.'

One sadness arising from the tightening of the drink-driving laws has been the demise of many rural pubs. In recent years we have lost The Old Smugglers Inn in Auchencairn and the Criffel Inn in New Abbey. When we resurrected the Hunt, we wrote it into our charter that it was part of our mission to support rural pubs – a directive that some of our subscribers have taken to heart more than others – and we have always tried to hold our meetings and fund-raising events in pubs.

During the time of the Reivers, it was common practice for criminals to make for the border at speed. The law gave injured parties the right of pursuit across the border. This was known as 'Hot Trod'. There is talk of Hot Trods again, as drink-drivers make for the border in the hope of being able to claim they are under a different jurisdiction, but I have not heard how this stands up in court.

All across the county, the farming neighbours are hedge-cutting. This makes me cross, as we are barely out of September and the fruit that is so vital for the birds to survive winter has not had a chance to ripen, let alone be eaten, and will now go to waste. They do this every year as a routine post-harvest job, so that there is seldom any fruit anyhow as most hedgerow species flower, and therefore fruit, on the old wood.

I think they are eccentric, as to me the delight in owning hedges is in the spring thorn blossoms, the blowsy summer roses, and the autumn larders heavy with hips and haws and old man's beard. And the reward is in the diversity of hedgerow birds that mostly nest in the bottom three metres and need good thick cover. They also need the blossom to attract insects on which to feed their young.

To me their behaviour is irrational, like having a garden where you prune all the shrubs, so that they never flower. On the other hand, they think I am eccentric for cutting the hedges every other year at most, and only in February when all the fruit has been eaten, because to them a hedge is a wild thing to be tamed, it needs keeping in check lest it encroach on any productive land or scratch their precious cars.

Its aestheticism comes from its form and its symmetry and its uniformity. Like cleaning your car on a Saturday morning, or mowing the lawn, it is something that has to be done to avoid letting the neighbourhood down. This attitude finds its expression in the 'lollipop hedges' that march across the fields, bare wooden trunks with carefully manicured bushy tops, like rows of bonsai trees. These are neither stock-proof nor helpful to wildlife, and will eventually die if not radically restructured, yet the idea of coppicing them and allowing them to bush up naturally from the bottom would be anathema to them.

The white settlers complain about the hedges if we do not cut them and then complain that they get punctures when we do. When we have coppiced hedges or cut and laid them, it has sometimes provoked a stream of invective about me 'ripping hedges out'. They would like to see the hedges tamed, too, but they still seem to come and pick all our sloes and blackberries every back end without any sense of irony. There will not be any meeting of minds on the subject anytime soon.

The humble hedge is what defines the British lowland landscape. We take it for granted and yet when we contemplate the view almost anywhere else in the world, except Ireland, it might be beautiful, but in a few moments we realise that something is missing, some ingredient that transforms our enjoyment of it from satisfaction to delight. Only in these damp islands do we exploit the conditions that allow our native trees and shrubs to be stuck in the ground and grow to form a stock-proof barrier that will last forever, if given a little attention from time to time.

I am a hedge fetishist. When I left the Army, a grateful government paid for me to undergo 'resettlement training', so that I would be of some use as a civilian. I chose to go on a hedge-laying course at Askham Bryan Agricultural College in Yorkshire. There I learnt how to cut through the trunks of hedgerow trees at the bottom, enough to push them over on their sides without breaking them off completely, and then bind them in to create a thick stock-proof barrier that will grow vigorously from the bottom. There is no finer sight than a newly laid hedge and, as a hunting man, also nothing more exciting to jump.

Hedges have been politicised from the word go. When landowners first started planting hedges to enclose the commons, and create the fields required for modern agriculture, there was uproar. In fact there were instances, including one famous incident near Kirkcudbright, where gangs of Levellers came and ripped them out in an early example of anti-capitalism. Then there was uproar again when my father's generation took some of them out, so that the newly invented big machinery could be used to grow crops.

My generation of landowners has been busy planting them again; on this estate alone, we have planted over four kilometres at the last count. Yet the received wisdom is that farmers are still busy despoiling the countryside. And it never occurs to anyone that the hedges are a colossal cost for farmers to maintain, in our case over £1,000 per year, let alone the ground that is lost to farming by the space they take up, something that our competitors overseas do not have.

To be fair to the Big State, the Scottish Government understands the issue and has used some of the EU grant money to persuade farmers to grow more hedges and to look after them in a more environmentally sensitive manner. The trouble is that they overcomplicate the schemes and this leads to more friction. Inspectors will come and measure the hedges, and if their satellite equipment provides a different figure to the farmer's measuring wheel, he will be made to feel like a criminal. Or there will be a difference of interpretation.

Vital time and emotion can be wasted arguing over a claim that currently pays the princely sum of 11p per metre. I wrestle with the problem, wishing that I was watching television with the rest of the family and not sitting in the office late at night to meet a deadline for my application.

Talk of a green Brexit fills me with equal measures of hope and dread. Hope that we might be rewarded for doing the right thing environmentally; dread that the environmental lobbyists and the vested interests within the civil service will make sure that any new scheme will be even more fiendishly complicated, and a further drain on farmers' time and sanity. What we need is for ministers to stand up and say that competing with the rest of the world on a free trade basis would entail ruining the British countryside, by ripping out the hedges again to create huge fields for robots to farm and cattle to be ranched; therefore, all farmers will be compensated for having hedges.

In return for this payment, there will be straightforward rules to ensure that hedges become fit for purpose as havens of wildlife. It needs to be simple without any requirement to claim money that never arrives, fill in forms or deal with inspections. I am not holding my breath.

⚜ ⚜ ⚜ ⚜

Throughout October, the shore starts to echo with the plaintive cries of waders. And flocks of knots and stints fly backwards and forwards over the sea in silvering murmurations. It is for us the second symphony of the year. The spring birdsong of the woods and fields is a distant memory, and now we wake to the haunting clarinet lament of the curlew. As many waders, particularly the curlew, are endangered species, it is always a relief to see them back. They have moved back from the uplands, where they went for the summer to breed.

When we lived partly in the Yorkshire Dales, I would fondly imagine that the ones we had nesting in our hay meadows were the same ones that wintered outside the House on the Shore. We would watch them as they flew round and around in circles during their courtship, piping strange primeval cries. Then, later, after we had waited for them to fledge before cutting the hay, sometimes we would see the curlew poults with their odd-looking, half-formed curved bills, like creatures in *Jurassic Park*.

Now that we live here full-time, I rarely see waders when there is not an 'r' in the month, with the exception of some oyster catchers, unless I am lucky enough to be invited to go and shoot grouse. For it is on the grouse moors that many of them breed and, being a keen twitcher, I relish a visit to a well-keepered moor as much for what I can see as for the shooting. Up on the moor, where the land meets the sky and the colour and the light make it seem like the inside of a rainbow, one feels doubly alive, braced by the wind and watching the cloud shadows chasing each other across the hillsides.

Crouching in a butt, scanning the horizon for the first covey, the eye is pleased by a carefully manufactured patchwork of purple heather, moor grasses, blaeberries and bents of differing thickness and colour. Here and there it is smoky grey from burning in the spring, or bright green with new regrowth where it is feed for grouse, hares and sheep alike, or a tired-looking autumn brown where it provides thick cover.

And, as a consequence, one is usually rewarded with sightings of other birds, golden plover flashing past, wheatears, and perhaps in the distance a hen harrier dancing on the breeze (they are not as rare as sometimes portrayed and much more likely to be seen where there is a healthy population of grouse).[38]

It should not be any surprise that what is good for grouse is good for most other species. The relentless assault on foxes, crows, ticks and worms by keepers, paid for by the proceeds of grouse shooting, provides a lifeline for vulnerable species like the curlew and the redshank. Yet, ironically, it seems that the Axis has grouse shooting in its sights now that they have their hunting bans. It is a soft target. The image of a fleet of Range Rovers conveying wealthy bankers up onto the moor is a toxic one, even if they are spending City money in some of the poorest regions of the UK.

---

38 The Game and Wildlife Conservation Trust (GWCT) has proved scientifically at Berwyn and at Langholm that there is a correlation between red grouse, hen harrier and wader populations.

The Axis strategy is plain to see. They hope to ban heather burning and moor drainage and, above all, to make 'wildlife crime' into such an issue that politicians are pushed by public opinion to regulate and eventually ban grouse shooting. If they succeed, the heather hills will be covered in sitka spruce and the effects will be heard across a silent Solway each winter.

We are powerless to do much to help the curlews here – their critical time is in the spring – except by ensuring that our livestock farming maintains a healthy worm population to feed them inland when the tide is in. And when our curlews leave the Solway for their summer breeding grounds, I always say a silent prayer for them, hoping that they will head for a well-keepered grouse moor somewhere and not the RSPB's upland reserve at Geltsdale, which is said to have a silent spring now.

The house is full of young people carrying clipboards, and I feel absurdly deferential as I ask for permission to enter my own home. The film production circus has come to town. There are seven 'trailers' the size of articulated lorries in the farmyard at Tallowquhairn, and there is a marquee on the tennis court where everyone, including us enjoyably, is eating. Over the last few days, a platoon of set builders has been in the house turning our home into someone else's, though disconcertingly some of our possessions are borrowed as props.

It is astonishing how many items have to be crammed into the set. It looks to my eye like a very disorganised antique shop, but when the camera has worked its magic, it will look just right. They turn up with highly skilled joiners, electricians, plumbers and decorators, and we find ourselves saying, 'While you are at it, you couldn't just fix this for us, could you?'

In his book about estate management, *Bearing Up*, Francis Fulford says that you should not worry about the ancestral pile crumbling, as something will always turn up. Films are proof of that and not for the first time I am very grateful that my great-grandmother's eye has given us a photogenic house, which occasionally gives us a very welcome bonus in the shape of a location fee, normally as the bailiffs are about to start calling.

This time we are masquerading as a Connecticut beach house and the Stars and Stripes are flying from a flagpole in the garden. John Paul Jones[39] would be pleased. I have been shooting (partridges, not movies) and I am wearing an old pair of plus fours. The young metropolitans in their jeans and sweatshirts give me a puzzled look as if to say, 'I don't remember there being a tramp in this scene.' Upstairs Glenn Close and Jonathan Pryce are having a bonk in our bedroom – this is scripted I should hasten to add – and I am relieved to say that it is not in our bed, which was rejected by the set dressers on the grounds of age.

I recall looking at the schedule and being amused that La Close has been booked into hairdressing for thirty minutes, earlier in the afternoon, to make her hair look 'post-coital'. I guess there must be a big market for sex for the third-agers. There is something hilariously incongruous about two seventy-year-olds grinding away, while all over the house technicians young enough to be their children are watching them on monitors.

I have arrived as they are starting another take and the whole house goes quiet. Everybody keeps looking my way and putting their fingers to their lips, and I watch the screen with suppressed mirth while Jonathan clambers onto Glenn and with much grunting and groaning simulates the act, rather perfunctorily if I may say so, before rolling off again.

I am asked if I would like to meet the stars and am ushered up onto the landing. Both actors are delightfully un-starry to talk to when they emerge from their – our – bedroom. Somewhere I have read that actors who play baddies are always the nicest and Glenn, the original 'bunny boiler', is proof of that and radiates warmth off-screen. She does not seem to be the slightest bit abashed at meeting her host while still in her bedclothes with post-coital hair, having just faked an orgasm in his bedroom, and I am very impressed at the professional way that she can flip in and out of a role.

---

39 John Paul Jones, founder of the US Navy and later Russian Admiral, was born on the estate in 1747 (not to be confused with the Led Zeppelin guitarist).

Over the next couple of days we talk more, and beneath those amazing cheekbones, she is clearly a down-to-earth countrywoman with a love of horses and dogs. She has her Cuban terrier on set with her, a bundle of mischief similar to a wire-haired Jack Russell. Filming one scene, it starts yapping enthusiastically and they have to cut mid-take.

When they have all gone, the same crew puts our house back together again and redecorates any rooms they have painted back to the colour of our choice. Sheri had been trying to persuade me for years that our bedroom needed painting so now, when I lie in bed gazing at the same ceiling that Glenn Close once looked at, I can say, 'Thank goodness I didn't allow you to persuade me to have our room painted, when the film company were going to do it for free. I knew something would turn up.'

It is so nice to be proved right.

One of the Brexit shibboleths is that UK farming is grossly inefficient, feather-bedded by subsidies, and a short sharp shock will boost productivity. But it seems to me that since the demise of the Milk Marketing Board (at the insistence of the EU) plunged the dairy industry into almost permanent recession, the dairy boys have been quite innovative to stay afloat. Unlike preceding centuries, there are few more revealing questions to ask a twenty-first-century dairy farmer than, 'How often do you milk your cows?'

Farmer Number One milks his fifty cows once a day. He follows the Norwegian system (as opposed to the Norwegian model we used to hear so much about). This entails leaving the calf on the cow and taking surplus milk once per day. His wife turns this into artisan cheese and yoghurt to sell at a premium in their farm shop, which they can do, being a small farm conveniently located near a major arterial route in a tourist area. The calves are also fattened, and the meat sold at a profit. They make a virtue of their cow-friendly dairy system as part of their marketing. They have little to fear from Brexit, as they have a successful niche product, and are less reliant on subsidies than others, but voted Remain as they are Liberals with Green tendencies.

Farmer Number Two milks his eighty cows twice per day, because he is an 'aye bin' (as in always been done this way). He milks in the dark at the beginning and end of the day and has another job as a delivery driver to make ends meet. They also rely heavily on his wife's income as the secretary at the village school, until the council closes it at the end of this year. Even when the milk price is good, he earns much less than the minimum wage from his farming, and frequently he has made a loss. He feels there is a risk that the end of the CAP and ultra-free trade policies could destroy family farms like his, but he voted Leave as he felt things couldn't get any worse anyway.

Farmer Number Three milks his one thousand cows three times per day, as they produce more milk that way from their 2.1 lactations on average. He achieves this by having a team of Romanians working in shifts for twenty hours in twenty-four. He reckons he is set to make a six-figure loss this year, but shrugs his shoulders and says he will make it all back in no time when the price per litre goes up by a couple of pence. He says he is in so deep with the bank that they don't dare pull the rug. His instinct was to vote Leave, but he was worried about the supply of Eastern Europeans drying up and the lack of Brits wanting to work, so he voted Remain.

Farmer Number Infinity has installed robots for his three hundred cows, so that they can go and get themselves milked when they feel like it. His cows live inside for twelve months of the year and all of his land is silaged now. He says less grass is wasted that way, although he has a twinge of conscience about the birdlife. He is also a bit concerned that he may start to receive less for his milk than his counterparts with 'free range cows'. He is a bit pissed off that the return from his dairy enterprise isn't pencilling out as his advisers said it would, but he enjoys his reputation as an innovator. He has the consolation of being able to set his farming losses against tax, as he has a number of other businesses, and is optimistic about farming in the long term. He voted Leave on principle.

Farmer Number Temporary Zero has Flekvieh cows, which are dual purpose, so he has turned them into beef suckler cows until the price of milk improves. Farmer Number Permanent Zero has sold all his cows and installed a 'concrete cow': an anaerobic digester. His farm now produces electricity rather than food. Their referendum votes were opaque.

✛ CHAPTER ELEVEN ✛

THE CRESCENDO of the autumn symphony is the arrival of the geese. We will just be starting to notice the toffee-apple smell of cercidiphyllum, and thinking about lighting fires in the evenings and wondering when the clocks go back; when *Pow!*, one morning we wake to the joyful, raucous sound of goose music and peel back the curtains to see five thousand of them on the shore.

It is another of nature's miracles. Geese have recently been seen by a pilot flying at 23,000 feet near Iceland. They seem excited to be back and intoxicated with relief at the end of their journey and so they gabble away at the tops of their voices, like a massive family reunion in the arrivals hall at Heathrow.

✛ ✛ ✛ ✛

The spectre of houses and cars crushed by fallen trees haunts me constantly. The thought of one of our trees causing a death is one that insurance can't erase. The Big State, unhelpfully, recently underlined landowners' responsibilities by making it mandatory to inspect roadside trees annually, to ensure that they are not in danger of falling. When I rang various forestry experts to see if I could pay them to do an annual inspection, they laughed and told me what I already knew: it is impossible to predict when a tree may suddenly give up its ghost and they weren't minded to take on a potential liability that was hard to insure. As a result, I conduct a rolling audit of the trees as I go around the estate.

It's an inexact science. Trees can be healthy one minute and near dead the next. Who is to say that if the ground is wet underneath, so that the roots have less grip, and a gale comes from a strange direction when the trees are in leaf and 'carrying too much sail', that any one of them might not topple over? Ivy, the death of stone buildings, is a contentious one in trees. Many people say it is harmless and often helps to keep trees upright;

on the other hand, it can sometimes make a tree top heavy. It certainly provides a rich environment for insects and birds.

I am reluctant to adopt the precautionary principle, evidently now being followed by various public bodies and quangos, of chopping down perfectly good trees because there is a slim chance they might blow over. But anything that looks dead, or dangerously 'on a lean', gets the chop and helps to fill the biomass boiler.

Today Wullie the tree surgeon, and his mate Ronnie and I, are looking at a young ash above Shore Cottage. It's an attractive proposition for harvesting — it must be about a hundred feet tall with a clean straight trunk, and no more than about fifteen inches diameter at the base, which is the maximum that the processor can manage. And it's growing on a steep slope, so maybe it's not as well-anchored as it might be. On the other hand, its crown is pleasingly symmetrical and it is starting to show that it has the potential to be a magnificent tree in its prime. It might be a good one to bequeath to future generations as a specimen tree. My grandfather's words echo in my head, 'A tree takes years to grow and only a few minutes to cut down with a chainsaw.'

'Do you think it would reach the cottage if it fell?'

Ronnie picks up a stick. 'Let's have a look.'

He walks off to one side and lines it up on the tree with the point of the stick covering the top of the tree and squints at it. Then carefully tilts the stick as if it is the tree falling towards the cottage.

'Yep, certainly make a mess of your roof anyway.'

Every day is a school day.

'Okay, better add it to the list then.'

✤ ✤ ✤ ✤

The politics of food are forced onto the news again. David Mundell, the local MP for Dumfriesshire, Clydesdale and Tweeddale, and Secretary of State for Scotland, has been confronted by an angry lynch mob at a local food bank. Viewing the footage on YouTube, I am shocked by the sight of a

British cabinet minister needing to be shepherded out of a side door to his car by police in the usually quiet Friar's Vennel, a street I know well, while a baying mob yells abuse at him.

It appears carefully scripted and, rather like the chorus in a school play, everyone seems to have one line to repeat. One man keeps shouting, 'Traitor!'

Every so often another, dressed like an extra in *Braveheart,* yells, 'Tory bastard!'

The majority repeat a mantra of 'Shame on you!'

Placards are waved. 'Break the Bedroom Tax!' and 'Down with Tory Welfare Cuts'.

There is an ugly undertone, reminiscent of another form of national socialism in the thirties. But to give him his due, Mundell appears unruffled and impassive in the face of the intimidation.

I have a gloomy feeling that these food banks are being written into history as part of a narrative of Tory misrule. There is a hope that balanced historians might see them in a historical context, as part of a tradition of charity stretching back through soup kitchens and so on, part of a philosophy of practical, tough love, a square meal rather than money for drink or drugs.

The facts might one day be picked over by economic historians, who might deduce that the price of food in real terms is relatively low compared to previous periods.[40] They might do a comparison with other countries and conclude that food banks are far from a British phenomenon. They might highlight statistics showing that the UK as a whole, though perhaps not Dumfries, is at or near full employment for those who are prepared to milk cows, or pick vegetables, or move to find work. In fact, they might postulate, Brexit was a reaction to the numbers of unfilled jobs in this country causing mass immigration.

Or will the dominant narrative be from social historians –

---

40 UK government statistics show that household spending on food is 10.5 per cent, the same as before the crash in 2007. In the 1950s it was a third.

social-ist historians – focusing on the headlines and the YouTube clips artfully manufactured by those who manipulate the mob? The juxtaposition of those two potent words, 'food' and 'banks', with all their emotional baggage of famines and bread riots, bank bailouts and wealthy bankers, and the 'failure of the capitalist system', makes the latter approach irresistible.

I would guess that there must be an historical correlation in rural areas between food poverty and poaching. But whether people are now so divorced from the countryside that they would no longer know what to do with 'one for the pot', or whether their palates have moved away from game, poaching seems to be at an all-time low. I have not heard landowners or keepers complaining about it for ages. Perhaps it is simply that pheasants are no longer worth anything, which rather supports the theory that in an historical context, food poverty is not as bad as reported, though no doubt utterly miserable if you are going hungry.

When I met with David Mundell as part of my research for this book, we talked about it. With his mild manner and softly spoken Dumfriesshire lilt, he is in fact the last person you would think of as a heartless Tory. He is genuinely self-effacing and, as the first British cabinet minister to come out as openly gay, compassionate. And it is this diffidence – almost unique in modern politics – that makes him the right man to present the face of reason and patient tolerance on behalf of HMG to a Scotland that now seethes with self-righteous anger. The more reasonable he is, the more the nationalists hate him, and it is why they demand his resignation daily.

He blinks owlishly, as he remembers the food bank debacle.

'The people running it were very upset. I had been invited along to see it and wanted to show my support. But food banks have been so weaponised [by the Left] that you can't have a reasonable discussion about them. There are complex reasons for people needing to use food banks. There has always been this type of support from, for example, the Church, and an attitude of helping, especially in rural areas. What I think they show is that there is less community cohesion now and that is why food banks have become more institutionalised.'

I guess that it must have been quite a shocking experience.

He gives me a look of weary resignation. 'It was rent-a-mob. They weren't locals, they had been bussed in for the day. Like at the weekend.'

I nod. There has just been an independence rally in Dumfries. The soundbite from the SNP was that it 'demonstrated the appetite for independence in Dumfries & Galloway', but eye-witnesses saw most of the marchers boarding coaches to go back to the Central Belt at the end of it.

'You get used to the constant abuse. It's relentless on social media. The SNP gives people licence to behave like that.'

I am struck by his quiet resilience.

We swap memories of the independence referendum that still casts a long shadow over Scotland.

'People across the UK don't realise just how intense it was. Much more so than Brexit, I thought. But Dumfries and Galloway voted two-thirds to a third to stay in the UK, by a greater margin in fact than voted Yes in Glasgow. Rural people played a very important part. The Yes campaign was very urban, and it came across that in an independent Scotland, the urban majority would prevail.'

He has never struck me as being particularly rustic, but he is in tune with the countryside.

'We are living in an increasingly metropolitan world. Outwith the Highlands and Islands, I represent the largest rural constituency in the UK. People in my office here in London simply don't realise that if I am in, say, Eskdalemuir, I can't be reached by text or email. Broadband is a huge issue in Scotland, it's partly topography and partly power supply.'

Which leads us onto Brexit and the implied threat to farming.

'I voted Remain, partly because I didn't want it all to kick off again ...' He means the independence 'neverendum'.

'Actually, I think Nicola Sturgeon made a significant misjudgement when she linked Brexit with independence. It ignores all the Leavers who are nationalists, her calculation was wrong, and those people were very influential in the general election.'

But if he was a Remainer, he is not a 'Remoaner'.

'Oh, we will be leaving. I think the Brexiteers have got to be accommodating. I mean, they have got what they want. I am supportive of a transition period.'

He represents Scotland on the relevant Brexit cabinet committees.

'I think we will get there, as we have at every milestone so far. The whole Cabinet has to sign off on it and I think they will. But you should not underestimate how difficult it is for the Prime Minister in a minority government.'

We discuss the threat of agriculture being used as a loss leader and our farmers being sold out in a new free-trading regime.

'I certainly don't underestimate how important farming is. As you know, the biggest centre of population in my constituency is Annan, and even there the economy is largely based on agriculture and fishing. I am very much of the opinion that farming should be supported. But it must be better than the CAP. It should be based on activity rather than land ownership, and on the wider contribution to wellbeing. It should be designed to keep communities going and more focused. We shouldn't support industrialised farming. I am someone who takes food security and food miles seriously. Lots of food is bought from countries where they can't feed themselves and we should recognise that.'

I am heartened by the knowledge that at least we have this quiet, decent man on our side.

✤ ✤ ✤ ✤

Autumn brings with it the Meet Card, now sitting on the mantelpiece. I am well aware of the hours of patient diplomacy by the Joint Masters that have gone into its production.

Today we are hosting a meet down on the shore below the house. Rosie is home and seeing her out on Chester, our coloured cob, is the icing on the cake. A meet always brings home to me hunting's universal appeal through Jaques' seven ages of man.

There are children spellbound. Then there are the adrenalin junkies of all ages and both (or should I now say all?) sexes, for whom hunting is all about the thrill of riding fast across natural country. Then there are the hound people, many of them on foot; they have probably walked puppies and have the satisfaction of greeting the hounds they've walked and watching them work in the field.

Watching gundogs work is one of the main reasons for shooting, but man's relationship with the canine world reaches its apotheosis in the hunting field. To breed a pack of hounds, carefully entering young hounds each year and training them to the point when they will ignore all other creatures and scent then chase a fox with deadly intensity – sometimes for miles, often without human intervention – is a special form of alchemy that is both art and science. Then there are the terrier men waiting on their quads, shotguns at the ready as they now double as the guns; for them the dizzying excitement of a hunt reaches its climax when there is a dig and the arcane challenges of working terriers underground is in prospect.

Finally, there are the foot followers, often old-age pensioners reliving past glories and assuaging the loneliness of widowhood by being part of a familiar community, when they follow in the car each Saturday.

Binding everyone together is the humour, the infectious laughter brought on by scaring ourselves stupid across a line of stiff hedges, or the *schadenfreude* when a local worthy lands in the mud. I remember once hopping off my horse for a pee behind a hedge, when one of the (many) pretty girls of the hunt rode past. 'Do you want me to hold it for you?' she tittered. I wasn't entirely sure that she was referring to the horse!

Seeing the work behind the scenes at the kennels, in committee meetings and at fundraisers, I realised the extent to which the rural community is enriched by the shared endeavour of maintaining the hunt. Friendships have been made that wouldn't otherwise have been imaginable across all ages and boundaries. As the field moves off up the beach, I can see landowners chatting to lorry drivers, BT engineers and relief milkers, all equals in the hunting field.

One day, Malc pointed out to me that if anything happened to either of us, we had a doctor, two nurses and a vet, and if it was terminal we had two joiners to make the coffin, an undertaker, still wearing his black tie under his hunting coat, and an Elvis impersonator to entertain the mourners. I don't think we have ever had a priest out with us, but in Yorkshire I hunted regularly with a clergyman.

✧ ✧ ✧ ✧

Fifty up. The sixth decade, oh dear; the NHS sends their idea of a birthday card in the form of an enrolment into a bowel cancer screening programme, taxpayer's money very well spent on reflection. The marketing fraternity take to the internet and the junk mail printing presses to send helpful advice on hair thinning, deafness, difficulty reading small print, incontinence, memory loss and other more personal failures.

For the landowner, it is a reminder that the hour-glass is starting to look heavier in its bottom cylinder, and the lawyer starts to perceive fee income from advice on 'starting to think about passing assets on'. It is clearly a lucrative business offering this advice. Sheri and I sit in sumptuously upholstered chairs around a polished table, gazing through vast glass walls across Edinburgh's roofscape from a reassuringly expensive height, in one of the city's most prominent skyscrapers.

It is a leap in the imagination from my first visits thirty years ago to a Georgian townhouse in the New Town and this is reflected in the fee. Lawyers charge by the minute. I sometimes wonder whether, if you sent them a Christmas card, they would charge out their time for opening it. When one of us asks a question, the other glares an ESP-laden look that says, you realise that question just cost us a hundred quid.

The lawyer, twinkly, charmingly and patiently, perhaps a tad too patiently for my liking, explains the deal. There are assets that form part of the business and attract inheritance tax relief and there are assets that don't. Over a certain threshold these will be taxed at forty per cent. He coughs slightly before delivering the bad news.

'The bad news is that since we last met, there has been a judgement that makes the case law on this less favourable in respect of the holiday letting property. If you let holiday cottages, you are no longer necessarily deemed to be running a business unless you offer some other attraction, such as a restaurant where your guests can eat.'

I digest this news as one would a smelly oyster.

'What? You mean … that can't be right … even the purpose-built log chalets?'

'I'm afraid so.' I think I detect a hint of satisfaction in the way he imparts this news.

I dug us further into debt to build the chalets, partly so that we had business assets that we could pass on without the Big State getting its sticky hands on them. How could anyone not think that we were running a business? I think of the hours Sheri and I have spent making up beds on Saturdays, cleaning up vomit and dog turds, and lugging pissed mattresses out of cottages. I think of the hours spent standing in the dark, my cheeks being whipped by horizontal rain, as I have tried to get boilers going again. I think of the midnight oil we have burnt administering bookings and uploading photographs onto websites via pulseless broadband.

I think of the mixed enjoyment of running a 'customer facing business' – of the time we have spent ensuring our guests get the most from their holidays, of calming hysterical women confronted by the indigenous insect life of Dumfries and Galloway, of the egregious Mr Baines, who banged on the door one night complaining that the heating had gone off at 10.30, because he and his family expected to wear T-shirts indoors at midnight, in November. Or the lady with OCD, who complained that the tourism leaflets in the basket were not in alphabetical order; complained about everything, in fact.

And then I think of the judge. Was he some legal fat cat, an appointee of the New Labour era? Had he ever had to worry about hospital corners on a freshly made bed, or filling potholes?

Looking further into it, it appears that there was some logic to the decision. It was a ruling on executors trying to claim relief on someone's second home being rented out for holidays, when not being used by the owner. I might have reached the same decision in that case. But the failure to be more specific in the judgement has potentially carted the rest of us. How is it, in our complacently perfect democracy, that a judge can subtly, perhaps even carelessly, alter circumstances beyond what elected politicians might originally have intended?

Inheritance Tax, or more correctly Bereavement Tax, since it is another burden that the bereaved have to carry, is used to raise money across the globe, but most heavily in these islands, where in Britain and Ireland it is still used as an instrument of social change. We persist in trying to prevent wealth fructifying in families and try to sweep it into the grasping paws of the state.

The advice is to take out lots of life insurance and then at some point hand over and live seven years. I hope that when the time comes, the thought of the Treasury getting its sticky mitts on our home will be enough to keep me clinging to life until it is safe to let go.

✢ ✢ ✢ ✢

The sheep arrive today. Apparently there are over one million sheep in Dumfries and Galloway, or four hundred and thirty per square mile, which makes seven sheep per person, the same as New Zealand, a staggering statistic when you consider how much of our region is covered in forestry, and a solemn reminder of how much of our economy locally is reliant on our woolly friends. There is a palpable gloom hanging over the industry at the moment. The majority of our sheepmeat goes to Europe, and the uncertainty of this market during the Brexit negotiations is getting on everyone's nerves.

Six hundred and fifty hoggs – young female sheep – come bounding off the back of McWilliam's lorry and go off to explore their new surroundings. It has become an annual ritual. I do a rough 'back of a fag packet' estimate of how many each field will take without the grass running out, and causing us the bore of having to move them. However, no plan will survive contact with our winter population of geese, who will eat the same grass, especially the 30,000 barnacles, who are protected.

We drive around dropping them off in groups of about fifty. I like looking at sheep, there is something deeply calming about watching them and the whole estate changes character when the cattle are housed, and the fields become more peaceful, pastoral places 'where sheep may safely graze'. I am less keen on having to deal with them; smelly, wilfully disobedient, scatter-brained, and prone to dying without reasonable excuse are only some of the ways I would describe them. Stockmen usually have a marked preference for sheep or cattle, and usually the latter.

'Sheep have one mission in life and that is to die. I cannae be doing with them. They dinnae even look good on a plate,' is the usual view of sheep from all farm workers save shepherds. Davie has enough and more to fill his day in the winter with the cattle, so I shepherd them myself, not that they take much looking after; and if the going gets tough, I ring their owner, who sends a man down with a couple of dogs to round them up and deal with any problems.

In my limited dealings with the lambs we have wintered, I have formed the view that the best type of sheep are other people's, though breed does come into it. We once made the mistake of wintering 'Blackies', horned Blackface sheep off the hills. They were forever getting their horns stuck in the fences, requiring me to get them out, usually skinning my knuckles in the process. These ones are polled, New Zealand Romneys, bred by our friends Marcus and Kate Maxwell. Romneys originated on the marshes of Kent, but were then genetically improved by those clever Kiwis – Kate is one – to be 'easy care' with good feet, and a remarkable desire to carry on living when compared to the rest of their species.

The money we get for looking after them over the winter provides a very welcome boost to our income, when the rents from holiday cottages start to tail off. Sheep are also great improvers of pasture. They are excellent grazers, eating almost any plant that grows in grass fields, so that the grass thickens up and we end up with a nice tight sward. Also, by two strokes of genius by our Creator, first, sheep will eat worms that affect cattle without any ill effect, and vice versa, so that alternating the grazing between cattle and sheep helps to keep the pasture free of parasites. Secondly, they will eat and therefore kill ragwort — a weed that is poisonous to cattle and horses — when it is in its early growth stages.

From now on 'looking the sheep' is an additional chore. Usually a pleasant one, but dragging a stinking carcass out after the foxes and badgers have been at it is always a low point.

✦ ✦ ✦ ✦

A *Farmers Weekly* survey reports that farmers are currently earning on average £12,600 per annum, against the public perception that they earn £43,000. I am forced to admit to Sheri that if we were to strip away the non-farm income on the estate, we would not be doing much better than average.

The figures are stark. It means that many farmers are earning much less than their employees and certainly less than the civil servants who come and inspect them. It is no wonder that many farmers voted Brexit, thinking that there was not much room on the downside. By coincidence, the price of wheat when we went into the Common Market in 1973 was £120 per tonne, and it would be close to the middle of its recent price range if it was £120 per tonne when we exit the EU in 2019.

It is hard to say whether the EU has exacerbated the situation or saved us from things getting worse. Even with the subsidy of around £25 per tonne, it is little short of a miracle that any of us is still in business. Is there any other profession that still earns what it did in 1973?

✦ CHAPTER TWELVE ✦

BY NOVEMBER the geese have an established routine. They roost out on the sandbanks, where we hear them chuckling at night; then at dawn, as the sun flares up behind the north Pennines and turns the sky into a Peter Scott study of orange and turquoise across the Solway, they form up on the tide line, like a medieval army cackling abuse at its opponents. Then suddenly – who gives the order? – they launch themselves at the shore, and as they come over the house, they wheel and fragment into skeins and rise up over the beech trees, heading off for their morning feed.

Walking the dogs later up on the barley stubble behind the house, we surprise a party of them. There is a magical soundless pause, followed by a roar like a rockfall down a mountain side as three hundred wings beat the air, and then a cacophony of honking and yapping as they lift and rise, buffeted by November gusts, and form their arrowhead. And all around them the other birds revelling in their flocks, perform acrobatics on the squally winds. The tableau of rooks, jackdaws and gulls tumbling in the foreground, with skeins of geese wheeling behind, is a tonic for the soul.

✦ ✦ ✦ ✦

In contrast to the Scottish independence referendum, when I knew very few people who voted Yes, the Brexit vote was highly contentious. After several heated dinner-party conversations, I was able to predict with some certainty where someone would be on the spectrum. The most intelligent people I know were all Leavers, as were the thickest, also the richest who could afford to gamble, and the poorest people who had nothing to lose. Those 'stuck in the middle' tended to be Remainers.[41] I admired David Cameron for calling the referendum and felt sorry for him being the fall

---

41 I hope my friends are not offended by this generalisation. They can amuse themselves by speculating on which category they and others sit in.

guy for previous prime ministers failing to do so, especially Major at the time of Maastricht, and Blair who had half-promised to hold one and who lost us the rebate.

From previous comments about the institutionalised officiousness of the Common Agricultural Policy, you may have deduced that I was a Leaver. In fact, when the time came, although my instinct was to leave the EU, when I weighed it up, I decided that maybe it was better to stick with the devil I knew all too well. The EU overall has an electoral incentive to protect farmers, which the UK does not. Also, none of us wanted to give the Nats another excuse for a referendum.

So, as it transpired, like most of my neighbours, I voted Remain, but without any great enthusiasm. The generational stereotypes were not reflected in our family. Dad's instinct was probably to leave, but he took soundings from all five of his children and their spouses, who were all Remainers. By contrast, the younger generation were more likely to be optimistic about our fortunes outside the EU and voted Leave, for which I admired them.

The image of a dyspeptic retired major choking on his porridge over the *Daily Infuriator* is an unattractive one and I try to moderate my reactions to events but, as Brexit unfolds, some of the Brexiteer rhetoric winds me up as much as the EU does. At the back of my mind is the spectre of the great agricultural depressions of the 1870s and the 1930s. I have just been lent a book[42] about the latter by my brother-in-law's father, John Holmes. It was so bad that there were negative rents: landowners paying tenants to farm the land to keep it in good order.

Within days there is the claim, 'Great news, Uruguay already wants to do a free trade deal with us.'

I groan.

'I'll bet they do.'

Uruguay has twelve million cattle or 3.8 per person. These cattle are no different from ours, except that they are on vast estates rather than

---

42 *Breaking New Ground: Norfolk Agriculture, 1914-1972* by Alec Dover, Coldbath Books, 2012.

small family farms, and tended by gauchos on a minimum wage of £1.20 per hour.

I have a vision of getting our team together.

'The good news, chaps, is that we are going to be trading with Uruguay now. The bad news is that your pay is going to have to be pegged to the Uruguayan minimum wage from now on. Oh, and those fancy new workplace pensions, they'll have to go.'

Not long after there is an article by Matthew Lynn[43] in the *Daily Telegraph*. He writes, 'Free trade benefits us even if the other country doesn't reciprocate ... Argentina's populist politicians love to impose tariffs that protect their industries, but that is no reason not to import their beef ... The UK is never going to be a major manufacturing power again. Nor is it going to have a major agricultural industry – small, crowded, damp islands can't expect to. We should spend very little time worrying about those sectors.'

Then Daniel Hannan writes an article[44] in which he describes us as 'post-agrarian' and says that we should not be worried that we now import forty-two per cent of our food. He advocates buying food from overseas and paying farmers to 'curate' the countryside.

Note the chilling phrase: post-agrarian. The smooth way that a metropolitan elitist seductively suggests that this tiresome 'one per cent of the economy' can somehow be airbrushed out of the way, while we import from the developing world and achieve the utopia of cheap food. It is a clash of 'anywheres' and 'somewheres'. It seems so obvious that it must sound unarguable in towns and cities, yet here in the countryside covering seventy per cent of the UK's land mass, where we are still very much 'agrarian', where farming underpins close to one hundred per cent of the local economy, it sounds childishly simplistic.

They must know, but choose not to acknowledge, that British farming produces the raw materials for a food processing industry that makes up

---

43 *Daily Telegraph* Business Supplement, 19 Jul 2016.

44 *Sunday Telegraph*, 6 Aug 2107.

fifteen per cent of the British economy. After all, why import raw milk when you can import butter or yoghurt made elsewhere? Why import live cattle to be slaughtered here, when you can import beefburgers, gelatine, bone-meal, leather and so on. They must know, but seem to have forgotten, that while farming accounts directly for one per cent of the economy, the industries that support farming – the fertiliser suppliers, the machinery salesmen, the marts, the agricultural builders and so on – account for over half as much again.

If you doubt me, go to an industrial estate on the edge of any market town and you will see rows of sheds dealing in the inputs for agriculture, or processing the outputs. They must know, but avoid acknowledging, that the British tourism industry, which accounts for ten per cent of the economy, relies on tourists seeing cattle and sheep in green fields and golden wheat crops waving in the summer breeze. They must know, but dodge the issue, that the British environment is a farmed environment and British wildlife is heavily dependent on, well, farming. The cowpats and the spilt grain in the fields are the building blocks for all our insects and birdlife.

Viewed from here, the economy is like a house of cards. Farming is a weak card, it is only the two of clubs, but it is right at the bottom holding up all the others.

The National Farmers Union likes to cite food security as a reason to keep British farming going. The National Miners Union used to argue the same thing, fat lot of good it did them. Brexiteers like to say, 'The U-boats are not coming back.' I was taught in some long-forgotten Army classroom that threat is the enemy's capability multiplied by their intent. How does that work in the modern age?

It occurs to me that whereas the Germans lost seventy-five per cent of their U-boat crews trying to starve us into submission, the capability bar seems to be lowered each year in the age of asymmetric warfare,[45]

---

45 The chaos caused by a Novichok nerve-agent attack in Salisbury in 2018 emphasises the point.

as technology hands more advantage to the terrorist. Is it possible that a dozen dirty bombs could disable the dozen or so major ports we rely on for importing our food, and drone attacks could simultaneously send thousands of tonnes of merchant shipping full of food to the bottom, before war has even been declared? What then?

We would have to regenerate our agriculture on a much smaller acreage to feed a much bigger population than last time. We would be growing vegetables on the hallowed turf at Lords and Wembley, if we have the seed. They say in the City that the period of greatest danger in markets is always when the people who remembered the last crash have retired. We are nearing the point when we will have no one left who remembers eating Woolton pies.[46]

A consultation paper thuds into my email inbox. The politicians are having another go at land reform and the various lobbying organisations, Scottish Land and Estates and the NFU, are urging their members to have their say; more midnight oil to be burnt defending our way of life. I had previously ignored such letters as we are 'owner occupiers' with no tenants, but they are now promoting the idea of community buyouts and diverting lottery and taxpayers' money into a Land Fund to assist them. In theory any land can now be blighted by the registration of a 'right to buy', though fortunately the European Convention on Human Rights prevents forced sales unless there is a public interest, such as a new motorway.

Land reform holds painful memories for my family. Both my father's grandmothers were Irish or strictly speaking Anglo-Irish, despite the Bagenals having lived there since 1580 and the Coopers since the 1650s.

Sir Nicholas Bagenal had risen to fame and fortune as Elizabeth I's

---

46 A pastry dish of vegetables widely served in the Second World War, when rationing and shortages made other dishes hard to prepare. It was named after Lord Woolton, the wartime Minister of Food.

'Marshall of Ireland', what in my day was the GOC. His son Henry, also Marshall, had the distinction of perhaps being the last general to be killed by an arrow hitting him in the eye, when he incautiously lifted his visor at the Battle of the Yellow Ford against his brother-in-law, the Earl of Tyrone.[47] The Bagenals' reward was 30,000 acres of County Carlow.[48]

The Coopers, on the other hand, had fought under Cromwell, and Cornet Cooper had so distinguished himself in battle against the O'Briens, that he ended up with Markree Castle and a large slice of Sligo.

Over the succeeding centuries, the Bagenals and Coopers had jogged along following the ups and downs of Irish history. Both families seem to have been benevolent landlords, who were therefore untroubled by the Troubles, and the Bagenals were early supporters of Irish Home Rule and Catholic emancipation. But this counted for nothing when it came to the various Land Acts of the late nineteenth century, which were a reaction to the callousness of some landowners during the Irish potato famines. The land was mostly compulsorily purchased by tenants and the ground rents on any remaining properties were fixed for all time by Parliament, so that by the time my father inherited Bagenalstown, the inflation of the twentieth century had eroded them almost to nothing.

But land reform in Ireland was nothing to the loss suffered by white farmers in Zimbabwe. My wife's family had gone there in 1890. In one of those quirks of fate, her great-uncle had met Cecil Rhodes at Oxford and followed him out to Africa to try his luck on the great trek north from the Cape. On reaching Mashonaland, he staked out an unoccupied patch of virgin wilderness south of the Zambesi and settled. And throughout the twentieth century, his descendants turned it into a model of agricultural and social administration.

Dams were built to preserve every drop of precious rain and the soil was carefully husbanded, so that it yielded as well as anywhere else in

---

47 This was a major historical footnote, as it caused Elizabeth I to despatch her favourite, the Earl of Essex, to deal with the rebellious O'Neills.

48 *Vicissitudes of an Anglo-Irish Family, 1530–1800* by Philip Bagenal, 1925.

the world, perhaps better, helping to turn Rhodesia and later Zimbabwe into a strong exporter. They grew roses for daily export to Amsterdam, as well as beef, cereals, vegetables and cotton. The farm supported over a thousand people and boasted a school and a hospital, and the workers were encouraged to have their own plots of land on which to grow mealies (maize).

Two generations answered the Empire's call and left first for Flanders and three decades later for North Africa, never to return. One of them, Sheri's grandfather Oliver Newton, won three Military Crosses in the desert before he was killed. A monument was erected to their memory on a high point overlooking Mashonaland.

If I could be granted a wish to revisit certain points in my life, one of them would be to go back and stay at Pimento, their lovely Cape Dutch-style house with its avenue of jacaranda trees, its wooded kopjes, and its weaver birds building nests around the swimming pool.

But it is all gone now, the fields are returning to scrub, the school and the hospital have closed, and the farm workers and their dependants have been driven off by ZANU PF thugs, to starve in the cities or flee to South Africa. My wife's family has been ethnically cleansed and a member of the ZANU PF establishment now occupies their home. Sheri's recently widowed aunt and her children just had time to shoot their horses and dogs before they left, to stop them falling into the hands of the mob. The war memorial has been desecrated, but still stands as a silent reproach to perfidious Albion – the Blair government, blamed by many white Zimbabweans for precipitating the land grab.

This was not a last-ditch stand by a die-hard British colonial family. They thought and still think of themselves as Zimbabweans; after all, they had lived there for five generations. They were 'progressive' in a correct use of the word, backing the liberal Garfield Todd against Ian Smith, employing African managers, and offering to give up a large chunk of their farm and help to establish black farmers on it; but only if it was done legally, in good order, and in accordance with the planned reforms. They harboured the hope that the British government would come forward with money, promised as part of the Lancaster House Agreement,[49] for a land reform deal.

Tragically, successive British governments procrastinated and finally in 1997 the incoming Blair government, trumpeting its 'ethical foreign policy', could not countenance giving money to colonialists and reneged on the deal. This refusal infuriated Mugabe, who then embarked on a ruthless and disorderly land-confiscation programme, which ended up bringing his country close to starvation.

After that uncalled for digression into family history, we return to Scotland. Proponents of land reform would no doubt be keen to highlight parallels with Ireland and Zimbabwe. The history of Scotland is no less bloody, and they would argue that land is concentrated in the hands of 'The Few'. The Scottish Land Commission, which sounds like something out of a Marxist playbook, bases its assumptions on the fact that half of the privately owned land in Scotland is in the hands of 432 families.

This fact is undeniable, although the 'privately owned' bit is routinely ignored by journalists, as are the vast acreages in quasi-public ownership via the Crown Estates, the Forestry Commission, RSPB, the National Trust, John Muir Trust and the MOD. And most of the estates in question rely on their owners pumping in money from other sources, as they comprise unyielding rock and heather in the Highlands, and are in many cases locked into long-term tenancies and crofts. Nevertheless, the disparity in wealth, always a precondition for revolution, is an uncomfortable one in the 'age of austerity'.

However, there are differences. We have not had a famine in Scotland, like the ones that provoked the Irish Land Acts (and also the repeal of the Corn Laws), since the mid-nineteenth century; although famines were a regular threat, and the wet summers of the mid-1840s caused equal misery

---

49 Named after Lancaster House in London, where the ceasefire was brokered that brought the civil war to an end in 1979, and paved the way for democratic elections and black majority rule. Land Reform was a key component of the agreement. Mugabe agreed to wait ten years and then British and American funds were promised to buy the white settlers out under a 'willing buyer, willing seller' principle. The money was never forthcoming.

in Scotland, when the spores of the potato blight blew across the Irish Sea.

Critically, unlike Ireland or Zimbabwe, the land has not been gained by conquest. Some of it may have been allocated by the Crown in what today may seem to us as rather dubious circumstances, particularly at the time of the Reformation, but the titles are legal. And increasingly, lairds are often now self-made men who have bought their estates anyhow.

Instead the Left, especially the Scottish Green Party, have carefully developed a doctrine for land reform that takes its philosophy from the Marxist dogma that 'all property is theft' and its history from the misery of the Highland Clearances. It is promulgated in books with titles like *The Poor Had No Lawyers*.

No reasonable person could deny the wrongs of the clearances, which now seem to occupy a place in Scotland's history similar to the Holocaust in Israel's and, like discussing the Holocaust, historians do so at their peril. However, viewing the clearances from the landowner's end of the telescope, it is clear they were faced with a serious problem.

In the early part of the nineteenth century, there was a dramatic population explosion. No one quite knows why, as there were no significant advances in medicine, and certainly not in nutrition. Peter Crookston[50] quotes figures from the Gairloch Estate, where the population rose from 1437 in 1801 to 4445 in 1831. This exposed the inefficiencies of the traditional run-rig system of agriculture and starvation followed.

Something had to be done, but it was the manner in which (not all) landowners responded to the crisis that was so wrong. Many reneged on the centuries-old, two-way loyalty implicit in the culture of *dùthchas,* that bound clansmen to their chiefs, but also signified a hereditary right to the place of their birth. They forced people off the land to make way for a more sustainable system of farming (financially, if not always environmentally), based on sheep. The displaced cottars were either coerced into crofts on the coast that were too small to sustain them, and a life of kelp gathering, or drifted away altogether into Glasgow or abroad. Ironically, many of

---

50 *Voices from the Hill* by Peter Crookston, CreateSpace, 2018.

those cleared went on to pursue their own clearances of aboriginal peoples in the New World.

Crookston's book focuses on the Mackenzies of Gairloch, who tried a different approach. Successive lairds kept people on the land by encouraging them to adopt modern farming practices and also, very entrepreneurially, by developing a fishing industry. It was incredibly hard and they only partially succeeded. One of them, Sir Francis Mackenzie, eventually drove himself insane trying to improve the estate, so that it could feed its people.

The iniquities of the clearances provoked the British government to act and Gladstone enacted the Crofters Holdings Act of 1886, which gave security of tenure and brought the clearances to an end. But land reform is still seen as unfinished business and to many people it is as if the clearances happened yesterday.

The Mackenzies are still there and although no clearance of any sort was ever carried out on Gairloch Estate, speaking to the current laird, John Mackenzie of Gairloch, it is clear that he is tarred with the same brush as every other crofting landowner in the Highlands. The crofting acts have caused a similar situation to that in Ireland. Croft rents are fixed by the Scottish Land Court, and in Gairloch's case at £10 per annum. Rent levels are so low that some estates don't even bother to collect it.

The crofters can buy their crofts at the (statutory) multiplier of fifteen times annual rent, and then, after a period of time has elapsed, sell them on the open market. An advertisement in the *Ross-shire Journal* in July 2018 offered an 'Excellent opportunity to purchase approx. 3.5 acres of owner-occupied croft land with fantastic views of Loch Gairloch ... a 5000-square-foot agricultural shed and garage. Potential for house site.'

Note the word 'potential'. If planning potential were remotely likely, the selling agent would no doubt have made much of it.

All this could have been yours for a fixed price of £120,000. The Gairloch Estate received around £150 for it. As John says, 'Someone is doing quite nicely out of this and it ain't the laird!'

But we are not in the Highlands and it is harder to argue that Lowland estates like this one are tainted with ancient wrongs. That does not stop people trying. History used to credit lairds like William Craik with being 'improvers', heroes of the Agricultural Revolution like Robert Bakewell and Turnip Townshend. But revisionist historians now argue that the improving lairds were guilty of clearances when they enclosed the land. They accuse them of causing hardship and mass emigration, when they broke up what Aitchison and Cassell call in *The Lowland Clearances*,[51] 'the fabric of Scotland's rural farming community, a peasant society engaged in a communal system of subsistence farming.'

Living here and viewing the archaeological evidence on the ground, I just don't buy it. Of all the people who have held this land since the Iron Age hunter-gatherers three millennia ago (in their fort behind our house), no one has left one-tenth of the mark left by William Craik.

In 1736, Craik inherited a windswept, treeless peninsula covered in bracken, heather and whins on the high ground, and rushes and goat willow in the low-lying bits. Eking out a Hobbesian existence were perhaps at most one hundred people in four or five 'fermtouns', a small cluster of buildings for the farm tenants, housed in smoky, turf-roofed cottages with dirt floors, unchanged in construction since pre-Roman times. They operated a run-rig system of arable farming with rudimentary tools on the in-bye land and grazed their cattle on common grazing. Archaeological digs show that cockles off the shore formed a large part of their diet. Malnutrition was rife.

The evidence of Craik's restless spirit is all around us. He turned the old fermtouns into model farm steadings and cottages with slate roofs. His stone dykes[52] built from huge granite boulders still stand and many of his land drains still function below the clay merse[53] that he transformed

---

51 *The Lowland Clearances: Scotland's Silent Revolution, 1760–1830* by Peter Aitchison & Andrew Cassell, Birlinn, 2016. The book grew out of a BBC Radio Scotland series.

52 It is one of the quirks of the English language that dykes are walls in some parts of the UK and ditches in others.

53 Marsh.

into productive farmland. He took Jethro Tull's ideas of crop husbandry to a new level, inventing new machinery, crop rotations and methods of soil husbandry.

There are records of his cattle being too large for the local abattoirs to hang up. And he built the church in Kirkbean with its laird's pew raised to one side at the front, so that he could see that all his tenants were there. He must have employed literally thousands of people to achieve all that he did. He certainly ripped apart 'the fabric of the rural community', but he replaced it with a far superior cloth, one that endured until mechanisation, and helped to create a rural middle class of grieves, merchants and craftsmen in the process.

Swift wrote in 1726, 'Whoever could make two ears of corn or two blades of grass to grow ... where only one grew before, would deserve better of mankind, and do more essential service to his country than the whole race of politicians put together.'[54]

By the time Craik died in 1798, the estate was probably capable of feeding a thousand times more people.

But, of course, Craik was motivated by enlightened *capitalism* and the land was no longer managed 'communally'. Hence the revisionism driven by an atavistic yearning for a prelapsarian state, where everyone can be a smallholder owning one cow that roams across the fenceless common, dodging the traffic and spreading disease as it goes. The Scottish Green Party is not known as the Iron Age Appreciation Society for nothing. I think the revisionism needs revising.

In the meantime, the Scottish Government supports high-profile community buy-outs. Some have been successful, others less so. They have generally needed large public subsidies at the expense of public services across the rest of Scotland, a case of supporting the few, not the many. And a frequent refrain from tenants of the new communities is, 'In the old days,

---

54 One of the frustrations of farming in the twenty-first century is that, ironically, trying to grow two blades of grass instead of one is often judged by public opinion to be wrong, though no less useful.

I just rang up the factor to have my roof repaired, but now I have to go and argue my case in a committee.'

In Ireland, so Irish farmers tell me, an unfortunate side effect of land reform was to preserve for all time a pattern of smallholdings that leaves its agriculture inefficient and reliant on subsidy. There is a whole genre of twentieth-century Irish literature devoted to the grinding poverty of small farmers as a result.

Of course, in Zimbabwe, the clearances and the starvation came after land reform.

Winter

+ CHAPTER THIRTEEN +

PULLING UP at the cattle sheds, I disturb the resident population of pheasants, who take off and swoop expertly through the main shed and out low over the silage pit. These are the ones with a high IQ, not something one normally associates with pheasants, who otherwise display a poultry-like gormlessness. They have worked out that there is a reliable source of food here and that it is the ultimate sanctuary, as we dare not shoot too close to the shed in case it stampedes the cattle. Seeing them picking around where some feed has been spilt, I am reminded that they were spread across the Roman Empire as farmyard fowl.

We have cattle going away tomorrow and I have a replacement ear tag for Davie to put in one before it goes. It seems a waste of money and plastic, when it is only going to be worn for a day before it goes to the abattoir, but they won't accept it without two tags. When I get to the crush, Davie is clipping their bellies. I don't distract him. The young bull in the crush is agitated by the clippers and threatens to kick them out of Davie's hand. It is the easiest way to get your arm broken, if you don't watch what you are doing, and an aching bone of contention between the farming industry and the abattoirs.

Their bellies need clipping so that the area where they make the incision to gut and skin the carcass is clean. Sound supply chain management would suggest that this operation should be done at the point in the chain where it is easiest and safest – at the abattoir once the animal is dead, as happens in other countries, not when it is leaping around in a cold, wet farmyard. But submissions to the Big Brothers (Business and State), on the grounds of health and safety, have hitherto fallen on deaf ears. Big Business does not want to absorb the cost and Big State either does not care, or does not want to go against his brother.

✦ ✦ ✦ ✦

About sixty acres of the estate is low-lying rush pasture close to the sea. It is difficult land to farm with its heavy clay 'man's land', capable of good yields of wheat in a dry year in periods when grain prices have justified the expense of maintaining the field drainage. But with wheat lower in real terms than almost any time in our history, I am happy to farm it for its wildlife, cutting mosaics in the rushes and grazing it with low densities of cattle, and receive a small payment from the EU for doing so. The real reward, though, comes in the form of the snipe shooting.

Whenever I organise a day's snipe shooting, I always think of General George. To say that he was a mentor would be taking it a bit far, as I only met him perhaps a dozen times, but Major General Sir George Burns, to give him his full title, was one of the people in my life who made the greatest impression on me. Colonel of the Regiment when I was a young officer, he was more of a grandfather, or perhaps a slightly rakish great-uncle, to everyone from the commanding officer down to the youngest guardsman. Whenever he visited the battalion, even in the most difficult circumstances, morale went up several notches. He had that rare gift of lighting up a room when he walked into it and making all he greeted feel special.

As a young officer, General George had been ADC to the Viceroy of India, the Marquess of Linlithgow, in 1938. Over a glass of port in the Officers' Mess, the smoke from his cigarette dying his grizzled walrus moustache a deeper shade of yellow and bringing a tear to his bloodshot eyes, he would tell us how he had not had to shave himself or tie his own shoelaces for a whole year.

When he had first arrived in the post, the Viceroy had told him that his first job was to organise a week's *shikar*, or hunting. He had set off on his reconnaissance and came to a village where there was talk of huge numbers of snipe. He walked the bogs himself and saw that the snipe were indeed very plentiful. With great excitement, he had organised for the vice-regal train to be loaded up with the vice-regal chefs and plenty to eat and drink. He had mobilised the vice-regal bodyguard and had sent signals redeploying a whole cavalry brigade to picquet the route and secure the area, and then they had set off.

'And do you know?' he said, with a mournful sense of the ridiculous. 'We shot six snipe all week.'

That is part of the attraction of *Gallinago gallinago*, the anticipation. They are more plentiful here now than I remember as a boy, probably because we have more grassland poached by cattle, and sometimes the bogs seem to be crawling with snipe, but at others they have an infuriating tendency to make themselves scarce at the critical moment. Like all waders, they are as happy out on the foreshore as they are on land, and we always try for snipe when the tide is in. They feed by sticking their long beaks into the mud, ideally into a cowpat, so conditions are best when they are moist – we do moist rather well in Galloway.

If the bogs are too dry or too much under water, then there is a disappointing lack of action, but when they come off in wisps with their piercing *scaap* echoing across the bog and climb steeply towards the guns, jinking as they go, there is no more testing quarry than the snipe. The beaters join in the excitement, shouting 'Snipe, Snipe!' as each one rises, so that the guns, Oliver and his friends, desperately look skyward trying to locate the birds, which look almost like bats when they come over at height.

My falconer friend Greg tells me that when he flies his peregrine over the same ground, they are apt to clamp down low in the rushes rather than risk flight, so it is interesting how they have adapted their defence measures to the invention of the shotgun. The smaller jack snipe, which is scarcer and protected, flies low in front of the beating line and pitches in again. Do they know that this is the safest way to react?

Snipe are notoriously difficult to pick, so the end of a drive invariably becomes a gundog field trial with guns, beaters and pickers-up hunting through the rushes together for the tiny birds. Eating them on toast a few days later, cooked whole with their bills bent through their breasts and wrapped in bacon, is one of the culinary treats of winter.

✣ ✣ ✣ ✣

The tractor groans over the ruts like a tank through no-man's-land on the way to feed the dry cows – the spring calvers whose calves have been weaned off them. It is an effort not to be jolted out of the seat and I am praying that the tractor doesn't get stuck in the unyielding mud, and necessitate a humiliating call for someone to come and pull us out. It's only December, but already the field looks like a bad day on the Somme. Better days on the same spot, standing waist-high in golden corn, or strolling across clover-flecked grass, now seem like a vision of peacetime during a relentless bombardment.

The winter feeding campaign has reached its attritional phase. I grimace at the thought of the damage being done to the soil structure with every spin of the wheels. The cows mill about expectantly, and I examine them critically for lameness or sickness, or, worse, signs of an abortion. We have had a few problems lately, when bits of silage have blown into their eyes and caused them to swell up. I am praying that this won't mean bringing a cow in for an injection into its eyelid.

At last I make it to the oasis of dryer ground where we are feeding them, and I drop the trailer off, so that as I pull away, there are twenty-five woolly beasts jostling around the trailer in a haze of steam. There is one cow for every feeding space on the trailer; any more and there is the risk of the cows barging each other and one of them slipping a calf. The empty feed trailer, when I get there, is axle-high in mud and the tow ring is well and truly buried. It is a tense fishing fumble with the tow hook to engage it, and there are a couple of false starts when the trailer lifts excitedly, only to slip off the hook and fall back down again. At last I see it on there, and I hear the satisfying clunk as the tow hook comes back up and engages; the return journey with a lighter trailer should be easier, and then there are just four more lots to feed.

'Out wintering' is the latest buzz phrase in the farming press. As well as obviating the need for investment in new sheds, the saving on bedding, on mucking out the sheds and spreading the dung is considerable. Added to which, the cattle are healthier and fitter for walking around outside rather than lying like couch potatoes inside, and they will be easier to calve as a result. Set against that, they eat more outside in the cold and wet to maintain themselves, and there is the cost of time and diesel and wear and tear on the machinery to consider; the mud consists of microscopic particles that get inside the wheel bearings and destroy them.

Then there is the impression that it gives to the outside world. There are few farmers who haven't received a visit from an SSPCA inspector after a call from a concerned member of the public. The inspectors invariably agree that the cattle look healthy and are well cared for, and besides, cattle sheds are a relatively recent innovation, but it leaves a nasty taste.

It all goes well in a dry winter, even when there are hard frosts or snow on the ground; the cows thrive and the extra straw we haven't had to buy means money we can spend on other things. But in a wet winter, when the BBC weather map shows bands of rain moving across the country in lurid green and blue patterns, the fields of Galloway turn to mud and our morale sinks even lower, as we think of the damaged land that may take several years to repair.

When we first started the herd, we had no option but to keep them outside. The dairy sheds my father put up in the early seventies had either collapsed under the great snow of 1996, or become so unsafe that we were unable to put cattle in them. With the help of an EU grant, I had built a shed to house the young stock and then gradually added to it as the years have gone by, so that now we can have around four hundred cattle inside.

This is the last winter we will need to keep stock outside. After scrimping and saving to build all this cattle housing, it will be just my luck if the weather shifts back to a run of dry winters again so that we can, but I will not be complaining if it does.

✣   ✣   ✣   ✣

Bumping along the West Avenue – it's time to do something about these potholes again – I see a vast rectangular object moving out of the Lodge. As I get closer, I see that it is a shiny new widescreen television, the largest I have ever seen. It is clutched at both ends by a pair of pudgy hands and is being propelled by plump legs, encased in what appears to be a black nylon tracksuit and a pair of fluffy slippers.

Ah, so they *are* flitting.

She sees me and adopts a demeanour of pitiful victimhood. 'Could you give me a hand with the telly, please?'

Unbelievable. I wind down the window.

'Actually, Iris, I think by rights that television should belong to me.'

She gives me a sour look and shakes her head as if to say, how could you behave so ungenerously towards me, what with my heart and all.

I drive on. There doesn't seem much to be gained from prolonging the conversation and besides, what was it Napoleon said? 'Never interrupt an enemy while they are making a mistake.' I chuckle involuntarily. The scene has proved a point and may even be the foundation for an important sociological theory. Let's modestly call it Blackett's Law. It is an infallible rule – now backed up by this empirical evidence – that the size of the rent arrears is in direct proportion to the size of the television. I could be ungallant and go on to say that there is also a strong correlation with the extent of the waistband of the tenant, but let's not go there.

The flit had been a while coming. Flits, incidentally, for readers in the leafier suburbs who have no knowledge of such matters, are when a tenant moves house suddenly with the intent of breaking contact with their creditors – the foremost of which will invariably be the landlord.

Over the next few weeks following the flit, letters will accumulate on the mat like autumn leaves: final demands from the purveyors of every known comfort, chiefly the aforementioned television and the commodious three-piece suite now awaiting a skip outside, summonses for non-payment of council tax and, perhaps what has clinched the decision to go, notices of intent to cut off all services to the cottage.

If the panel of wise men and women who advise the Governor of the Bank of England want evidence of the levels of indebtedness in the economy, they could do worse than ask private landlords to send them regular measurements of these piles in feet and inches. They are an excellent barometer of the relative stupidity and irresponsibility of lenders and borrowers alike.

After a while, the Big State and his nauseating brother Big Business will cotton on to the fact that the doves have flown and search around for another victim: the landlord. TV Licensing will start to send me threatening letters, as will the utility companies, and the council will be after me for council tax – charged at double the rate on an empty property, regardless of the difficulties of re-letting a cottage that now needs a thorough renovation.

Relations with Iris and her brother Barry had been worsening steadily. There had been the unfortunate incident of the disintegrating lavatory. It had collapsed under the elephantine weight of one of them, presumably mid-operation. They had insinuated that it was my fault that the offending appliance, installed several years before I was born at a guess, was of such shoddy workmanship and inferior quality that it had failed so spectacularly. And they had asserted boldly and with much invective that the liability for replacing it rested squarely with the landlord. I, on the other hand, was of a mind to take a different view, though I ended up paying all the same to defend the moral high ground and to comply with the Big State's 'Landlord's Repairing Standard'.

Then there was the matter of the rent. It had been paid regularly for a number of years and then dried up. I knocked on their door politely and then progressively more assertively to demand payment. They followed the predictable programme of feigned confusion, promises, excuses, evasiveness, and complaints about the property: 'By rights you should be paying us to live here, the state it's in.' And, finally, non-speaks.

The last straw, as far as they were concerned, came when I successfully managed to persuade the Big State to pay their housing benefit directly into our bank account. I had been to the relevant council department and stated my case. The bored civil servant (such a misnomer in his case), after some prompting from me, had admitted that, in general terms, the regulations did state that the landlord was entitled to request direct payment after several months' arrears. But he was unable to discuss the specifics of any case, and this appeared to give him satisfaction, without the express permission of the individuals concerned. 'We are bound by data protection legislation.'

I proffered a consent form to Iris and Barry and it seemed their inability to earn a living by working was not due to an awareness of their self-interest. Iris grabbed it, announced that she would be taking legal advice, and disappeared behind the door. The form was never seen again.

I was in that position so often engineered by the Big State – Catch-22.

Finally, I rang the council, this time the Crimestoppers hotline.

'Hello, is that Crimestoppers?'

'Yes, can I help?' A friendly, solicitous tone.

'Oh yes, I have a crime to report.'

'Right, well I will just take down some details.' Enthusiasm. 'Can you tell me about it.'

'I have reason to believe that some people are claiming housing benefit fraudulently.'

'I see.' Hesitation. 'Can you give me a bit more information?'

'Well, to my certain knowledge they are taking housing benefit from the government and not passing it on in rent.'

'And who might you be?' Less friendly now.

'I'm the landlord.'

'That's not a crime.' Firmness bordering on rudeness.

'What?'

'That is a civil matter and we don't get involved in these type of situations.'

'So you don't think fraud is a crime.'

'No, I'm not saying that …'

'Look, we can have this conversation on the front page of *The Standard*, or perhaps you can be kind and have a word with the housing benefit office for me.'

I got the rent paid, but the arrears were another matter. After a short deliberation, I went through the motions of obtaining a court order and this precipitated the flit, as I guessed it probably would.

When I broke into the house later that night, the electricity had been cut off. The walls were lined with wax dolls of every description leering crazily at me in the dark. I beat a hasty retreat. On my next visit in daylight, I found that the dolls and anything else of any value had been spirited away. Poking around in the favela of sheds they had erected in the garden, I deduced that they had been supplementing their benefits by trading on eBay, as there were job lots of Christmas cards, Engelbert Humperdinck CDs, cuckoo clocks in boxes, and other esoterica stacked up ready to sell. I left messages on their mobiles, but never heard of them again.

Being a landlord gives one a front-row seat for the daily drama of the welfare state. For years we had relied on the steady flow of housing benefit to provide rent from the estate cottages. These had once all been full of farm workers but, since increasing mechanisation of agriculture and the advent of arable contractors, they now provide vital income to underpin the mercurial returns from farming. Housing benefit seemed to provide a guaranteed income for landlords and many seized the opportunity, so that in large swathes of rural Scotland, estates now provide more 'affordable housing' than the local authority. As the housing benefit has not risen in line with rents for the last twenty years or so, it has become progressively less attractive.

For years it was like living in a reality TV show about 'Welfare Britain'. We had a succession of tenants who arrived displaying a disabled badge in their cars, nursing a 'condition' that had put them permanently 'on the sick', like a 'Blighty wound' in the First World War.

There was Gary, whom I saw one day hobbling down the pavement in Dumfries to sign on at the benefits office. It was a pitiful spectacle, as he hauled himself along, hunched over with a withered arm, dragging one leg. It was also an astonishing sight, as he had proudly told me only the day before that he had been up on his roof and cleaned out all the gutters.

Or there was Stevie, who was seemingly unable to work, but kept his garden in an immaculate condition and had a large Portakabin dropped off in his driveway for his 'workshop'. It was still there when he left and was only disposed of with considerable effort and expense.

For the first few years I saw myself as a benevolent landlord, the type who would never 'put anyone oot'. But as I had to deal with more properties left in appalling conditions, after months with no rent, I took a harder line. The final straw came with two middle-aged ladies named Beryl and Brenda. The two of them lived together in a state of perpetual grievance. We all assumed, not that it bothered anybody, that they were gay in the modern sense of the word, but gay in the original sense they were not.

They flaunted their drudgery as a shield against the world and their body odour was such that people would go to extreme lengths to avoid sitting near them on the bus. The cottage was rapidly becoming a slum, and the neighbours said that they could often hear a dog barking inside, but had never seen it being taken for a walk. The rent arrears built up and any attempts to negotiate were met with sullen obstructiveness.

I checked the lease and saw that they were not complying with any of its provisions and served notice, giving them the stated period to move out. Nothing happened. So I consulted a lawyer in Dumfries and proceeded to obtain an eviction order. The day arrived for the hearing.

My brief greeted me cheerfully, 'Have you done this before? No? Well, this should all be fine, with a bit of luck they won't turn up to contest it.'

It was our turn and we were ushered into the courtroom, where I learnt to my dismay that not only had they turned up, but the procedure is for the landlord to sit next to his lawyer at a table below the sheriff, opposite the tenants on the other side of the table with theirs. I bid them good morning and got a scowl in return, so I stared fixedly at a point on the wall behind them.

All seemed to go according to plan, until their lawyer stood up. To my untutored eye, he looked sharp. He exuded confidence and the way he flicked his gown back over his shoulders and deployed rhetorical flourishes made me wonder where they had found him. The thrust of his advocacy seemed to suggest that somehow it was all my fault. Apparently, I had been remiss in not complying with sub-section seven of section 'c', of something-or-other.

My lawyer tugged me on the sleeve and bent round to whisper in my ear, 'I'm awfully sorry. I think we're buggered.'

My heart sank. Would this mean years more of having to avoid looking at Beryl and Brenda's beards, while I reasoned with them? I was mystified. Clearly a lease no longer did what it says on the tin. As he carried on detailing my administrative shortcomings as a landlord, I ran through possible contingency plans in my head, and was briefly considering selling up and moving away ourselves, when he concluded his peroration and sat down.

We all looked at the sheriff, who from the twinkle in his eye appeared to find the whole situation rather more amusing than either party in the dispute.

'In this case,' he began, 'the law might say that the tenants are in the right, because the landlord has not served notice correctly and therefore their right to continue living at the property has been disturbed unjustly.'

He paused for effect.

'On the other hand, it might reasonably take the view that the tenants have not been complying with the lease regarding the upkeep of the property and the keeping of a pet without the landlord's permission, nor have they been paying the rent for some considerable time. I therefore find in favour of the landlord.'

There is a God after all.

When they finally moved out, I went into the cottage; and promptly ran back out again and threw up in the garden.

We accepted no more tenants on housing benefit after that, unless they were pensioners or had an obvious disability. To be fair to the tenants, in those early days, the cottages were mostly unmodernised, any heating was by a back boiler behind the coal fire, and there was no insulation or double glazing, but the rents, while barely higher than the cost of maintaining the properties, were fair. But as we did the cottages up, one by one, we put the rents up and sought good tenants, who would look after the cottages and pay the rent on time.

As I write, touching wood, we have not had an empty property or any bad debts for years, and we genuinely like all our cottage tenants, who have become good friends. Often, they have brought useful skills with them, so that we have a joiner, a mechanic and a stonemason living here now. It is, after all, one of the best perks of the job that you can choose who your neighbours are.

The Scottish Government has since changed the law to make it even harder to evict tenants. Landlords are now treated as potential criminals and have to pay a fee to be put on a register, so that any shortcomings on our part can be reported by the tenants and investigated by the Big State. There is apparently a blacklist of 'rogue landlords', but it is illegal to publish details of bad tenants.

⁺ CHAPTER FOURTEEN ⁺

JANUARY. WALKS at this time of year become litter patrols. All but the beech leaves have disappeared, leaving every twig revealed, and I find myself leaning into the hedges to pick black 'witches knickers' – fragments of silage wrap. I don't mind picking up agricultural black plastic, in fact I consider it a duty to clean up after ourselves. I get annoyed about all the other rubbish, but pick it up anyway. Normally it's on the verges, shorn of their summer froth of umbelliflora and revealing all manner of curiosities, and the pick-up accumulates a collection of beer cans and crisp packets on the floor, which I keep forgetting to transfer to the bins.

Today there is a balloon blowing about under the dyke at the top of the Borron Bank. Suppressing a sigh, I stoop to pick it up and then pause. It has a message:

Hope this follows you Richard
High up in Heaven
Alan F

It feels a trespass to pick it up and consign it to the rubbish. Who was Richard? And who, for that matter, was Alan F. What was their relationship? The heart-shaped balloon and the pink ribbon indicate something more than friendship. Was it the love that now dares to speak its name? Or a more casual acquaintance? Probably the latter, or he wouldn't have added an F. I imagine a graveside with a reading of Auden's *Funeral Blues* and Richard's grieving friends releasing balloons as the coffin is lowered.

I hesitate, then sadly prick it on a briar and put it in my pocket. Its job has been done. It has provided some catharsis and comfort, or not, and it hasn't followed Richard high up in heaven, not all the way anyway, and now litters our fields and threatens to end up harming wildlife or livestock, or to blow out to sea and end up inside a whale.

I feel a killjoy seeking to deny people the simple pleasure of releasing balloons or lanterns into the sky. City folk wouldn't understand and think that I was being a whinging farmer, but it is becoming more of a nuisance, and I seem to pick up more fallen symbols from birthdays, weddings, civil partnerships, funerals and bar mitzvahs every year. And when the wheat ripens in the summer and the whole place turns into a tinder box, releasing lanterns seems plain daft.

Yet there is nothing quite like a message in a bottle, or written on a balloon, for bringing the outside world in.

⚜ ⚜ ⚜ ⚜

As Hunt Chairman, it was agreed that I would be the spokesman for any media stories. My first introduction to what we have learnt during the Trump presidency to call 'fake news' was a headline in a local newspaper, 'FOX TORN TO PIECES', with a story alleging that an anonymous woman had been 'horrified' to find a dead fox 'ripped to shreds ... in an area of the town by the war memorial.'

Apparently, 'what made it suspicious was the fact there were a lot of hoof marks in the grass around the carcass.' There was a photograph of dubious origin purporting to show fox remains and a statement from 'national animal welfare charity' the League against Cruel Sports, saying that they had been 'inundated with calls'. Fortunately, unlike the editor of the newspaper, the police had seen through it and issued a statement, saying, 'The incident is not being treated as suspicious,' yet the paper still published it.

We scratched our heads. Could it be true? Yes, we'd had our Boxing Day meet in the market town in question, but we had then ridden several miles into the hills to hunt, and although we had dug and despatched a brace of foxes, there was no way that we could have been responsible for a dead fox in the centre of the town. It was definitely a deliberate smear. It was our first indication that the League was out to get us after eight years of being left alone.

Our opponents have complete mastery of the media and, in the post-truth era, statements from hunt spokesmen and the Countryside Alliance are like Polish Cavalry being pitted against German tanks. Over the last two decades, I have observed with deepening gloom the way that the Axis has conducted a ruthless media campaign.

Even the agricultural story editor of *The Archers* seems to have been involved. A few years ago, after the announcement that David Cameron was going to push an amendment to the Hunting Act through the House of Commons to help Welsh sheep farmers control foxes, *The Archers* developed a storyline about stray foxhounds chasing sheep into a burn. You could not make it up.

As I write this, there has recently been an incident in Clapham, south London. A fox had gone into a house through an open French window on a hot June night and bitten a woman on the arm as she slept in bed. What is striking is not so much the story, but the sixteen (out of seventeen) comments at the bottom of the online article denouncing it as fake news.

It appears that foxes are incapable of doing anything wrong and we are now so far post-truth that the victim, Miss Jodie Nailard (22), is clearly thought to be a secret agent for the Masters of Foxhounds Association. If only the MFHA could be credited with such ruthless deviousness.

It is wretchedly depressing. You don't want to stoop to their level, but how do you fight the battle for public opinion with one arm tied behind your back?

Snow is forecast. The farming community becomes anxious. Cattle shed roofs are particularly susceptible to collapsing under a big weight of snow. And dairy farmers can have the heartbreak of pouring milk into the slurry tank, because the milk tanker can't get in to collect. If it is accompanied by a prolonged freeze, the drinkers may stop working in the sheds, and we will have several hours added to the working day watering the beasts in troughs with fire hoses.

The anxiety is palpable on the bird table outside the kitchen window, as a succession of small birds stocks up on vital food, much like the housewives of Dumfries baring the supermarket shelves. It is one of the joys of winter, curling up for a few minutes on the window seat with a mug of hot chocolate to watch. There is a pecking order, the long-tailed tits are shyest of all, while their cousins the coal tits and blue tits dart in and out, giving way to the great tits.

They are trumped in turn by the chaffinches and siskins, who are then driven off by the nuthatch. He scarpers when the woodpecker arrives and all of them fly up into the branches to wait impatiently while the squirrels come in for a feed. I could sit watching the squirrels for hours. They are surprisingly different, ranging in colour from blonde to dark red and they can be almost grey, which gives rise to false sightings of their nemesis, though there is no mistaking the tufty ears.

In the event, the snow gives the hills a good coating, but we have only a light dusting. The Solway is like a fjord, with snow on the Lake District forming a white cliff, then the cloud comes down and there is a strange, unfamiliar white isthmus on the other side. In late afternoon the sky turns an icy green. As the snow melts, Criffel takes on a marbled effect, white and black and brown, like the rump of a large dapple grey horse.

✤ ✤ ✤ ✤

The Dumfries and Galloway Constabulary no longer exists, and all policing is now coordinated by one centralised Police Scotland. A recent incident made me question the wisdom of this policy.

I had given two old boys permission to go and shoot the geese, which were damaging a field of wheat. A fifth columnist in the village, who dislikes shooting, saw them and rang the police. They treated it as a firearms incident and despatched two armed policemen from Glasgow, eighty-eight miles away. They spent several hours driving around the parish looking for the two old-aged pensioners with shotguns. When they emerged from their hide carrying a goose, a short conversation ensued. It was confirmed that they had shotgun certificates and the landowner's permission, so the police got back into their car and drove eighty-eight miles back to Glasgow. I hope there were no bank robberies that day.

This incident could not have been envisaged prior to 1997. Has the world gone mad?

✢   ✢   ✢   ✢

Veganuary, the media are pushing it hard.

From a letter in the *Evening Standard*:

> Do you know it takes 1800 gallons[55] of water to produce one pound of beef? It was the shocking environmental cost of meat that helped me turn vegan.

The politics of food are convoluted and suppurating with contradiction. I have noticed that those on the Left, those heroic defenders of the working man everywhere on the planet but in the British countryside, will try to avoid eating British food, if at all possible. Not for them a large bloody steak and chips with the pick of British seasonal veg glistening with butter. Islington Man eats rice from the paddy fields of Indochina, lentils from the plains of India and, if meat is eaten at all, tofu or some other 'meat analogue' made from genetically modified soya grown on former rainforest land in Brazil.

All the ingredients are irrigated using vital water supplies on continents that are said to be running out of water, then brought halfway around the world by carbon-propelled transport. They are unsullied by British farming hands and generally grown by Big Business on the other side of the world and therefore not tainted by the landed interest, otherwise known as family farms, in this country. This taste for the exotic naturally boosts British imports from the developing world.

By contrast, if British farmers have the temerity to export food outside

---

55 Take this statistic with a large chunk of salt; I am merely quoting what I read.

Europe, we are accused of 'food dumping', of foisting grass-fed beef and lamb onto the populations of the rest of the world, displacing would-be cowmen and shepherds in sandy deserts and steaming jungles.

Some foods are politically correct and others not and, as a beef producer, it sometimes feels as if I can't open a newspaper without reading an article urging consumers to avoid eating the stuff. It is dispiriting to come in bruised, aching and stinking of dung to open the *Daily Infuriator* and find that the calves I have been wrestling with all morning, in order to put beef on a grateful nation's plates, are health-destroying, planet-warming, polluting and bad all round. It seems I am really no better than a Colombian drug baron, but without the helicopter, the sultry mistress, the gin palace moored in the Caribbean, and the billions stashed in a Swiss bank account.

That eating beef is bad for you and bad for the environment is fast becoming a truism without ever having been true. An anti-capitalist doctrine that identified beef cattle with the enemy has spread from the more far-fetched pages of the *Guardian* via the BBC into the mainstream. It feeds off atavistic memories of the Enclosure Acts and images of all those mean-faced cattlemen in cowboy films forcing those nice Mexican shepherds off their land.

Prophets of doom with large research grants in second-division universities pronounce that it is 'inevitable' that we will have to give up eating beef, if we are to save mankind. Millionaire pop stars use their social media following to propagate helpful tips to avoid destruction by eating meat only once a week. For those of us poor demented souls who scratch a pitiful living from rearing cattle, it seems that we are fated to be on the wrong side of history, doomed.

Yet, if you are prepared to look at the facts objectively, and hear them without interruption from one with a 'vested interest' on the capitalist side of the argument, it makes no more sense to give up eating beef and lamb than rice or lentils, much less probably. The environmental argument against meat is based on dodgy science.

It has been proved beyond doubt that, if you cut down acres of

Amazonian rainforest and then cover those acres with grazing cattle, and then take the offspring of those cattle and move them by smoky diesel trucks to a feedlot, and then fatten them with irrigated cereals and genetically modified soya, before slaughtering them and exporting them to be eaten by greedy, undeserving people in rich western economies, then (and only then, but the 'science' doesn't mention that) it will be harmful to the planet.

No distinction is ever made, or allowed for, between beef grown in parts of the world where there is insufficient water for cattle to be grown naturally without concerted human intervention, and the north and west of Britain where increasingly, with our wet climate, it makes little sense to grow anything else.

A scientist with no biases or preconceptions, faced with the problem of how to produce the most food from a patch of land in Galloway, using the least resources and with the least impact on the planet, might briefly and humorously consider rice as the best crop to soak up 'the breezes and the sunshine and soft refreshing rain', but would then swiftly discount most cereals, legumes, pulses and brassicas as impractical; before coming up with the brainwave of establishing a rich green carpet of grasses and nitrogen-fixing clovers – one that might last forever if looked after, or at least eight years before it loses vigour and needs re-establishing – and putting cattle and sheep on it.

He might agonise over the amount of methane produced by the cows as they fart and belch their way around the pasture, but he would then be reassured by the fact that the vegetation was going to die back and rot at some stage, giving off gas anyway. Not only that, but these harmful effects are counterbalanced by the volume of greenhouse gas that is re-absorbed by the pasture, which acts as a 'sink' for it, in one of those virtuous cycles that make one think that our creator must have been a very clever chap.

In fact, this is how herbivores have managed to roam the world's grasslands in far greater numbers since prehistoric times without the world exploding like a ruptured gas canister. Being a conscientious chap, he is also concerned that the cattle are using water to sustain themselves and to grow, and he may even calculate how many litres of water it takes to grow each kilogram of beef, but then he will conclude that the rainfall in Galloway is bounteous and as most of it flows into the sea anyway, allowing some of the water to go through the beasts of the fields, so that it is sprayed back onto the land as fertiliser, can only be a good thing. He may also conclude that the land is less prone to erosion if it is kept in grass, rather than ploughed up for arable crops.

If he is really diligent and willing to suffer great discomfort in the name of science: he will forswear eating meat himself for a given period of time and subsist entirely on a diet of baked beans. Then he will calculate the energy and water required to grow the baked beans, and the harm done to the planet by frequent cultivation releasing greenhouse gases from the soil into the atmosphere. Next he will measure his daily output of harmful greenhouse gases and multiply it by the number of people on the planet, currently 7.2 billion, to work out the sum total of the greenhouse gases produced by the world going vegetarian.

Being a rational chap, he will conclude that it is a lot of hot air and for a variety of reasons he will not become a vegetarian, not least in order to save the planet.

There is also a wicked deceit about the exclusive focus on the meat itself. Islington Man forgets that the bone-meal used to fertilise his allotment would have to be produced artificially at an environmental cost. And glue, and jelly babies and a host of other products. He wears plastic shoes and garments made from synthetic fibres from the petrochemical industry, so that no global-warming ruminant has died to clothe him.

He is blind to the irony that he is doing huge damage to the environment by doing so. Whereas leather shoes and woollen clothes will biodegrade in landfill sites naturally, his man-made accoutrements will be there forever, and each time he washes his clothes, a microscopic layer of plastic finds its eel-like way to coat the floor of the oceans.

The anti-meat brigade never takes into account the tallow either. This useful product formed by rendering down all the excess fats can be found in soap and increasingly in biodiesel. Tallow burns more cleanly and efficiently than plant oils and provides a saving of ninety per cent of greenhouse gases against fossil fuels.

And all that is before we even consider what comes out of the back of each animal. The organic farming, so lauded by the veggies, would be virtually impossible without muck from cattle. And from my limited observation here, the cornerstone of all our wildlife seems to be the cowpat with its rich insect life.

So, when you hear someone say that you should not eat beef to save the planet, you should take this advice with a piece of salt, and say, 'No, that's wrong, the advice is that you shouldn't eat beef that isn't British and specifically beef that isn't grown in a DG2 postcode.'

If the Campaign for Random Accusations against Pastoralists – I'll spare you the acronym – doesn't get you on the environmental argument, they can always get you on health. There is some truth in the assertion that if too much grain is fed to beef cattle, then some of the benefits of eating it are negated. And, as British beef farmers, we have perhaps been too slow to capitalise on our ability to grow grass-fed beef, which is rich in healthy Omega-3 fats, possibly because we have become lazy about marketing, while we have relied on the cushion of subsidies. This void has been filled very effectively by the veggies, as we are all susceptible to those health stories that the media like to run on slow news days.

Far less prominence is given to research highlighting the benefits of eating meat, which some believe should be branded a super food. Professor Tim Noakes is one brave soul, who has risked ostracism in academia for his research on the human gut. A prominent sports nutritionist who previously championed carbohydrates, he now says we should eat less carbs and more saturated fats. He links the rise in type two diabetes to eating too many carbohydrates. Noakes believes mankind's evolution during the end of the Ice Age, when we had to eat meat as we could not grow much else, means that we are supposed to be carnivorous. And, certainly, our teeth would seem to support that theory.

And, on the environmental argument, far less prominence in the media is given to experts like Zimbabwean wildlife biologist-farmer,

Allan Savory.[56] In the sixties, Savory made a significant breakthrough in understanding what was causing the degradation and desertification of the world's grassland ecosystems and developed a way to restore the land to health using livestock as his primary tool.

For centuries we believed livestock were a major cause of desertification, but Savory's research showed that the cause lay in how those livestock were managed. His solution involved mimicking the behaviour of the formerly vast herds of wild grazing animals he had witnessed as a young biologist. He devised a simple method any pastoralist can use to move massive amounts of carbon and water from the atmosphere back to the soil, and begin reversing thousands of years of human-caused desertification – on the scale required, which no technology imaginable can accomplish. In the process, he showed we can feed more people.

As will have become painfully obvious to you, dear reader, I am not a scientist, but I think there is enough evidence out there at least to counterbalance the ever-louder nostrums of vegetarianism. There is a need for balance and Matt Ridley, who is a scientist, points to research on food-feed competition. That provides a rule of thumb that says it is okay to eat animals, if they have not been eating food you can eat, though this is complicated by the useful work that cattle do in processing by-products like straw and vegetable tops into food.

He also cites emerging research that shows that if the world started going vegetarian there would initially be a beneficial effect on greenhouse gases, but that it would rapidly go horribly wrong as we struggled to replace the protein from other sources without any organic fertiliser to do it with. And he points out that whilst methane levels in the atmosphere were rising in the nineties, possibly due to a leaking Russian pipeline, they are not going up much now.

Perhaps, if we are to continue with the old-fashioned Pravda-esque idea of having a state broadcaster, the Beeb might consider a bit of balance. I look forward to Frune, when fruit farmers get scared out of their wits

---

56 https://www.savory.global/institute/#our-strategy.

by lurid stories about the evils of eating fruit, and Ocarbter, when arable farmers lose sleep over reports that carbohydrates should only be eaten on the third Thursday of the month.

Incredibly, the Scottish Government appears to have swallowed the propaganda whole. Their Climate Change Consultation Paper talks about a net zero target for carbon emissions by 2050 and blithely states: 'A net zero ambition would mean the end of viable livestock farming in Scotland.' So that's us screwed then.[57]

✤ ✤ ✤ ✤

As winter drags on, we start mucking out the cattle sheds about every six weeks and pile it high in field middens. It is one of the big winter jobs and we usually get contractors in to do it. It can take a couple of days with one man on a telescopic handler and two men hauling it away. Goodness knows how they managed before mechanisation. Where there's muck, there's brass, and these days also regulations.

The big story a few years ago was the proposal to tax our muck heaps. We were living in Yorkshire at the time and I was writing a column for the equestrian supplement of a local paper, *Northern Horse*, known to its sole columnist as *Northern Whores*. I did my research and contacted DEFRA. The helpful girl at the Department for the Eradication of Farming and Rural Affairs told me it didn't apply to horse manure, although 'if the horse waste is mixed with other controlled waste (*such as, believe it or not, straw*), then it is considered as composting and should be registered, free of charge, with the Environment Agency as an exemption under paragraph 12 of Schedule 3 of the 1994 Regulations.'

I checked to see if it was the first of April, but sadly it wasn't.

---

57 Lest you think I am being complacent, the beef industry is working on plans to improve nutrition and genetics so that, all things being equal, greenhouse gases from beef cattle are reduced. The farming press is full of the news that food additives can reduce flatulence by twenty per cent but this good news has so far been ignored by the mainstream media.

✦ CHAPTER FIFTEEN ✦

THE SCOTTISH Government has its knickers in a twist again about the average age of farmers. It is now approaching sixty and thirty-six per cent of farmers are old-aged pensioners.[58] Its stock remedy is to spend money on eye-catching initiatives to attract new entrants. The sad facts are that it needs more fundamental reform to make it a financially attractive profession. Most farmers have been unable to spare the cash to pay into a pension scheme over the last few decades and are therefore unable to afford to retire. And the younger generation have watched their parents struggle to earn a decent living from ceaseless toil, and are not in any hurry to come home.

As Oliver is now away working in London, I am frequently asked, 'Do you think he will ever want to come home?' A generation ago, the assumption would have been that he would be itching to take over, and the question about our handover would have been phrased as 'when', rather than 'if'. The SNP's tax plans and their focus on the redistribution of wealth are also having an effect, but – and this was predicted – not in the way they had hoped.

The wealth is being redistributed alright, but outside Scotland, as young entrepreneurs choose to set up shop abroad. The grannies of Dumfriesshire could charter a plane to visit their grandchildren in Hong Kong and Singapore, they are so numerous. And some of the generation now retiring are choosing to remain domiciled elsewhere for tax reasons, treating any Scottish properties as second homes.

The age profile may also be because their tenancy reform measures have meant that few estates want to take the risk of letting land, and this has meant that young farmers are finding it hard to get on the ladder. Ironically, by siding with tenants against wicked landlords, they have hit the person who needs most help, the keen young farmer starting out with

---

58 Scottish Government Annual Labour Statistics, 1 June 2016.

a few sheep on annual grazing lets, who now needs to take on a small farm.

The average age statistic is probably unreliable, as it masks the fact that there are a number of farms where there are two generations working together, and the business remains in the name of the older one. However, it is worked out on a constant basis and therefore the fact it has been going up for as long as I can remember should make the politicians stop and think. The big question is, how are farmers who are not far off being OAPs going to be able to respond to any drastic reforms post-Brexit?

✢ ✢ ✢ ✢

We are driving through the wheat lands of south Oxfordshire to go to a family christening. The wheat looks fit, it is coming through the winter well, and I shudder at the thought of our waterlogged ground at home. But the absence of trees and hedges, and consequently birds, is dispiriting and I would not swap farming there for here.

Driving through West Hagbourne, we grind to a halt. There had been diversion signs on the outskirts of the village, but the Backseat Driver had been insistent,

'Ignore them, they won't be working on a Sunday. Come on, push on, we are late.'

We are greeted by the sight of a large woman in a quasi-official yellow anorak standing in the middle of the road. She is arguing with the driver of a Mondeo, who has been coming from the opposite direction. It appears that the driver has dragged an orange plastic barrier out of the way in an attempt to drive through, and the woman, perhaps the chair of the local residents' committee, has dragged it back again.

Looking around, I guess what has happened. There is a mini-digger parked up by a village hall and a pile of hardcore. No doubt a plant operator is due to arrive later, probably on Monday morning, to manufacture speed bumps or wheelchair friendly pavements, or some other civic convenience.

In the meantime, this village Hampden[59] is asserting her authority by keeping the Queen's Highway closed, and therefore her street peaceful for once, because the council has issued a blanket road-closure notice.

The Backseat Driver gets out and remonstrates. These things are much better handled woman to woman. There is much gesticulation and I hear the words, 'Ooh, DON'T …YOU … DARE. This is an official road closure.' The inference is that the anorak will lie in front of the cars, rather than allow us to flout the regulation.

We retreat with our tails between our legs. Driving round by a side road, we meet the Mondeo coming the other way and shake our heads at each other in resignation.

'Damn.'

'What is it?'

'We should have asked, "Are you the hag in Hagbourne?"'

Not for the first time, I thank my lucky stars that I don't live in a village in the south of England.

✛ ✛ ✛ ✛

The Axis would argue that you don't have to kill wild animals to appreciate them, and I get that, but to me merely watching wildlife is like seeing a play from the back of the theatre, whereas pursuing field sports is like being up on the stage; stirring the birds from their trees and the roe deer from their hiding places, feeling the adrenalin and interacting with the quarry species in a very personal way. It doesn't get any better than a good day's hunting; it is the sporting equivalent of performing grand opera, or headlining at Glastonbury.

It is an iron grey Galloway day, cold enough to lift our spirits without being uncomfortable. The morning sun has broken through the clouds, so that there is a dazzling light display on the sea below us and, in the

---

59 *Some village Hampden, that, with dauntless breast, the little tyrant of his fields withstood …* , Thomas Gray, 'Elegy written in a Country Churchyard', 1751.

distance, we see the mountain fortress of the Isle of Man. There is hope of a good scent and an air of expectation, as we mill around on a hill above Dundrennan, while Andrew puts hounds into a thick covert. Hip flasks circulating, we tighten our girths and exchange light-hearted banter.

Malc's horse is lame, so he is on foot and wanders among us, ready to run like a beagler. Paddy knows what is afoot and will not stand still, so we circle as if at the start of the Grand National, his ears pricked as he listens intently for any indication of a fox as the guns on their quads roar into position.

The guns are often keepers who have come to appreciate the value of the hunt in their fox control arsenal. Even if no foxes are found, having a pack of hounds through the coverts may yield valuable intelligence for future use about the location of earths, as they will often 'mark' at the entrance of any hole that is being used. Keepers are frequently surprised at being shown holes they never knew existed by hunt staff.

Seeing guns out on a hunting day still makes me uncomfortable, whatever the law may say. Philosophy lecturers like to teach ethics by placing their students in hypothetical situations. So, place yourself outside the covert with a shotgun, with the hairs standing up on the back of your neck and your heart in your mouth, as you wait for that fleeting moment when you can take a safe shot.

Traditional venery mimics natural selection by culling the weak in the manner that nature intended, when the fox was chased by larger predators. The fittest foxes escape. For the others, death by hounds is instantaneous and rendered painless by the endorphins released by flight. Shooting is indiscriminate and not always instantaneous. And there was no such thing as a wounded fox before the politicians introduced guns into the hunting field. Do you obey the law and shoot the fox, or do you obey your conscience and allow him to take his chances and try to evade the pack?

Andrew starts his exhortation, 'Try on! Try on!' and a couple of notes on his horn. A cock pheasant rockets out of the wood and climbs high over the valley, before setting his wings and gliding down towards the cliffs.

'That's a good bird,' says someone.

Then from the depths of the wood there comes a single, deep, excited note, and then another. Then a breathless pause and several more as other hounds hit on the scent.

'They've found.' The field goes quiet as we all strain our ears. Paddy is dancing on his toes now, waiting for the off. We edge closer to Piet, the Field Master, so that we can get away in the first echelon.

The scent must be as good as we dared hope. The woods now echo with a riot of noise that goes first this way then that, as it hurtles around the covert like an express train.

'There he is.' A fox shows itself briefly, then darts back into the covert, and moments later we see hounds tumbling clumsily out of the wood and then back in again. They appear to be heading uphill onto a long bracken bank.

'Come on, we'll get round the other side,' says Piet, as he kicks his horse into action and we speed towards a gap in the wire fence where there is a solid timber hunt jump. Paddy takes it in his stride and I let him have his head, so that he flattens out rhythmically into a fast canter across the springy turf, and I stand in the stirrups, crouched forward to keep my weight off his back. Above us, still in cover, hound music soars and crashes like the 1812 Overture.

Next comes a wall – a tall, solid, unforgiving Galloway dyke made of granite boulders. I check Paddy so that his hocks come underneath him, and we bounce twice before I let him go two strides out. He clears it by a foot and at the top of our flight, in a burst of exuberance, kicks his hind legs up behind him like Nureyev, so that I am nearly pitched out of the saddle. Our blood is up now, as we race away downhill towards the next fence, a low rail down onto a steep bank of bracken and whins.

We need to do a small, neat jump here, so that we can immediately turn right-handed onto a sheep track that runs along the top of the bank. Battling with Paddy on the run in, I shift my weight from side to side to unbalance him and slow him down, but we are still going too fast. I should circle him away from the jump and come back in at a trot, but I hold him, seemingly motionless, as he pauses, then jumps.

We take off like the 11.30 New York flight from Heathrow and go up, and up. Below us the ground falls away with alarming rapidity. Then we are coming down again and I feel him stumble on landing; his head seems to disappear from in front of me, and I am being scraped over the pommel of the saddle and down his neck. The ground rushes up towards me.

'Oh God, this is going to hurt.'

Darkness.

'Is he dead?'

'I don't like the look of it, he's not moving.'

'Has someone gone to catch the horse?'

'Yes, Malc's gone.'

Fragments of conversation come and go as if overheard in the street.

'He's got a pulse anyway.'

'Don't move him, in case he's broken his back.'

I can't tell whether this is a dream or whether it is real, and I just can't wake up.

'Can you hear me, my love?' An angelic voice. 'Can you open your eyes for me.'

I open my eyes and promptly close them again; the world seems confusing and I want to go back to sleep.

'Listen, Jamie, I want you to wiggle your toes. Can you do that for me?'

Good idea. I wiggle my toes and nod. Thank God, I am not paralysed.

Gradually I come to and my rescuer, fortuitously an off-duty nurse, says, 'Just lie still, poppet, the ambulance is on its way.'

Soon Malc appears with Paddy. I start scrambling to my feet.

'No, you are not getting back on, you were out cold for several minutes. You are going straight to hospital,' says my rescuer.

'Well, I might as well ride Paddy then,' ventures Malc, 'so at least he doesn't miss out. Can you pass me his hat?'

I told you the Bells are descended from horse thieves.

'Might as well pass me his flask as well. They will only confiscate it in hospital. And better have his car keys.'

Shameless! Malc and Paddy set off and I go back to sleep again.

The ambulance crew want to know where my hat is.

'We would have cut the straps on it if you had it, so that you couldn't wear it again.'

I nod and think of my mother. In the vanity of youth, I had always hunted in a top hat until I got married and then Mum and Sheri had ganged up and forced me to buy a jockey's crash hat. Maternal instinct is a wonderful thing; I would be dead had they not done so.

When we arrive at the Dumfries Royal Infirmary, the ward sister wants to know what I have had to eat and drink.

I rack my brains.

'Porridge at about eight, then a few sausage rolls and a slice of fruitcake at elevenish.'

She nods, 'And to drink?'

'A couple of glasses of port at about eleven.' A slight frown plays across her features. 'Then just the odd swig after that: bramble whisky, cherry brandy, damson vodka, maybe some sloe gin, that sort of thing.' She looks concerned and scribbles something down on a clipboard.

I have my brain scanned and then I am put to bed and sleep like the dead. Hours later, Malc comes to pick me up. The same ward sister discharges me.

'Now you are to go straight home and have a good night's sleep.' Then her eyes seem to moisten and a gooey maternal look comes over her. 'And do try and stay off the alcohol, if you can, dear.'

The League Against Cruel Sports has taken to sending covert 'monitors' out to film hunts. Video 'evidence' is then spliced together in the style of the German propaganda film maker Leni Riefenstahl to try to get a conviction. My respect for huntsmen grows daily as they keep calm and carry on, hoping that one day sense will prevail. I once had dealings with the League and had a measure of respect for them.

As a schoolboy, in a bid to stir up controversy, I asked them to come and speak to the school's Agricultural Society, of which I was the secretary. Richard Course, their chairman, and Jim Barrington, both serious-minded people and genuine animal lovers to their vegetarian fingertips – limes, not watermelons – came and spoke reasonably, if somewhat misguidedly in my view, and we listened courteously before we politely agreed to differ. Years later, I read that both of them had changed their views on hunting and joined the Middle Way Group.[60]

Richard Course was to write in 1998:

> After thirteen years of discussing and debating this issue, I found it impossible to ignore the truth and facts about hunting. I have come to despise the League Against Cruel Sports even though I was its chairman, simply because these people know as well as I do that the abolition of hunting will not make any difference to the welfare of foxes, hares or deer ... To abolish hunting is to say: 'You must not kill pests by the relatively quick kill or escape method of hunting, but you can kill by other methods that cause a lot more real pain and suffering.'
>
> When one asks, 'Why?' the only truthful answer is, 'Because I do not like the fact that you get some enjoyment out of it.' Frankly it does not matter whether a man in a slaughterhouse enjoys his job or hates his job. Normal people enjoy their Sunday roast and their bacon for breakfast. It really is as simple as that.

Sadly, the watermelons have since taken over.

---

60 The Middle Way Group proposed that hunting should be allowed to continue with regulation.

✤ ✤ ✤ ✤

Good Morning Vietnam. It struck us like a sledgehammer that soon Oliver
and Rosie would have left university and have twenty days holiday a year
instead of twenty weeks, so we needed to make the most of it. The four of
us are backpacking. Brought up on films like *Apocalypse Now*, I am awestruck
by the way the Vietnamese 'commie gooks' are teaching us a thing or two
about capitalism. It must be very confusing for the old people – what
terrible atrocities must they have seen? There they were, living on two
grains of rice a day in tunnels in the jungle for all those years with Uncle
Ho, inspired by a Marxist dream, and now what? Seemingly unfettered
capitalism and a top rate of tax of thirty-five per cent; and for the ageing
American GIs revisiting their terrified youths, what was it all for?

The streets of Hanoi are buzzing. We expected to see bicycles, but
everyone has a moped, especially the girls who ride around in tight skirts,
with drumstick nylon legs and court shoes. The traffic is such that it is
probably slower getting around than in the bicycle age and they all wear
masks to protect their lungs without any sense of irony. How long before
they are back on bikes?

The streets are refreshingly free of multinational chains and there is
an absence of monopolies; there are no supermarkets. New businesses
are springing up everywhere. There is no sign of any loafers – everyone is
busy – and no lonely old people sitting on park benches. All are engaged
in the great game of life. There are some people sleeping rough in Ho Chi
Minh City, but no more than in British cities, and they are at least sleeping
by their means of support: their rickshaws.

Even in the middle of nowhere, the Wi-Fi is better than at home.
Education has to be paid for and consequently is valued highly. Rose, the
highly efficient receptionist in our hotel in Hoi An, speaks flawless English;
I realise with admiration that it is her third language.

Doubtless I am looking through rose-tinted spectacles and there are
children who need 'lifting out of poverty' and other 'ishoos' but, wherever
we go, people seem happier than in any other country I have ever visited.

The future belongs to Asia and I come back feeling that, by contrast, we are an old country on the way down.

Our friends Rob and Maggie divide their time between Scotland and Hong Kong, which has been part of communist China since 1997. I asked them recently what it was like living in a communist country. They laughed and said simultaneously, 'Which country do you mean?!' The top rate of tax in Hong Kong is fifteen per cent, so that middle-income earners have to work four times longer in Scotland on the same salary to make the same amount.

✤ ✤ ✤ ✤

Nothing brings home to me the visceral love of hunting in rural communities more than funerals. It is striking how often hunting is mentioned in eulogies as being one of the most important things in the dead person's life, even if they have died aged ninety, having not been on a horse for forty years. And the hunting community always turns out in force and grieves as an extended family.

We were gathered in Lockerbie for Rupert Morgan's funeral. Rupert was much loved, a man without an enemy in the world and widely respected as a cavalry officer, farmer and, particularly by me, as our point-to-point chairman. Father Edward Corbould, a monk from Ampleforth, delivered a homily in which he praised the way Rupert supported hunting, 'because he knew instinctively that it was a way of bringing people together', then our friend Gordon Dickie gave a very moving eulogy.

He finished with these lines from *The Irish RM*:

> What followed was, I am told, a very fast fifteen
> minutes; for me time was not; the empty fields
> rushed past uncounted, fences came and went in a
> flash, while the wind sang in my ears, and the dazzle
> of a morning sun was in my eyes. I saw the hounds
> occasionally, sometimes pouring over a green bank, as

the charging breaker lifts and flings itself, sometimes driving across a field as the white tongues of foam slide racing over the sand; and always ahead of me was Flurry Knox, going as a man goes who knows his country, who knows his horse, whose heart is wholly and absolutely in the right place.

We all had lumps in our throats the size of gobstoppers.

Spring

CHAPTER SIXTEEN

BY WINTER'S end, I find myself longing for the departure of the sheep, much as I enjoyed their arrival. The grass needs to recover if we are going to have anything to feed the cows when they most need it in the spring, as they are recovering from calving and need milk in their bags. The geese will be around for another two months yet and it will be hard to avoid them baring it, but 'grass gets grass', and we need to do all we can to ensure there is a bit of depth in the sward for when the sun finally allows us some warmth in the soil. Also, if I am honest, I am beginning to find their ovine foibles tiresome.

So we have agreed on the end of February for the end of the grass let. Some sheep graziers have a nasty habit of going incommunicado at this time of year, so that they can snatch a bit more of our grass and save their own at home, but Marcus has always been as good as his word and arranged to take them away on time.

The gather is a complicated business. It starts several days before the arrival of the lorries. I need to concentrate them in large groups in the fields where the gateways are sufficiently dry and hard for the sheep to cross – they are fussier than other animals about getting their feet wet – otherwise it will be a long and frustrating day. Despite our best efforts, there always seem to be a few pockets of sheep where they should not be.

I have been watching one of them along the burn side. We have fenced a water margin as part of one of our environmental schemes – paid for by the EU, but for how much longer? – and the resulting strip gets grazed in the winter, then left all summer for the birds to nest. I thought I had got them all out of there, but there is one refusenik, who must have been hiding under a bush when I had moved them. It is always much harder to move animals on their own and I could wait for the shepherd to come with his dogs, but I think, och, we'll be fine, there will be few enough hours of daylight to complete the job without wasting time on a single sheep.

I can see her up the far end grazing quietly. If I leave the gate open and get between her and the burn, I should be able to run her along the fence, so that she turns through the gate when she sees the gap. On second thoughts, I walk up out of sight on the field side and climb over above her, just to make sure that she does not spook and go the wrong way. So far so good. As I round the bend in the burn, she sees me and sets off in the right direction. This is going to be easier than I thought; who needs dogs?

She is a strong lamb with a good thick fleece, and she has put on a lot of meat in the last few months – perhaps staying here by the burn has helped her foraging and she is not so daft after all. A shaft of sunlight breaks through the cloud and lights up the first primroses dotted among the snowdrops on the far bank of the burn. Somewhere in the Cavens woods I can hear a woodpecker, that early harbinger of spring, and I congratulate myself on being here now, by the burn, when I might be staring at a computer screen in a dreary office somewhere.

There is something comforting about carrying out a task that has been executed without modification since biblical times. Searching for lost sheep gives one a virtuous self-image as the Good Shepherd, and the therapy of looking after animals always seems to release a few happy endorphins, even if one's efforts are seldom reciprocated by sheep.

It occurs to me with a twinge of fascination tinged with regret that, after twelve millennia of sheep farming, I might be the last generation to be doing this. It is already possible, and probably more efficient, to use drones to look for lost sheep and some farmers are already investigating using them instead of dogs to gather sheep.

I have a vision of my dotage.

'Are the grandchildren coming this weekend, darling?'

'Yes, I think so, why?'

'I want to gather the sheep up and I need them to operate the drone thingy on the laptop.'

The sheep seems to get what is expected of her and settles into a steady trot along the fence line. By staying at forty-five degrees behind an animal, ensuring that they can see you behind them, rather like being able to see a lorry driver's wing mirror, one can normally control their speed and direction. We edge closer to the gate. It was placed there because it is by the corners of two fields for ease of moving stock in and out, but this has put it in the middle of the fence that runs parallel to the burn.

I am hoping that she will see the other sheep and want to turn in when she gets there, so I slow the pace down to give her time to have a good look. She slows to a walk then stops level with the middle of the gateway. This is always the tense bit, like waiting for a fish to take. She looks around as if weighing up her options, then snatches at a clump of grass and chews ruminatively. She won't be hurried. I dare not move a muscle. With deliberate slowness she takes a step, then another, into the gateway, then stops and looks around.

Who knows what, if anything, passes through a sheep's head. Maybe she has remembered that there was some especially tasty grass down the far end, or maybe she feels she needs a bit more exercise, perhaps, and this is an uncomfortable thought, she is enjoying toying with me; in any event she decides at that moment to turn away from the gate and sets off at a sedate jog down the bank of the burn.

Bitch.

No plan ever survives contact with the enemy, still less sheep, as von Moltke nearly said. Decisive action is required, so I sprint round in a wide arc to turn her, but she is alert to this and speeds up, her head thrown back with disdain. There is nothing for it, but to follow her down to the end and turn her round for another attempt. When we get there, I think perhaps I might be able to catch her in the corner and lift her over the fence, but she is too fly for me. Maybe it is just as well for my back.

So up we go again, this time her leading me in and out of the trees where some willows are growing horizontally, and I stumble on a root and graze my hand as, half-falling, I put it down on a branch to catch myself. Scrambling to my feet, I look frantically for the sheep; we are perilously close to the burn here, but she has kept going and is now near the gate again.

'Please go through it. Please. No, not that way, that way. No, don't you dare. No. Oh bollocks.'

She carries on up the bank. I realise that I am out of breath and my back feels prickly with sweat under my fleece. Perhaps I should concede defeat and wait for another opportunity. But some inner stubbornness tells me that I must carry on, that I can't let a ten-month-old sheep get the better of me. Grimly, I trudge up the fence line again to bring her back. The sheep is starting to lose her cool as well. She keeps stopping and half-turning before carrying on. I should stop and allow her to regain her composure, but I want to end it and so I keep pushing her, foolishly, as she then turns towards the burn and calmly walks down the bank and into the water.

It's the sheer perversity that gets me. She probably wouldn't cross a puddle in a gateway, but here she is doing doggy paddle. She swims across to the far bank and tries to scramble out, but it is too steep and she falls back. There is nothing for it but to try to get her out. Stepping gingerly into the burn, I am relieved to find that the water does not quite reach the tops of my wellies. Shit, spoke too soon.

First one then the other boot fills with water. It makes me gasp with the cold, but then there is that delicious warming feeling, thank God for Neoprene. The burn is in spate and it is an effort to stay upright even in knee-high water. It takes me a second or two to get my bearings and, as I look around for the sheep, I see that I am in an unaccustomed riparian world quite different from the one three metres up the bank. The noise of the water shuts out the outside world and the trees form a tunnel above me.

My eye is caught by a flicker of movement and I see a small, wren-shaped, brown bird with a white front, not much bigger than a chaffinch.

It is jumping from stone to stone on a spit upstream, bobbing its upturned tail in a delightful manner. It is a dipper. I have never seen one on the estate before and I am happy to trade my wet feet for this vision of innocence. The dipper is a born optimist. It builds its nest on a rocky ledge on the river bank in springtime, in the hope that the water level will not rise again.

I wrest my attention back to the sheep. She is about twenty yards downstream, hanked up in a hawthorn branch. Gingerly, I wade down to her, ducking to avoid low branches; not low enough, as one knocks my cap off. I catch it and, pleased with my reflexes, put it in my pocket – now for the rescue.

'Got you now.'

I wedge one foot between some rocks and brace my legs to stay myself in the fast stream. It may be my imagination, but the water level seems to be rising. She is well and truly caught and I curse as a thorn pricks my finger and covers my hand in blood; it mingles with the greasy lanolin of her fleece, as I pull the hawthorn off, her wool coming off in great swatches and hanging on the branches.

'Oh well, good nesting material for the birds.'

I keep thinking I have her free but, in her struggles, she keeps entangling herself again. Finally, I push her off into the current, holding her by a fistful of wool on her rump to try to guide her downstream, until we can find a break in the steep bank to climb out.

The water is definitely going up and I realise that we have just passed a junction where one of my neighbour's ditches comes in from the left. There is no prospect of turning round and going upstream, as the current is too strong and we are now being bounced along by the water. I am soaked to the skin and haven't realised that it is nearly up to my crotch. We need to get out before we are pushed too much further downstream, or we will be bobbing around in the sea in a few minutes. Then I see a gap in the undergrowth. The bank is a bit lower there, and I think to myself, there isn't going to be a better chance.

Carefully, I steer her into the bank and manoeuvre myself round to the downstream of her. She has become completely passive now, like when a tired horse stops pulling.

'Here we go, lass, soon have you out.'

I put one hand under her throat and one under her belly and heave. It is only then that the awful realisation dawns on me that wool is one of the most absorbent materials on the planet and, in her soaked condition, she weighs perhaps three times as much. Lifting a dry hogg up onto the bank would be hard, and this is right on my limit. I pause and push her against the bank to keep her still, while I think about it.

Lifting my head from the task, I realise that it must have been raining for some time. Soft spring rain, barely more than mist, has soaked my head and shoulders and it makes me recognise how hot I am, hot and cold, and how out of breath. I can feel my pulse throbbing at my neck and there is a strange electric taste under my tongue and in my throat.

'OK, let's do it.'

They say there is some superhuman force that can be summoned in times of need by extreme focus. It is used by weightlifters and karate experts and people who walk on burning coals. Well, I need it now.

I push and pull and drive her up the bank, lifting her with my knees as well as my hands, and inch by muddy inch we scramble up out of the water, until at last we lie on the grass panting. My chest is heaving and my neck feels as if it is about to burst. The lamb is now a fragile, muddy bundle of rags. The awful thought occurs to me that we both might die and be found here together.

I picture a breathless young reporter on Border TV news, 'No one will ever know what possessed this happily married father of two to bring this sheep to this remote beauty spot, or what happened here. Police say that there were signs of a struggle, but they are not looking for anyone else in the course of their enquiries.'

The print media will trot out the usual range of platitudes and innuendo to build a picture. 'A close-knit rural community' will be 'shattered' by the news. Neighbours will talk of a 'family man', who 'kept himself to himself'. Journalists will feel it is germane to the story, under the circumstances, to mention that the dead man was an Old Etonian.

Local people will retell the story, punctuating it with that useful Scots word 'seemingly', and it will be further embellished as word spreads. Wifeys at bus stops will shake their heads sadly, and say, 'Puir wee soul, what was he thinking?' Acquaintances in London clubs will snort into their port, and say, 'Well, he was a sheep shagger after all!' (I should explain that a derogatory eighteenth-century nickname for my regiment is 'the sheep shaggers', for reasons that need not detain us here and are in any case lost in the mists of time.)

'No, sheepy, it can't end like this. At least one of us must live.'

I look down and see that her eyes are glazing over, and she is curling up at the edges.

'No, you bloody don't. You can't die now.' Frantically I start pummelling her chest. The boundary between life and death is vanishingly small in sheep and I have seen heart massage work well on them before, and soon she pulls herself together.

'Come on then, let's go and find that gate.'

I tuck one hand under her chin and push her along, clutching her like my most prized possession now. Fifty yards to go, but it's not over yet. Whether the tree root has been growing there for some time naturally, or whether Fate has placed it there in order to test my fortitude, it is there, and it gets me. Sprawling headlong in the grass, I let go of my sheep and she runs in fear. I scramble to my feet and go after her, but she is not coming back. She stops briefly, turns to give me one last look, and runs down into the burn again.

I never did find her. I ran up and down the bank looking, but she just vanished. I even began to wonder whether she had ever existed, whether she had been some diabolical incarnation or a hallucination. But no, she was real, alright; the greasy sheep smell on my hands was unmistakable. In all probability, she had achieved every sheep's only mission in life, and died. And I had lost.

✤ ✤ ✤ ✤

Andrew and Bean are ploughing in Graham's Hill. The rich chocolate soil is coming up again for the first time in two years. I look anxiously at the base of the furrows for any panning, but to my relief it looks crumbly and the clods don't look too shiny. The 'green manure' mix has done its work well and the roots seem to have improved the soil structure, on top of the good work it has done fixing nitrogen from the air and putting nutrients back into the soil.

A flight of pied wagtails come and show their appreciation. They tumble across the furrows in search of insects, like leaves being blown on the stiff March winds. Although some of them are resident, these are clearly birds of passage that have jetted in from sunnier climes, possibly even North Africa. Perhaps two of them will be the ones who take up residence on our lawn. I imagine them peeling off from the others, 'Well, here we are, this is our stop. Have a good summer if we don't speak and we'll see you in the back end.'

I am pleased to see them again, apart from the robin they are perhaps the tamest of all our birds, and they are cheerful companions. They seem to be on the increase, which is encouraging considering they eat only insects.

Lack of insects is becoming a preoccupation in the media. It is undeniable that windscreens are no longer spattered with tiny corpses. It's very likely that the pronounced fall in swallow populations we have noticed here is for lack of insects, as they feed on the wing on their long migrations. With my arable farmer's hat on, I am uneasy about the role agriculture has played. All that spraying is bound to have an effect and there is some, but only some, truth in the ritual vilification of 'modern farming practices'. Ironically, mainly because they are not modern enough, as GM crops would allow us to spray much less.

But with my livestock hat on, I am certain that reintroducing stock has caused a dramatic increase in our insect numbers. There are always many more insect-eating birds concentrated around where there are cattle or middens. In fact, the most damaging aspect of modern farming practices may be the absence of muck on arable-only units, something for the increasingly vociferous anti-livestock lobby to ponder.

It can't all be gloom and doom either. The record numbers of grouse in recent years would not have been possible if there had not been healthy populations of insects to sustain the chicks during the critical early days, something that keepers can do absolutely nothing about. And the extraordinary plagues of different types of insects on the estate some summers, to the astonishment and consternation of urban visitors, give grounds for optimism that insects can regenerate very quickly given the right conditions.

The NFU 'Brexit Roadshow' is in Castle Douglas. The union has spent months working out a blueprint for Brexit and I am interested to hear what they think. My expectation is that we will wargame various scenarios ranging from no deal in Europe and a 'hard' Brexit, through to us remaining virtually unchanged, and a range of options with and without subsidies.

The presentation is jaw-droppingly complacent. The message is that the industry cannot afford any change to the status quo and therefore the union has planned on this basis. The line on Brexit seems uncannily like Nicola Sturgeon's and there are sideswipes at the right wing of the Tory party.

Afterwards I ask the presenter if he is really sure that there is not going to be a 'No-deal Brexit' and we are not going to have big changes imposed on us. He looks at me as if I am mad and I receive a lecture on how many farmer suicides there were in New Zealand.

I hope to God he's right, or we are going to be in for one hell of a shock.

We went for a winter break to Cuba, desperate for some sun to recharge the batteries after a long Scottish winter, and on a tight budget we found an all-inclusive holiday on the internet. The Caribbean for less than going to Lanzarote – what was not to like?

Actually, we did like it very much. The hotel was a bit scruffy, but the white sand and Caribbean sunsets were just what we needed, and the birdlife was wonderful. Grackles courted on the rafters at lunchtime, flirting outrageously with their long black tails, and hundreds of sparrows roosted in the lobby in the evenings. We had not been sure what to expect, but the country gave a superficial impression of being open for business and keen to embrace tourism.

The bar had a life-sized, carved wooden model of Ernest Hemingway propping it up in one corner. The hotel was full of Canadians, who were – and they would be mortified to hear me say this – carbon copies of Homer and Marge Simpson. Inside the hotel, it could have been any other beach resort in the world, but for a few obvious deficiencies. The first night we asked for a gin and tonic.

'I am sorry, we have run out of tonic.'

'No tonic? When do you think you will have some?'

Shrug. 'I don't know, maybe a few months.'

Ginger grows plentifully in the Caribbean. 'Rum and ginger ale?'

'Sorry, no ginger.'

The hotel staff were polite, charming and friendly but always reserved, as if they carried some terrible secret inside them.

It was only when we hired a driver for the day, and Francisco took us off to explore in a turquoise 1954 Chevrolet, that we gained a true picture of the country. The leather seats were a bit patched, but the air-conditioning worked, and we felt like John Travolta and Olivia Newton-John as we sprawled on the back seat. It had been converted to run on a Hyundai diesel engine and kept going for six decades. In Cuba, the mechanic is king.

The only other traffic consisted of a few tourists being driven around in vintage American cars; no petrolhead am I, but even I gawped at a spectacular 1949 Red Plymouth. Nearer the towns we saw Soviet-manufactured Ladas and Trabants.

'People who work for the gooberment,' said Francisco, jerking his head at them.

Otherwise the roads went for mile after mile through acacia-studded scrub and the only other road users were local people in carts, being pulled by pitifully thin horses and mules, and the occasional tractor that looked like a museum exhibit.

The land looked fertile.

'Does no one farm this land, Francisco?'

'People ask the gooberment for papers to farm the land, but ...' Shrug. 'They want us to be poor. Everyone has to earn the same.'

Francisco pointed out his house and we asked if we could stop and look. Home consisted of a wooden shack with a half-acre patch of maize at the back, a few chickens and a pig in a wooden cage. His farming model was to grow enough maize to keep his two horses alive, so that they could pull carts for tourists. The car was rented, and he spoke of it as if it were one of the most important business assets in the country. I imagined its original owner, some American businessman, throwing the keys to his houseboy as he left in a hurry; and the car being carefully nurtured as a breadwinner ever since.

Francisco described how he and his family had to lie on the floor of the shack during a hurricane. Next door, he was building a four-room, breeze-block bungalow, block by block. It had taken him six years so far and it was still not wind and watertight.

'The land belongs gooberment; they let me have the land for free, but I have to build house. It is difficult saving to buy materials.'

Continuing on with our journey, we arrived in the city of Holguin. There were vast Soviet-style government buildings facing a huge concrete sculpture to heroes of the revolution. Walking through the streets, we saw open sewers, empty shelves in shops, queues for groceries, and churches. It was disconcerting, as in other respects it felt as if we were in Spain, or Portugal. The people look Hispanic. There are pictures of the Pope everywhere, and it made me wonder how the Roman Catholic church has not countered communism in Cuba, like it did in Poland.

Taking Francisco out for lunch in a tourist restaurant, in a fishing village on the coast, we quiz him about what he gets from the Big State, in return for paying them all his income in tax above a certain level.

'No, we don't get sick pay; if you are ill it is very hard for the family. Education is free, but shoes for my daughter are very expensive. Hospital is free, but drugs you have to pay, and they are very expensive. You get a pension at sixty-five.'

'How much is it?'

Sad shrug. 'Ten pesos a month. Older people who can remember, say life was better before revolution.'

We returned to our hotel chastened. The world sees Castro as a card and Guevara as a good-looking charmer. Looking at yet another mural of Castro, I think, 'Fidel, you bastard, you are nothing but an old fraud. You had no right to inflict this on these people. I hope in whatever circle of hell you are in, they are turning up the heat.'

I wonder about the other guests in the hotel and imagine them back in Toronto.

'Yeah, Cuba is not so bad, food was great and they all drive around in Cadillacs. Now where are those cigars we bought?'

Trying to leave Cuba through immigration is a masterclass in socialist bureaucracy. There is no queue for the booth next to Sheri's. A girl wearing lieutenant's pips waves her finger negatively and indicates the sign, wheelchair only. I look around pointedly for the absence of disabled people and put on my quizzical expression, but no dice. Rules are rules.

I go next door and a lovely girl second lieutenant bids me look at the camera, while she studies my passport with a serious look.

'Where are you staying?'

Jesus, what does it matter, now that I am leaving? I give her the name of the resort.

'Who are you travelling with?'

'My wife.'

'Where is she?'

I lean forward conspiratorially and speak slowly, 'In the next-door cubicle. Can you give me a Cuba stamp, please?'

She gives me a cheeky grin, as if to acknowledge that it's all a joke really, and she stamps it for me.

The airport departure lounge has Wi-Fi, and the code is 'cubawifisucks'; someone has a sense of humour. The departure lounge is called 'The Last Waiting Room'. Let us hope not.

Everywhere in the airport shop, there are Che Guevara mementoes. Books called *The Sayings of Che Guevara*. Che looking like Elvis with cigars and sideburns, Che looking like Jim Morrison with long hair, Che with AK-47, Che with golf club. Che Guevara was born in 1928 – would he be dribbling in a Havana old people's home on a pension of ten pesos a month now?

The Left seem to have bagged the word 'progressive' as a way of describing with approval any policies that move us leftwards. Likewise, any shift in the opposite direction is described as a 'race to the bottom'. A trip to Cuba might make even the Corbynistas question this polarity.

* CHAPTER SEVENTEEN *

THE 'BLACKTHORN winter' in March is often the worst of the year, except this time even the blackthorn has stayed in hibernation. There is snow lying along all the hedge backs and dykes. The view towards Criffel looks strangely familiar, like an interpretation of the landscape by a radical young artist, with bold white squares on a green background.

The 'Beast from the East', as the latest meteorological phenomenon has been dubbed, has deposited drifts of sand in the yard. At first, we wonder if they are what remains of the snow and think that perhaps the snowstorm from the East has brought sand from the Mongolian wastes in its grasp, but it turns out that there has been a sandstorm on the shore. One consolation is that the view from the house is breathtakingly beautiful, as seeing the snow-capped Lake District mountains reflected on an ice-blue Solway is like looking at the Himalayas across Lake Phewa.

✧ ✧ ✧ ✧

The news on the political front is depressing. The noose around hunting's neck is being tightened. Like a thunderbolt out of a clear blue sky, we were hit by a 'review' of hunting by the Scottish Parliament back in July 2015. For ten years we had been left alone. Hunting had been 'triangulated' by the politicians. It was a dirty secret, banned but not banned. This satisfied all but the most rabid antis in the towns and allowed country folk to carry on 'shunting'[61] not-quite-as-normal. If there had been widespread popular discontent with this state of affairs, then you would have thought there would have been demonstrators with placards every time we showed our faces in public. There were not. The Minister for Wildlife in the Scottish Government, Dr Aileen McLeod, said that the Scottish Government

---

61 A hybrid of shooting and hunting to reflect that we are now gun packs.

'had no plans to revisit the Hunting Act', but a few days later all that had changed.

David Cameron had tried to push an amendment to the Hunting Act in England and Wales through the House of Commons. Unfortunately, this was sold in the media as 'bringing the law into line with Scotland'. Doubly unfortunately, the West Lothian question still dogs English politics. The SNP had a convention that they would not vote on legislation affecting only England and Wales, and reportedly a gentleman's agreement with the Tory Chief Whip that they would abstain on this vote. But the temptation to shoot Cameron's fox was too great and they changed their minds and made the vote impossible. In order to justify this shameless opportunism, Nicola Sturgeon made out that she had been unhappy with the way that hunting was working in Scotland, and by coincidence had just arrived at the conclusion that it needed reviewing.

Lord Bonomy was asked to conduct the review, and predictably his remit was purely to look at the issues of numbers of hounds and enforcement, rather than whether the use of guns was appropriate. Bonomy endorsed the need to use a full pack of hounds for effective fox control, rather than just two. However, as a retired law lord, he was concerned to tighten the law. He recommended a system of monitors to oversee hunting. Sinisterly, he recommended reversing the burden of proof, so that anyone tried for illegal hunting would be assumed guilty until proved innocent. And he thought the government should look at extending vicarious liability, whereby, if anything goes wrong, the landowner could be held responsible even if not actually present.

The Scottish Parliament is unicameral, so there is no House of Lords to scrutinise this terrifying legislation and rein in the authoritarian state. The pace is driven by the six 'watermelon' Green MSPs for whom no one voted directly,[62] but who nevertheless hold the balance of power at Holyrood. As it rumbles through committee, the League Against Cruel

---

62   The Scottish Parliament comprises constituency MSPs and 'list MSPs' voted in under a form of proportional representation. The Green MSPs are in the latter category.

Sports is given equivalence with the Countryside Alliance. Tellingly the new code of practice will only apply to the nine mounted packs and not the 'feral' gun packs that operate on foot.

It is a very worrying time for our team at the kennels. Every time they go out, they risk prosecution under a law that is hard for humans to understand, let alone canines. A recent ruling by a sheriff rested on the interpretation of a fox being chased on a forestry track as not 'in cover' and therefore illegal. And there is an unspoken fear that the politicians will make hunting too difficult, so that eventually we have to stop and they will lose their jobs.

The whole thing is like a bad dream. I imagine the kennels with no horses or hounds, the hound show rosettes in the tack room gathering dust and old meet cards fading on the walls. Any restriction on foxhunting still seems as bizarre to us as it would to a Glaswegian, if a Tory government imposed a ban on football. It seems extraordinary that our democracy can have become so skewed.

There is a feeling that we have arrived at one of those periods of change in history like the middle of the nineteenth century. It was then that the phrase 'one nation' was coined. In his novel *Sybil*, Disraeli examined the gap between the wealthy elite and the working classes. He lamented that they were 'as ignorant of each other's habits, thoughts and feelings as if they were … inhabitants of different planets'. The gap between rich and poor is still there, unfortunately, though nothing like what it was in previous centuries, and is being addressed or exploited by politicians of all hues.

But viewed from the backwoods, it is clear that two extra dimensions, not visible in 1845, have developed to prevent us being one nation. In those dimensions there are now two very discrete and distinct nations: rural and urban, and private sector and public sector.

Those of us out in the sticks like to quote G.K. Chesterton:

We only know the last sad squires rode slowly towards the sea,
And a new people takes the land: and still it is not we.
They have given us into the hand of new unhappy lords,
Lords without anger or honour, who dare not carry their swords.
They fight by shuffling papers; they have bright dead alien eyes;
They look at our labour and laughter as a tired man looks at flies.
And the load of their loveless pity is worse than the ancient wrongs,
Their doors are shut in the evening; and they know no songs.
We hear men speaking for us of new laws strong and sweet,
Yet is there no man speaketh as we speak in the street.
It may be we shall rise the last as Frenchmen rose the first,
Our wrath come after Russia's wrath and our wrath be the worst.
It may be we are meant to mark with our riot and our rest
God's scorn for all men governing. It may be beer is best.
But we are the people of England; and we have not spoken yet.
Smile at us, pay us, pass us. But do not quite forget.

It has been quoted *ad nauseam* by columnists since 1997, when Tony Blair's victory unleashed the full power of the Big State on the countryside. This has been felt most particularly in Scotland, where a socialist administration has focused on the countryside with disproportionate weight, partly because it can, as all things rural are devolved matters, and partly to avenge 'ancient wrongs'. But the rural people of England, or for that matter Scotland, have not spoken yet, barely squeaked. We just simmer.

Revolutionary talk is the preserve of the hard Left, the far Right, extreme nationalists and nutters. Nevertheless, we have a dream. It doesn't involve smashing shop windows or burning flags.

It goes something like this.

We all send our tax demands back to HMRC with a polite note saying that there can be no taxation without full representation and an assurance that the money is going to be spent wisely. Then we quietly remind the nation that the countryside does matter after all. We stop sending milk to the dairies and put it in the slurry tank instead. We keep the grain and the beasts on farm, so that the flour mills, the breweries, the distilleries and the abattoirs cease production, we turn off the wind turbines and anaerobic digesters and divert the water down the burns instead of through the hydro-electric turbines.

We stop sending timber and straw to the power stations and stop the flow of grains and tallows to the bio-fuel plants. We close all holiday accommodation and announce that the countryside is closed until further notice and while the nation panics about empty supermarket shelves and power cuts, we take a few days off and engage in rural pursuits, the old way. Battered Volvos with greyhounds in the back will be sighted on motorways on their way to coursing meetings. Hounds will meet by war memorials in market towns, before drawing ancient coverts. Apple-cheeked farmers' wives will saddle up cobs outside West Country inns to see the staghounds work their magic up on the moor.

And if the Big State doesn't like it, people will say, 'Haven't you heard? We're not part of your country anymore.'

And we will all send a letter of explanation like this one to 10 Downing Street and Bute House:

Dear Prime Minister / First Minister (delete as applicable),

> *You may know that like many other rural folk, I have suspended paying my taxes for now. This letter is official notification of my intention to suspend my citizenship of the British and Scottish states until further notice, while we sort things out. I stress that my loyalty to Her Majesty the Queen is undimmed and I still think of myself as British. It's just that in the meantime my little corner of the Kingdom has become semi-detached. Think of us as a sort of Crown dependency, like the Isle of Man. We are very happy to offer reciprocal freedom of movement and a free trade agreement so that day-to-day life can continue.*
>
> *I am very sorry that it has come to this, but I think you will understand that things couldn't go on as they were. It had been dawning on me for some time that your country is no longer my country. I felt*

*utterly disenfranchised and impotent. You politicians took us for granted,
you didn't value the food we produced, or the woods and hedges we cared
for. You thought you knew best about how we lived our lives and you used
us as a political football when you needed something to kick.*

*That thing about 'the ancient insanity of governments, governing too
much',*[63] *well, you politicians just went too far. And the further you went
the more we seemed to pay. I never thought I would say that Marx was
right: 'Democracy is a form of government that cannot long survive, for
as soon as the people learn that they have a voice in the fiscal policies of
the government, they will move to vote for themselves all the money in the
treasury, and bankrupt the nation.' Well, we are going to jump ship before
it happens. There is no point in paying taxes into a black hole and you
won't get another bean out of me until you learn to balance the books
and shrink the state to a size we can afford.*

*Nor was it right that laws affecting rural people should be made
by people in cities with no knowledge of what the effects are. 'The most
certain test by which we judge whether a country is really free is the
amount of security enjoyed by minorities.'*[64] *Well, you are about to find out
what a big minority we are, even if you did carve us up into small bits.
You made a big fuss about the democratic deficit in Europe, but ignored
the gaping one at home.*

*That nonsense over electoral boundaries had a lot to do with it. It
just wasn't right that rural people's votes should count for less than those
of their urban counterparts. No taxation without representation, that's
always been the deal. If there is one thing that I have learnt from dealing
with your civil servants, it is that unless something is 100 per cent right,
it's wrong, it's a binary world now.*

You people seem very keen to devolve power to cities with their new

---

63 Apparently Robespierre said this, a man who then unleashed a reign of terror, but let that
    pass. But the only reference I can find is in my former Eton tutor and History master Michael
    Kidson's commonplace books.

64 *The History of Freedom in Antiquity* by John Acton, CreateSpace, 2018.

mayors, so why not devolve power to the countryside? Let us decide within our own communities whether we want to allow foxhunting, or whether we want to allow the culling of some of the major predators to preserve our wildlife. Devolution for Scotland was all very well, but it made us rural folk even more at the mercy of the urban majority. Whatever made you stop there?

Perhaps it's unfair to blame you. It was those pesky Normans who made such a mess of things by centralising everything. Those of us in the Middle Kingdoms between England and Scotland bore the brunt of it then and we still do. So, for now, we are going to walk away. Please don't send the tanks in, that would be boring for everybody and make a scene in the world's media, and I doubt whether you can afford to lock us all up anyway.

Yours more in sorrow than in anger,

But, of course, we won't do anything of the sort and nor should we, for it's not for us to undermine the rule of law. And we are all part of the client state now, either through the old ties of patronage, or the new dependency on the state for granny's hip replacement, and for our single farm payment, when it eventually comes. It would be a strategic error anyhow, as the vacuum would be soon filled by the Mob. It is there now in waiting, nurtured and stoked by Corbyn and Sturgeon and the others.

It has air supremacy on the twitter-sphere and has made huge areas of the media no-go areas for the likes of us. It extrudes noisily every now and again, in marches and rallies and outside food banks, to remind us that we need to keep paying it, and throwing it red meat, if we want to preserve our way of life.

And so we will muddle on, hoping that things will turn out not too badly, and we will keep our heads down, and take comfort from the natural world to help us to cope with the madness of the temporal one in this age of incredulity.

✠ ✠ ✠ ✠

Springtime. And all around the estate, trees and shrubs go off in a firework display that amazes us as much as if we have never seen it before: white cherries and hawthorn, and here and there the shocking purples and pinks of rhododendron and azalea. It is historically when farmers throw off the cares of winter and take their rewards for the hard work done in the rest of the year. Somehow it all seems worth it when I walk across the estate, thrilling at the sight of the new crop of calves chasing each other in the afternoon sun, and marvelling at the greenness of it all. My confidence seems to grow with the grass and the cattle as they pile on the weight again after the lean months. Yet, perversely, it is also now the most stressful time of the year.

Cashflow is everything. Turnover is vanity, profit is sanity, cash is reality, so the saying goes. And I keep thinking of accountancy lectures at Business School, where it was drummed into us that businesses go bust because they run out of cash, not because they are unprofitable.

It is becoming an all-consuming obsession. It is several weeks before I have any fat cattle to sell and harvest is months away. Paying the wages each week is becoming a worry and bills start piling up in my office. It keeps me awake at night and there is a large butterfly lodged somewhere between my heart and the top of my colon. I sit down and tot up the creditors on one side of the page and the debtors on the other. We are owed more than we owe and I start chasing the latter in order to pay the former.

It is disconcerting to find that the Scottish Government owes us over ninety per cent of the debt. There is in excess of £50,000 outstanding in various subsidy payments, some of it from five months ago. It is unedifying to be chased by Her Majesty's Revenue and Customs for an overdue PAYE payment, when the Scottish Government is sitting on our money in another part of the national bank account. The words banana and republic spring to mind.

I wrestle with the Scottish Government website. If our website was like this, we wouldn't have any customers. It has clearly been designed by someone with zero empathy for the people who have to use it. The website has cost £178 million so far[65] and doesn't work. As a result, the payments are still paid months, sometimes years, late. By the time it does work, we will have left the EU and a new regime will doubtless require a new IT system.

It makes me all the more cross when I think how much money must have been spent on rebranding it. The website used to say Scottish Executive at the top of it, with the Royal coat of arms. Then the SNP came into power and called themselves the Scottish Government, something I don't recall ever voting on. Everything now has the Saltire at the top and *Riaghaltas na h-Alba*, which I presume must be Gaelic.

The standard history of Galloway[66] tells me that Gaelic was 'the speech and culture of the upper classes of Galloway in the twelfth century'. The SNP normally goes in for toff bashing, so perhaps this rare concession should be welcomed, but I suspect most farmers scratch their heads in incomprehension when they see it and in fact, asking around, it seems most people assume that it is Polish, which is apparently now Scotland's second language.

I see that there are five tranches of money. Four of them say 'anticipated' against them; you can say that again. The other says 'ready'. I know that every other farmer is in the same boat, but I tell myself that it is the squeaking wheel that gets the oil, and it is my duty to my creditors to try to get the money for them as soon as possible.

I force myself inside to spend a couple of hours listening to a clunky version of a Mozart piano concerto, while one department after another puts me on hold. The Dumfries office passes me to the Edinburgh office, and a girl answers. She is friendly, but I detect a resigned timbre in her voice. She has had this conversation many times before.

'I'm afraid I can't give you a date for payment.'

'But it says anticipated on your website.' It has said that for five months and we both know that.

---

65 This is an Audit Scotland figure from June 2017. It will now be much higher.

66 *Galloway: A Land Apart* by Andrew McCulloch, Birlinn, 2000.

'Yes, but unfortunately that doesn't necessarily mean it is about to be paid.'

'Okay, but what about the beef calf scheme? That says "ready"; is that better than anticipated?'

'That is better; it means that it is ready and nothing should hold up payment now, but we don't have a date yet.'

'So what's to stop you paying it? If I have a bill to pay, I just pay it.'

'Ah, I can see from a customer's point of view, you think a word is literally what it means, but it doesn't mean that.'

'What about this one? It says "awaiting deadline".'

'It needs to progress from "awaiting deadline" to "ready for payment". It's in a holding area at the moment.'

'What's stopping it?'

'That's something the IT team are looking at. The payments haven't been processed from the Government's point of view; there has to be a timeline. You see, payments have to go through a number of stages.'

'So I see.'[67]

✤ ✤ ✤ ✤

Andrew the agronomist produces the eagerly anticipated results of the soil sampling. It is five years since I have had them done and I study the maps as intently as I would X-rays of my own body. Each field has four maps: one for potash, one for phosphate, one for magnesium and one for pH. I have learnt to look upon our soil as a kind of bank account. Take too much out without replacing it and it soon becomes overdrawn. Conversely, if you invest in it, over time the increased fertility will yield interest in the form of bigger crops for less input.

'Look after your land and your land will look after you,' is the old saying. For years as an arable-only farm we took crops off, including the straw to sell to produce vital income, and scrimped on adequately

---

67 In case you are wondering, this was a real conversation. We no longer need parody.

replacing potash and phosphates, allowing the pH levels to become too acidic. Since converting to a mixed farming regime, we have had muck to put back on and I am anxious to see whether our fertility has improved.

The maps[68] show coloured blotches to indicate the levels; where it is low it is a chilly blue, high is bright red, good levels are reassuring greens and golden harvest yellows. I am relieved to see that we have at last turned a corner and the bill for lime and bagged fertiliser is set to come down. We have yet to see any more money in our pockets, but the tests confirm that we have more capital tied up in the soil.

The maps tell a story. When we first started this exercise, you could see where the boundaries of the old fields were before they were amalgamated in the seventies. The fields furthest away from the old dairies were less likely to have muck in the old days, because of the hassle of hauling it by horse and cart and forking it out by hand. I can also see fertile hotspots where we have had field middens in recent years. The huge variety in soil types is also reflected, from the clay down on the Carse to the sandy loams at the south end, and everything in-between. Some are better at retaining potash than others.

I never cease to be astonished by the power of muck. Spreading ten tonnes to the acre on our fields each year is giving them most of their fertiliser needs and also putting vital organic matter into the soil. This helps the drainage in wet years and moisture retention in dry years, as well as giving back all sorts of healthy bacteria. The worms and insects will all be having a lovely time and this will be helping the birdlife. I notice every year as we limp towards the end of winter, how birds seem to concentrate around our muck heaps for food – pairs of mallard, pheasants, starlings, rooks and jackdaws.

I simply cannot understand how public opinion has somehow got into its head that crops are environmentally good and livestock are bad.

---

68 The maps are also digital and control the fertiliser spreader on the back of the tractor via satellite technology, so that each part of the field gets the right amount and no more; a dramatic leap in precision farming previous generations could not have imagined.

Without the livestock to produce the muck, we were completely reliant on mineral granules for potash and phosphates to spread on the land. They produced no goodness for the soil apart from a slight alteration in the chemical mix and no feed for the worms. The soil itself became thinner each year without the organic matter to bind it together, and the fertility leached out more quickly as a result. The arable farming press is full of woe about flat-lining, or in many cases declining, yields and the nostrum 'we have perhaps only another hundred harvests left in the soil' is becoming commonplace.

Certainly on this farm we were heading into a downward spiral until we put the cattle back on. Organic farming would only produce a fraction of our food needs without organic fertiliser, i.e. muck. In a vegan world, the only sources would be human sewage sludge, which can't be used on crops for human consumption and runs the risk of poisoning the soil with harmful chemicals from lavatory cleaners, or 'green manure' from effectively leaving large portions of the world's surface fallow each year to regain its fertility.

Rachel Carson articulates in *Silent Spring*, far better than I can, why I think we need muck to put on our soil:

> The soil exists in a state of constant change, taking part
> in cycles that have no beginning and no end … Subtle
> and vastly important chemical changes are constantly
> in progress, converting elements derived from air
> and water into forms suitable for use by plants. In all
> these changes living organisms are active agents …
> teeming populations that exist in the dark realms of
> the soil … Perhaps the most essential organisms in the
> soil are the smallest – the invisible hosts of bacteria
> and threadlike fungi. Statistics of their abundance take
> us at once into astronomical figures. A teaspoon of
> topsoil may contain billions of bacteria.

✤ ✤ ✤ ✤

There is devastating news on the squirrel front. Squirrel pox has been found in Dumfries. The keepers of Dumfriesshire have been fighting an heroic battle against the greys. There are frequent sightings of the American intruder all around us. Each sighting triggers the hit squad with traps. The fear is that fifth columnists or useful idiots are letting the captured greys out. It had been assumed that the two species were co-existing, because the greys did not have the pox, but no longer it seems. The advice is to stop feeding the red squirrels to avoid spreading the disease. With a heavy heart, we take down the squirrel feeder.

The announcement that pine martens are to be introduced into the south of Scotland to help control grey squirrels depresses morale further. These reintroductions have a way of ending badly. Friends in the Highlands confirm that the idea might work as the reds, agile enough and clever enough in the sitings of their dreys to escape pine martens, can coexist with them, though they all say, 'But you don't want pine martens.' I have a gloomy feeling that we could end up with no red squirrels and pine martens; they are the scourge of small bird and mammal populations.

The Axis loves introducing more predators. It is part of what Owen Paterson calls the Rousseauist fantasy of re-establishing some imagined primordial landscape. The classic tale of a bad reintroduction concerns the sea eagles up the West Coast. [69] Sea eagles originally lived on fish, as did the crofters. The fish ran out, probably because of the EU Common Fisheries Policy, and the crofters came to rely on their lambs, as now do the sea eagles. These mega-predators will even take deer calves and as sea eagles grow more densely populated, they are causing the golden eagles to go into decline. There is no agreement on how many sea eagles is enough. The Big State is in denial and will not admit that it has got it wrong. Meanwhile there is talk of a looming beaver problem on the rivers of Perthshire with landowners adopting a scorched-earth policy to stop them spreading.

---

69   The saga is well documented in *Voices from the Hill* by Peter Crookston, op. cit.

Matt Ridley makes the eminently sensible comment that most reintroductions would be okay, as long as the reintroduced species is not protected; that way its population cannot grow to the point where it becomes a nuisance.

The grey squirrel is one introduction that we can all agree was tragic. Two friends, Bertie Ross and Alistair Mathewson, are involved in a charity set up by the Prince of Wales[70] to save the red squirrels. They are developing contraceptives to feed the greys and, in time, hope there will be a squirrel pox vaccine for the reds. It is a race against time.

I just hope the population on our peninsula can hang on long enough.

---

70 Donations please to the Red Squirrel Survival Trust, www.rsst.org.uk.

+ CHAPTER EIGHTEEN +

ANGUS THE boiler man arrives to have a look at the Aga cooker, which is playing up. He is incensed because the council has closed the road from Canonbie to Newcastleton along which he travels regularly. The forestry lorries have damaged the 'cundies' (culverts) with the weight and he acknowledges the need for the work.

'I just wish they would fix the potholes at the same time, but they don't.'

What is really annoying is that Cumbria Council has also closed the long way round, so that the Debatable Land has ground to a halt.

'Can they not just talk to each other?'

It's a parable of modern life along the Anglo-Scottish border.

Of the portfolio of extra jobs that keep us afloat, while still allowing me to be master of my own diary and able to respond to farming crises, writing has provided the escapism. One day I am making silage at home, the next I am in London lunching with David Cameron.

Cogitating on the challenges facing rural life, notably Brexit, from the parochialism of our peninsula, I decide to see whether I can get a helicopter view of some of the issues by talking to those in the Westminster bubble. I remember the feeling of revelation in the Army, when I would sometimes visit a superior headquarters to be given the 'big picture', and I would feel less of a mushroom for a while.[71] I contact our ex-premier thinking that, although now out of power, he will have a good view of what is going on, and, very generously, he asks me to lunch at the Carlton Club.

I have never been inside the Carlton Club before, traditionally the

---

71 Army slang: mushrooms are kept in the dark and fed on shit as, so they generally believe, are soldiers.

nearest thing the Tory Party has to an Officers' Mess. Although I have a vivid memory of the night it was blown up by the IRA in 1990. I had been dining in the basement of Pratt's two doors away, when I heard what I knew straight away to be a bomb go off, though there were a number of theories advanced around the table as to the source of the bang. This was confirmed when a few minutes later a young policeman came rushing down the stairs to try to evacuate us and an elderly peer said, 'I used to eat down here in the Blitz young man and we were safe then and I am not going to allow the IRA to move me now.' So we stayed put.

It is a year since we last met, when he had helped me launch my first book on Michael Kidson,[72] a man who had a big influence on both our lives, not long after the bruising experience of his sudden departure from office, and he seems far more relaxed and chipper about life. We walk past his portrait into the dining room. Cameron still looks absurdly young for an elder statesman and the portrait is a reminder of how youthful he was in office. It is an excellent likeness by Johnny Jonas. In contrast to the other, more staid, portraits of Tory prime ministers around the walls, it is of a young man in a hurry, striding across Downing Street, red file under his arm, eager to make a difference to the world; a reminder that he was the future once.

'Slightly unnerving walking past it and I am going to have to look at it for the rest of my life and be reminded of how old I am getting,' he says. It is his very own picture of Dorian Gray.

We compare writing experiences and I feel rather inadequate hearing that, contrary to press reports about writer's block in the shepherd's hut, he has almost finished his memoirs, and is about to start the editing phase. This while pursuing his own portfolio of roles that includes launching a billion-dollar, UK–China investment fund, and being president of Alzheimer's Research UK. One is apt to forget in saloon bar banter about our politicians what enormous capacity many of them have.

---

72 *The Enigma of Kidson: The Portrait of an Eton Schoolmaster*, Quiller, 2017, available on Amazon and from all good bookshops.

I am itching to ask him about Brexit. Does he regret calling the referendum? Is it frustrating watching someone else negotiating in Europe? What would he do? But I have a feeling this is off-limits.

'I am guessing that you don't want to embarrass your successor by talking about Brexit?'

He grins apologetically, 'Yes, in fact I am publishing next year, partly for that reason.'

He seems genuinely interested to hear how my farming business is going. He was probably the only prime minister since Sir Alec Douglas-Home to have had any sort of empathy for the countryside.

'I started out as an angry rural backbencher standing up for my constituency, but feel today that the countryside is really quite robust. Village life is popular. Farming has good years as well as bad ones and many rural economies are strong. The Hunting Act was wrong, it went into areas of our national life where you just shouldn't go in government, and I really don't think it is working in practice.

'I was worried about the Heythrop while I was in office, because they were targeted by the antis the whole time, partly because I lived in their county. I thought we could help the Welsh hill farmers by amending the law, so that they could use more than two hounds to control foxes if appropriate. Unfortunately, our plans were briefed to the newspapers too soon and that alerted everyone and the SNP, who were sort of squared away then weren't and pulled the plug.'

This brings us onto Scotland. We are all getting heartily sick of the 'neverendum' and I wonder if we should have another vote like Quebec to kill it once and for all, although the last vote was horrible, and there is little appetite for going through the unpleasantness of it all again.

He nods. 'I cared deeply about the Scottish independence vote. Yes, there is the Quebec precedent, but I don't think any Westminster government should agree to holding another referendum. I mean, I was absolutely clear with Alex Salmond; I said, "It is a vote made in Scotland, it is on your timing, and on your question." He described it as "once in a lifetime" and we shouldn't go back on that.'

He adds, 'Frankly, Nicola got her timing wrong by making such an issue of a second referendum just before the snap election in 2017 and it cost her.'

I tell him of the deep anxiety mixed with excitement about Brexit in the farming community; it could be an opportunity or a huge threat.

He looks pensive about that for a moment. 'Of course, it is a concern, but we seem to be heading towards a softer Brexit.[73] The realities of pressure from business and the parliamentary arithmetic make that seem more likely.'

I wonder to myself whether, ironically, after all the fuss of Brexit, we will actually end up roughly where he was trying to position us in his negotiations over our relationship with the EU, but no doubt that will come out in the book. I ask him where he is on protectionism versus free trade. You don't find many New Zealand farmers who want to go back to subsidies.

'Yes, that's true, but the New Zealanders went through hell and back to get there. Do you want that? Could you survive without subsidies?'

I shook my head, 'Not without being able to sell my produce for a lot more. Although I think we could try a New Zealand-plus model.'

'I certainly saw that subsidies were very important to my farming constituents. We had all that business when Margaret Beckett was at DEFRA and they made a mess of it, so that bankers with a couple of fields all got paid and the genuine farmers had to wait months. I think food security is important, but it is a question of degree. Also, there are areas where we need to improve our agriculture. Why are we so bad at value adding? Why did we homogenise our food products, while the French did so much better at continuing to add value by having local cheeses and so on.'

We discuss the idea of a new deal between farmers and others living in the countryside. He sympathises with that approach, 'I'm a big fan of better access, more footpaths for the ramblers and so on.'

---

73 This interview took place in June 2018.

I am intrigued that even out of government, he views life from the centre ground. Despite his Bullingdon image, he does always think of the many rather than the few. I guess it's what made him the Tories' best election winner for a generation.

I ask him whether he thinks the countryside is now in such a minority in our democracy that it is almost impossible to act in its interests. He disagrees.

'I think the badger cull is a good example of where our party can still work for the countryside. I was the British prime minister who agreed the cull. It cost me a lot of political capital, but I was prepared to pay the price, because I saw that it needed to be done. Labour would not make a decision on it and it was spiralling out of control. But in the end government did do it. It is difficult, though, all that sort of thing. At least we still have geographical constituencies, so that MPs have a formal bond with their rural constituencies. If we had gone to proportional representation, we would have lost that.'

Walking back up St James's Street after our lunch, I realised how much the country is missing Cameron's sunny optimism.

Next up is Owen Paterson. He has what must be the best office in London on the corner of Parliament Street, with a panoramic view across Parliament Square of the Palace of Westminster. The House is in a febrile state. The Remainer rebels – the so-called Ag-Grieved, after their leader Dominic Grieve – have managed to move the dial back towards a no-leave scenario. Owen is a leading Brexiteer, so I imagine it is like calling in on Richard Cobden in the House of Commons in the months leading up to the repeal of the Corn Laws. He has just returned to work after breaking four bones in his neck, when his horse fell with him, and I can imagine him fuming with impatience in his hospital bed while Brexit has rumbled on without him.

He has just hosted a meeting of the Brexiteers in his office and he glances at his phone as we speak, while texts ping to and fro with the latest voting calculations. There is excitement in the air and I detect a buzz in him that I remember from being on operations in the Army.

'I'm afraid I can't give you long, as everyone is due back in here shortly.'

He is optimistic that, despite the recent setback, Brexit will happen. In fact, he has an infectious optimism and a clear vision of what British farming should be like post Brexit.

'It's quite simple. Those sectors of British agriculture that can thrive on world prices without subsidies – East Anglian barley barons, Scottish raspberries and so on – should be left to get on with it, free to embrace the latest technologies and grow their businesses. But there are parts of the UK where you cannot survive on the production of food alone; so farmers should be paid for providing public goods, soil and water quality, biodiversity, animal welfare, etc. That way we preserve our landscape on which our tourism industry worth £30 billion per year depends.

'So, we copy New Zealand on the one hand, where they allow food production to thrive unsubsidised, and Switzerland on the other. The Swiss have a fantastic system of support where they give far more generous subsidies than the EU to farmers who graze the high Alps with cattle and sheep and maintain their iconic landscape. Outside the EU, we will be able to do all these things far more simply without interference.'

I wonder where that leaves me, will I be stuck in the middle? Farming at sea level on goodish land, but neither a barley baron with high yields and economies of scale, nor a crofter up a hill somewhere able to be portrayed as needing handouts.

'No, you'll be fine, as everyone has marginal land, which will attract subsidies for public goods. And you will find that you will make adjustments and diversify into what you do best, whatever that might be. Look at what happened in the Adelaide Hills when the Australians removed subsidies. They had an inefficient dairy industry: some stayed in dairying and became highly efficient, others diversified into tourism, and many of them created world class vineyards.'

I share my concerns about what happened to the rural economy at other times when free trade has been tried. I sense a little impatience with this dim-witted Galloway farmer who has wandered into his office, but his reply reveals his passion for farming, and he has clearly thought it all through,

'Look, the repeal of the Corn Laws was a "good thing" in inverted commas. Reducing the cost of food by ten per cent will have a dramatic effect on our economy. Yes, there will be a shake-up and some people will get out, but we will come through it much better and agriculture will be able to let rip. We are being held back by the EU. Do you know that India is a big importer of Scotch whisky? The industry calculates that, if we were free to do a trade deal, and could persuade the Indians to reduce the import duty from five hundred and fifty per cent to thirty-seven per cent, the extra demand would be bigger than Scotland's entire output of whisky is currently.'

That would be a game changer for Scottish agriculture and I digest this thought, as he carries on.

'And we could increase our productivity; the precautionary principle is stopping us using GM, and they are trying to ban glyphosate and 'neonics'[74] in the face of all the science. Just wait and see what happens to the bees when they go back to pyrethroids. And we'll cut out the bureaucracy.'

I nod, agreeing that is why so many farmers voted Brexit.

'Yes, I know you have had a bad time of it in Scotland with your payments system. England had exactly the same problem and I said to my opposite number, "Come to DEFRA and learn from our mistakes." But he thought he knew it all, and look what happened; typically arrogant of the SNP.'

I ask him about the badger cull, in which I knew he was heavily involved.

'I was invited to Somerset recently to look at the new flood drainage

---

74 Neonicotinoids: chemicals used on oil seed rape and other crops, said to be harmful to bees, although the science is contradictory.

scheme I had launched on the Levels,[75] and I was touched by farmers coming to the public meeting to thank me quietly for the very significant reduction in bovine TB since the cull. I cannot understand why DEFRA is not publicising it more. It was such an obvious thing to do; it had worked everywhere else, with badgers in Ireland, possums in New Zealand, and so on. Do you know the Americans sealed off affected counties in Michigan and culled all the white-tailed deer? I went out there and the American chief vet said to me,' – he puts on a Boss Hogg accent – '"Mister Paterson, tell your government that bovine TB is a zoonosis[76], we do not tolerate zoonoses in the United States."They were quite right, there have been cases of bovine TB spreading to humans in this country. It was hard, though. I received more death threats when I was at DEFRA than I did when I was Secretary of State for Northern Ireland.'

I am struck by his enthusiasm and he is clearly frustrated that he was reshuffled out of the rural brief before he could see things through.

'I tried to put a study in place to see what would happen to ground-nesting birds when the badgers were removed, but whether that happened …' He shrugs. Our time is up, as the Brexiteers are gathering to plot their next move to try to ensure that it is their vision that is adopted for the British countryside.

Reflecting on my meetings with Dave and Owen, I see the two sides of the Tory party. They are both countrymen, both completely genuine in their desire to help the rural economy, but with very different prescriptions. Cameron, typical of the one-nation Tory, wanting to help the countryside, but doing it by tacking carefully into wind from the centre, always thinking about the electorate and the art of the possible. He would take big gambles when he thought he could win, but mostly try to nudge

---

75 The flooding of the Somerset Levels in 2013/14 deserves a book of its own. The Levels flooded because, it is widely believed, the Environment Agency had prevented vital dredging of the rivers and man-made drains in what Paterson calls *laissez-faire* Rousseauism. He had been the Secretary of State for DEFRA and took the flak, but also took the measures required to prevent it happening again.

76 A disease which can be transmitted to humans from animals.

things in a favourable direction; cautiously sceptical on Europe, wanting to finesse keeping us trading in Europe with a degree of protectionism, but not bound by too many European rules.

Or Paterson, Rees-Mogg and the other Brexiteers, conviction politicians, they follow in the tradition of ideological Tories, free traders in the nineteenth century, anti-appeasers in the thirties or the early Thatcherites in the seventies. They have mastered the technical detail and embraced the science. They revel in being out of step with their party, because they believe history will prove them right.

Despite the temptation to wrap myself in the dogma of one side or the other, it occurs to me that both prescriptions would probably work well enough for me and my little platoon, as long as they were applied carefully. The fear is that through the machinations of party politics in the UK and intransigence in the EU, we end up with a fudge that combines the worst of all worlds.

My trip to London has given me a better understanding of some of the issues, but I am still a mushroom. The only consolation is that everyone else from Mrs May downwards seems to be as well. The picture is as opaque as it was in the Brexit referendum, perhaps rather more so, now that it is complicated by the uncertainties of a hung parliament. While in London, I go round the Summer Exhibition at the Royal Academy with Sheri. As usual we struggle to find very much that we would enjoy seeing on our walls, but we find the art thought-provoking. The judges obviously prefer the communication of ideas and clever techniques to aestheticism.

Predictably Brexit has provided the subject for a number of the works, though the artists can't seem to throw much light on it either. There is one entitled 'Brexit', of someone's cat (called Brexit) sitting on a Union Jack cushion. Another one has a photograph of some angry women with placards saying, 'We want our country back.' Someone else has submitted an architectural model entitled 'Homage to Brexit'. The graffiti artist Banksy has submitted a UKIP poster that says, 'Vote Leave', but it has a heart-shaped balloon stuck to it so that it reads, 'Vote to Love'.

I fall to musing over what would happen if all 650 members of the House of Commons were asked to submit a piece entitled 'Brexit'. My guess is that their creations would reveal they have very individual views of it. Leavers would submit paintings of sunlit uplands and cartoon strips of Superman. Remainers would stick urinals on the wall and paint apocalyptic images with skeletons. Both sides might focus on the process, rather than the end state, and submit pig's ears suspended in formaldehyde and plaster buttocks, and clever videos of people walking forwards, but not actually going anywhere. It seems to be all things to all men, and our politicians are no exception, and there is the rub. It allows Monsieur Barnier, the wily EU negotiator, to play on our divisions.

I am acutely aware that I have calves that will be going to the abattoir after we have left the EU. I am also increasing our borrowing to erect more farm buildings. Are these going to be paid for by increased profits, as British agriculture, freed from the shackles of the EU, 'lets rip'? Or will they become rapidly redundant like my father's old dairy parlours, mothballed while we stagger along as we did in the thirties, trying to earn money from second jobs, unable to compete on world markets, as we 'dog and stick' the farm with everything in grass, reduced labour, no winter feeding and only a simple, summer grazing regime? Or is there going to be no change after all?

I reflect that my calculation is much the same as it was before the vote. The answer is still 'it depends'. It is like one of those matrix-style contingency models beloved by business schools. Down one axis is the final outcome: No Brexit – Degrees of 'Soft' Brexit – Brexit on WTO rules. Down the other axis is the implementation as it affects farmers, ranging from great opportunities or full support, to devil take the hindmost. We might end up with a soft landing from a hard Brexit or a hard landing from a soft Brexit, or innumerable other permutations. There is just no way of knowing.

Overlaid on that is a further Scottish dimension, as much will depend, as now, on how the devolved administrations interpret the new regime. The Scottish Government's response so far seems to be to pretend it isn't happening and commit to keeping subsidies until 2024, which at least gives us a buffer period.

✤ ✤ ✤ ✤

London is undergoing its own revolution. Black taxis drive round with their lights on, like birds circling above the Serengeti in the dry season. Taking a trip in one invites a monologue on the unfairness of 'doing the knowledge', paying for a cab licence, and then being undercut by Uber, as he takes us south of the river by what we suspect is the long way round.

Coming back the other way, we take an Uber. The driver is Kenyan with a Glaswegian accent. He flies down from Paisley each week and couch surfs in London while he drives his cab, which he rents. We are humbled by his drive and ambition.

Are we farmers seen in the same light as black cab drivers?

I rather fear we might be.

✤ ✤ ✤ ✤

Euston holds special memories for me, of starting adventures by mounting the sleeper north. The sharpest of these are of going home for half-term from school. Boys from Scotland would be granted Scotch Leave and we would converge on the station's central hall like escaped prisoners of war and share various comforts for the journey ahead: cans of Carlsberg Special Brew, half-bottles of whisky, cigarettes and, during a cherooty stage I was going through, Hamlet cigars.

The intoxicating spirit of freedom will always be associated with the raw taste of whisky swigged neat from the bottle and the rich smell of cigar smoke exhaled through an open sleeper compartment window into the cold night air. Alas the Stranraer Sleeper has long given up the fight against the airlines and been done away with – although you still can't actually fly to south-west Scotland – and you can no longer open windows on trains.

The modern experience holds no pleasures for me. The station authorities play a game. In the Army, when we were moved around the world by the RAF – or Crab Air, as we called them – it was called 'rush to wait'. Euston has devised a variation on this called 'wait to rush'. It involves withholding information about the platform for the Glasgow train until the very last minute.

As usual I have not reserved a seat, so I join the throng of Nor'westers craning our necks at the digital display, ready for the off as soon as the platform is announced. Then it is a sharp-elbowed scramble down the ramp and onto the platform for a game of musical chairs to see who can get the last available table seat with a laptop plug-in. The Wi-Fi is so slow as to be functionally inoperable anyhow.

The train is hopelessly overbooked. This is a regular occurrence on the West Coast Mainline. You would think they might recognise that the great advantage that rail travel has over flying, or going by coach, is the ability to match supply with demand by sticking on an extra carriage without any need for extra staff. And one might assume in the age of algorithms that they might be able to predict that if they did nothing, then the end of every carriage would be depressed by disconsolate people sitting on their suitcases. I wonder whether HS2 will crack this problem, but I wouldn't bet on it. We pass several sidings full of redundant carriages.

Members of Parliament, especially urban ones, should be made to sit on the train between London and Glasgow and write down everything they see out of the window. It is impossible to believe that agriculture accounts for only one per cent of the British economy.

* CHAPTER NINETEEN *

TODAY I heard a cuckoo calling behind the house, the first I have heard from the garden since we have moved home. It is a moment to savour and celebrate and my heart swells with pride. I may be deluding myself, but I think it is very likely that its presence is an endorsement of our stewardship of the estate. The cuckoos need small birds to nest in the area so that they can lay their eggs; our creation of nesting habitat for pipits and flycatchers and other chosen species will have helped. They also need a plentiful supply of caterpillars for the young cuckoos to grow, and here also I feel we have been making progress.

Critically, they need protection from predators and the Larsen trapping we have been doing has kept the crows and magpies to a minimum. I can't wait to tell John, who has volunteered to do the trapping. We are catching less every year, proof that we are controlling their numbers.

It is all the more effective for the efforts of our neighbour, Jeremy Culham, who also traps on Southerness Golf Course. One of the great treats of spring is a round of golf to the magical singing of the larks hovering above the heather. It is vital work. If we lose control of the corvids, some future Vaughan Williams will never know the sound of 'the lark ascending'.

The traps are cages with either a crow or a magpie in with some food and water. The traps work on the birds' territorial psychology during the mating season. Put in the right place, the birds will see the intruder as either a threat, or perhaps a potential mate, and go and land on the cage – then the spring action traps it inside. They can then be despatched humanely or put in other traps. Fifth columnists and useful idiots for the Axis of Spite sometimes come and release them, so we now have tags with a licence number on them, which we get from the police, to demonstrate that it is being done within the law. Despite this, people still let them out and the extra bureaucracy, though designed to be helpful, brings with it the fear of prosecution for non-compliance.

✠ ✠ ✠ ✠

The Brexit vote has prised the lid off Pandora's Box again as far as Scottish independence is concerned. Far from being a 'once in a lifetime' vote, indyref2 is firmly back in the news. Sturgeon appears to be adopting the strategy followed successfully by Parnell in promoting Irish independence in the nineteenth century: being a constant irritant to the British body politic, so that the English eventually wish to be shot of us. I notice with dismay that the postcodes of guests coming to our holiday cottages show a much lower proportion of English people. Do they think they will not be welcome? Is the Scottish brand now tarnished in their eyes? I can't find it in me to blame them if it is, but it worries us sick whenever we have a vacancy in a cottage. It makes me even more determined to argue for a separate identity for Galloway. The SNP's obsession with independence is costing us.

We spend more of our time wrestling with unseen algorithms in cyberspace to try to manage our marketing through the big online agencies. These are nearly all American. After inventing the internet, how come we Brits were so crap at exploiting it? Uncle Sam must now trouser at least ten per cent of the British holiday cottage turnover. Now as well as the Big State troll, we imagine that we are working for a twenty-six-year-old computer nerd on a beach in California, who effortlessly rakes off a hefty percentage while he sips his piña colada. I have a horrible feeling that part of the reason why we pay so much tax, is because he does not.

✠ ✠ ✠ ✠

Spring is above all a time to look forward. The dealer has a fresh deck of cards and the new season's crops, including the new calves gambolling in the fields, will pay or not according to chance, regardless of what has gone before. Spring 2019 will bring with it an extra dose of hopes and fears.[77]

---

77 Assuming that Brexit has not been reversed or postponed between now and then.

Brexit is viewed by country folk with a mixture of excitement and deep anxiety, and the talk is all about opportunities and threats.

Reading up on what the politicians are thinking, I am struck by the curious lack of, well, vision. Here is a once-in-a-generation chance to reset British agriculture. But they seem timid and lacking any blue-sky thinking. I am worried that the policymakers have not hoisted in exactly what radical restructuring of the whole economy would be required to keep the rural economy going in a non-subsidised, free trading environment.

My bank manager and my accountant always reassure me that, of all the many sets of accounts they see from farmers each year, ours usually show more profits than most. Yet if you strip away the subsidies, our accounts would show a loss most years. It is a big risk; nearly every other country subsidises its agriculture, so it is akin to unilateral disarmament.

Having lost my vote to remain, I thought the ideal solution, if it could be made to work in our very different circumstances, might be to try and break free from the dependency of subsidies and opt for a New Zealand-plus model, and this does seem to be what the Brexiteers would like to implement once the transition period is over. A few months ago, I had jotted down in a notebook what I thought would be required to make it work, and I dug it out recently to see how it compared with what we are hearing from Whitehall and Edinburgh.

Currency

The New Zealanders manage without subsidies, partly because they were able to devalue their currency. As agriculture accounts for over a third of their economy, there was the political will to do whatever it took to make it work. But could we or would we make this happen? The UK economy, with its large trade deficit, might suffer from terrible inflation if we devalued the pound enough for us to be competitive. The City of London gives us an artificially strong currency, as international money buys sterling to be invested. So much depends on relative currency levels. I am dismayed to see that this is not even discussed in any of the policy papers as far as I can see.

I would have hoped to see some simple support mechanism whereby, if the pound rises above a certain level, compensatory payments would kick in. Otherwise British farm workers risk losing their jobs, simply because the relative currency levels mean that they are paid much more than South American gauchos, and this makes us uncompetitive. You could counter that by saying why should farming be made a special case – why should it be different from manufacturing industry? But the answer to that is, what manufacturing industry? Can we really afford to export our farming in the way that we have exported large chunks of our manufacturing base?

Supply chains
We could make up a lot of lost subsidy simply by allowing farmers to keep a larger share of the profits in the supply chain. Currently our suppliers and the big retailers take most of the profit, leaving farmers to sell at less than the cost of production. This works okay, because the subsidies make up for it. In non-subsidised parts of the world, farmers pay less for inputs like machinery and fertiliser. But farmers would need to be able to form powerful cooperatives like New Zealand's *Fonterra* to be able to stand up to the big cartels at either end of the chain. Fairness in the supply chain is partially addressed by the Groceries Adjudicator, but the NFU would like to see its powers bolstered. Again, this doesn't seem to be on the agenda.

Deregulation
My experiences with a still-born shellfish farm made me realise that rebooting the rural economy might need a bonfire of regulations and quangos to allow us the freedom to innovate and diversify without too many constraints. We would also need the burden of form-filling and box-ticking to be drastically reduced. Allegedly Michael Gove said that he would have succeeded at Education, if he had got rid of the Department for Education completely and set schools free.

Will he do the same for farmers? Britain barely had an agriculture department before the wartime command economy; in theory, Brexit removes the need for such a big one now. There has been lip service paid to reducing bureaucracy, and there have been announcements about reducing the number of inspections, something that was happening anyway. But talk of a 'Green Brexit', and the way that our civil service might implement the Swiss side of the model, suggest a depressing continuation of measuring and form-filling in order to demonstrate 'public benefits'.

Capital

When they axed subsidies in New Zealand, the price of land fell by fifty per cent, before slowly going back up again. This might not necessarily be a problem for farmers who don't want to sell, and it might even help them to buy more land. Although it would be a tragedy for any farmer forced to sell up at rock-bottom prices. But what are the banks to make of this if their security is suddenly halved? In my experience, changing direction in a farming business eats money. Faced with a capital drought from a banking sector that might no longer see farming as a safe bet, we could be unable to take advantage of Brexit, simply because we couldn't borrow the money.

Again, there is silence from policy makers on this contingency. One idea might be to kill two birds with one stone, by allowing every farm to build some houses to help solve the housing crisis. This could easily be achieved without despoiling the countryside, as long as they are contiguous with existing buildings, or in woods. And it would give the whole rural economy a shot in the arm with small builders benefiting. The money freed up, at no cost to the taxpayer, could be seen as a one-off injection of capital into the farming industry to allow it to adjust and invest. But is there the imagination to do this, and the will to see it through, against the twin threats of capitalist nimbyism and anti-capitalist nihilism?

Trade deals

The Kiwis have been very successful at free trade deals with the rest of the world. The difference is that, when they negotiate, food is at the top of their agenda, as it forms the bulk of their exports. For us it will be the other way around. The UK will have to prioritise services and non-food goods, and the temptation will be to allow cheap food imports from the New World in return for access for other things. In a recent talk at the Farmers Club, an American diplomat made the point that the US electoral college means that a sizeable majority of senators represent rural constituencies, whereas the reverse is true of British MPs, and that fact will have a bearing on UK/US trade negotiations.

We would need to make a concerted effort to favour farming and find clever ways of promoting British farm products, perhaps by inducements so that Scotch whisky is made with all Scottish barley, in the same way that New Zealand sauvignon is made with New Zealand grapes. Otherwise flogging whisky to the Indians is of no benefit to the countryside at all.

Green opportunities

If we want our countryside to stay looking beautiful, we cannot afford to industrialise our farms in the way that the New Zealanders have done. But so far talk of a 'Green Brexit' seems to mean more of the environmental schemes the EU has been doing anyhow. They are silent on producing green energy, which might help to stimulate demand for our crops, probably because most Brexiteers are climate-change sceptics. And I feel a really bold Secretary of State would insist on high taxes on plastics and man-made fibres for clothing as a compensating measure.

This would have a dramatic effect on the price of wool and leather and bring crops like flax and hemp back into play, as well as helping developing countries to grow sisal again. If we are going to pay less for food, why not pay more for fibres? After *Blue Planet*, I can't think there would be much opposition to this. Outside the EU, continuing with glyphosate to allow 'min-till' and allowing genetically modified crops[78] would certainly have environmental benefits, but I wonder whether the (Luddite) green lobby is just as strong in the UK as it is in Europe.

---

78 Glyphosate (or Round-Up) allows us to avoid ploughing. We can spray off the weeds rather than burying them with the plough and this keeps the fertility in the topsoil and prevents worm mortality. Genetically modified crops need less spraying. Planting blight resistant potatoes would do away with sixteen passes with the sprayer each summer!

But of course, if we stay too closely aligned to the EU, all bets are off.

And we will never know whether breaking out of the existing model of subsidy dependency would have worked or not. Though doubtless we will spend the next decade discussing it.

✤ ✤ ✤ ✤

The measuring wheel bumps along the rutted earth. Each bump threatens to throw out the accuracy, but I reckon it is still more accurate than pacing it out and I don't have GPS on my phone. I know in any case that in a couple of months there is likely to be a young civil servant measuring the very same field, with a pack on his back containing a more state-of-the-art GPS system, with an antenna coming out of the top of it. And, however carefully I have done it, he will then come up with a different measurement, because, as he will explain, his kit takes its bearings from no fewer than three satellites. As I will have come up with a slightly different measurement down two sides of the field and then squared the error, he will imply that I have been trying to cheat the system by putting in a false claim.

This disagreement will cause my single farm payment to be held up for months while other civil servants work out what penalty to apply to this misdemeanour and this will throw my cashflow into chaos. When the matter is finally resolved, more of my hair will have fallen out and gone grey and the EU will have saved about £13.50, which is less than the cost of the civil servants' time, let alone mine.

The Big State has yet to learn one of the first rules of business: 'Do not spend pounds to save pennies.' I have suggested that as there are about the same number of civil servants working in agriculture as there are farmers, it might be simpler to allocate us all our own commissar; then he or she could do the measuring in the first place and there would be no discrepancy. But this caused great offence when I first mooted it, so I have stopped suggesting it.

The British countryside has never been more measured. Land in

England, south of Cumbria and Durham, was famously measured for the Domesday Book, land in northern Britain hardly at all, and then only sporadically over the centuries, either when it changed hands for money, or when the landowner forked out for an estate map. In fact, I know of a hill farm sold in the sixties that turned out to be several acres smaller when this new mania for measuring came in during the nineties.

Now we seem to revise the measurements of our fields every year, or at least every time the Big State procures another measurement system. It depends whether you use a method like my wheel, which takes into account all the ups and downs, or you use a satellite which treats the land as being flat. Which is right? I am blessed if I know. I suppose there will come a point when scientific endeavour arrives at a definitive point when measuring can't get any more accurate. But then there will always be wet bits coming and going in fields, or new fences, or tracks made by the machinery, and there will always be room for arguments over whether those areas should be included or excluded.

Brexit offers us an opportunity to break this paradigm. Is this the last time I will be doing this? I have my doubts.

✤ ✤ ✤ ✤

The Scottish Parliament has introduced minimum pricing for alcohol. Part of me thinks this is a good idea. It might persuade people to drink in pubs again and Brian, the manager of T.B. Watson, the excellent wine merchant in Dumfries, tells me that it allows him to compete with the supermarkets again on some of his cheapest lines. It is just that it is of a piece with the miserable, 'North Korea without the humour' puritanism of the new regime. The SNP appears convinced that we are all raving dipsomaniacs and is determined to stamp out any *joie de vivre*. You would think that if they really wanted to persuade voters of the merits of an independent Scotland, they would promise free drinks all round.

American historians of the Prohibition era tend to argue that this type of legislation usually has unintended consequences. One of them is that we pull off the motorway at Carlisle to buy drink for a barbecue, something we have never done before. The nice lady in the hooch aisle in Tesco tells me that they are being run off their feet by thirsty Scots.

The Tartan Curtain is not a customs border, although presumably it would be if Mrs Sturgeon had her way, and so this smuggling is overt and legal. The residents of Dumfries had already taken to shopping in Carlisle by the Sprinter, the optimistic euphemism for the train that runs between the two towns. They can now be heard clinking as they disembark.

Smuggling was critical to the local economy in the eighteenth century. Employment was created either in running the contraband, or in the forces of law and order. And Robert Burns could afford to write poetry on the back of his day job, or probably night job, as an exciseman in Dumfries.

It is thought that William Craik could afford to pay for all his improvements at Arbigland with profits from brandy smuggled across the Irish Sea from the Isle of Man's duty-free ports. Certainly the cellars of the big house are several times bigger than you might expect. Craik took the precaution of also being a Commissioner for Excise, so there was little danger of being caught, although an exciseman's report on a seizure near here stated: 'I would not go so far as to say that the Laird of Arbigland was involved, but many of his horses and servants were present!'

Sometimes on a moonless night, I imagine hearing muffled oars in the bay, and once, arriving home late from Yorkshire with Rosie's pony in the trailer, I had a strong feeling that I was not the first person to be leading a pony up our drive at midnight.

Today the water diviner comes. I am not sure what to expect, maybe some sort of witch doctor. My hopes are riding on him. Our water bills have been going through the roof, since deregulation forced us into the arms of billing companies who make the Kray twins seem philanthropic. And we have nearly five hundred thirsty cattle – hence the idea of a borehole, which appropriately came to me while I was in the bath. Craig the borehole engineer speaks very highly of him.

When he gets out of the car, Andrew the diviner turns out to be a regular-looking Aberdeenshire farmer. He sets off with divining rods and I wonder whether this is not something I could have done myself. I fancy myself as a dab hand at finding water pipes by dowsing with a couple of rods made from old coat hangers.

'Surely he will be finding lots of drains just below the surface?' I say to Craig.

'No, it's weird, he is focused on the streams in the aquifer twenty metres down. He is terrible at finding drains.'

The aquifer is what remains of a desert of windblown sand that sat on the equator in the Permian Period, two hundred and fifty million years ago. Conveniently, it has been compressed into porous sandstone that now sits right under the estate. Andrew walks backwards and forwards over the points where his rods cross and makes a mark with his heel each time, then he pulls out what looks like a large wishbone of hazel and confirms it. The last one is the best.

'That will be it there and the water is flowing in that direction.'

I look sceptical, so he tells me to try with the wishbone. Nothing happens.

'Here, hold on to one end of it and put your arm round my waist, and I will hold the other end and we will try it together.'

This time when we cross the mark, I feel the wishbone pulling my hand strongly towards the middle with invisible force. It is witchcraft.

'I reckon that's an eight,' he says. 'That's much better than the others.'

'But that one was a seven.'

'Ah, but my scale goes like that,' he makes a V with his arms.

Craig explains, 'His scale is logarithmic … exponential.'

Andrew grins. 'That's the word. The only thing I passed at school was the gate on the way out.'

I am very glad that was the case, as they might have educated the magic out of him.

✢ ✢ ✢ ✢

May is perhaps the loveliest month here. The vulgar yellows of early spring have given way to the cerulean haze of bluebell and the bright white drifts of garlic flowers in the beech woods. Shelducks are courting on the beach and nesting in holes in sandy fields along the coast. The swallows are all back now and the lawn is once again patrolled by pied wagtails, while their cousins the yellow wagtails bob along the rocks on the shore.

Above the froth of cow parsley, the hedges are bursting with life, and death, as the sparrowhawks scythe along the lanes, motionless in their speed, hoping for an unwary yellowhammer. A passing raven rattling its deep *kronk* is escorted by small birds, like RAF Typhoons shadowing a Russian jet across the Baltic.

The garden becomes a sumptuous technicolour, surround-sound, epic movie, as birds sing operatic love songs from first light, fall in love, mate, fight acrobatic duels with other suitors, mate again and nest. Each foray into the garden now produces alarm calls from unseen birds watching from the mass of foliage that wasn't there last time we looked.

Goldfinches had always seemed to me to be at odds with nature. British birds should be LBJs – little brown jobs – not garish combinations of black, white, yellow, buff and red, the sort of bird a child would draw if let loose with a full set of crayons and a sketching pad. Seeing a charm of them at a distance, feeding on some thistles, always lifts the spirits, and helps one to accept the thistles in the hedgebacks, where the sprayer doesn't venture. Seeing a flash of gold as they fly over on a dark winter's day gives a heart-warming glint of sunshine. But seen up close, feeding on the nyjer seed outside the kitchen window, one can't help thinking that the Almighty must have been experimenting with magic mushrooms when he created that one, a preposterous clown of a bird, at odds with its surroundings.

But this spring it all made sense and I have had to concede that goldfinches fit into the universe with a beautiful elegance. There is a goldfinch nest above the back door. High up near the eves where the fuchsia – whoever thought fuchsia could climb? – intertwines with a climbing rose and the wisteria rambling sinuously from the other side of the door. It is a perfectly judged nesting site. Seen surreptitiously from a bedroom window, the hen goldfinch can only be seen with the left side of the brain, like one of those trick pictures made from coloured dots.

She has picked a spot not far from the eaves, across from where the swallows provide a constant distraction for any predator with their noisy comings and goings at their gravity-defying mudball, stuck to the wall above my dressing-room window. Viewed from above, the white and red on her head blend with the pale pinkish white of the fuchsia candles and the red petals of the rose. The black bits mimic the shadows, and on hot afternoons, while she waits anxiously for the sun to disappear behind the chimneys, as she stands and fans her wings to keep her eggs cool, the yellow flash along her side looks very like the rose leaves with the sun coming through them, and the black is like the leaves' dark undersides.

It is not the goldfinch that has an imperfect understanding of life, it is I.

Epilogue

Dusk in June,
Somewhere a cow bellows the knell of parting day, insistently.
Bats take over from the swallows,
Foraging the heavy air, thick with fumes of elderflower and rose,
And the last blackbird gives way to the owls.
A fox barks along the bank and the pheasants cock-cock up to roost.
The woods are black save where a candle of white foxglove burns brightly.
I am wrapped in green, the trees have grown all the leaves they can this year,
The silage pit heaves with bounty,
The corn glows green gold in the fields down to the sea,
And the bulls will soon be going out again.
It will be a fine day tomorrow,
All will be well.